THE GREAT TREKS OF THE ALPS

The TOUR DU MONT BLANC Handbook

by
Andrew McCluggage

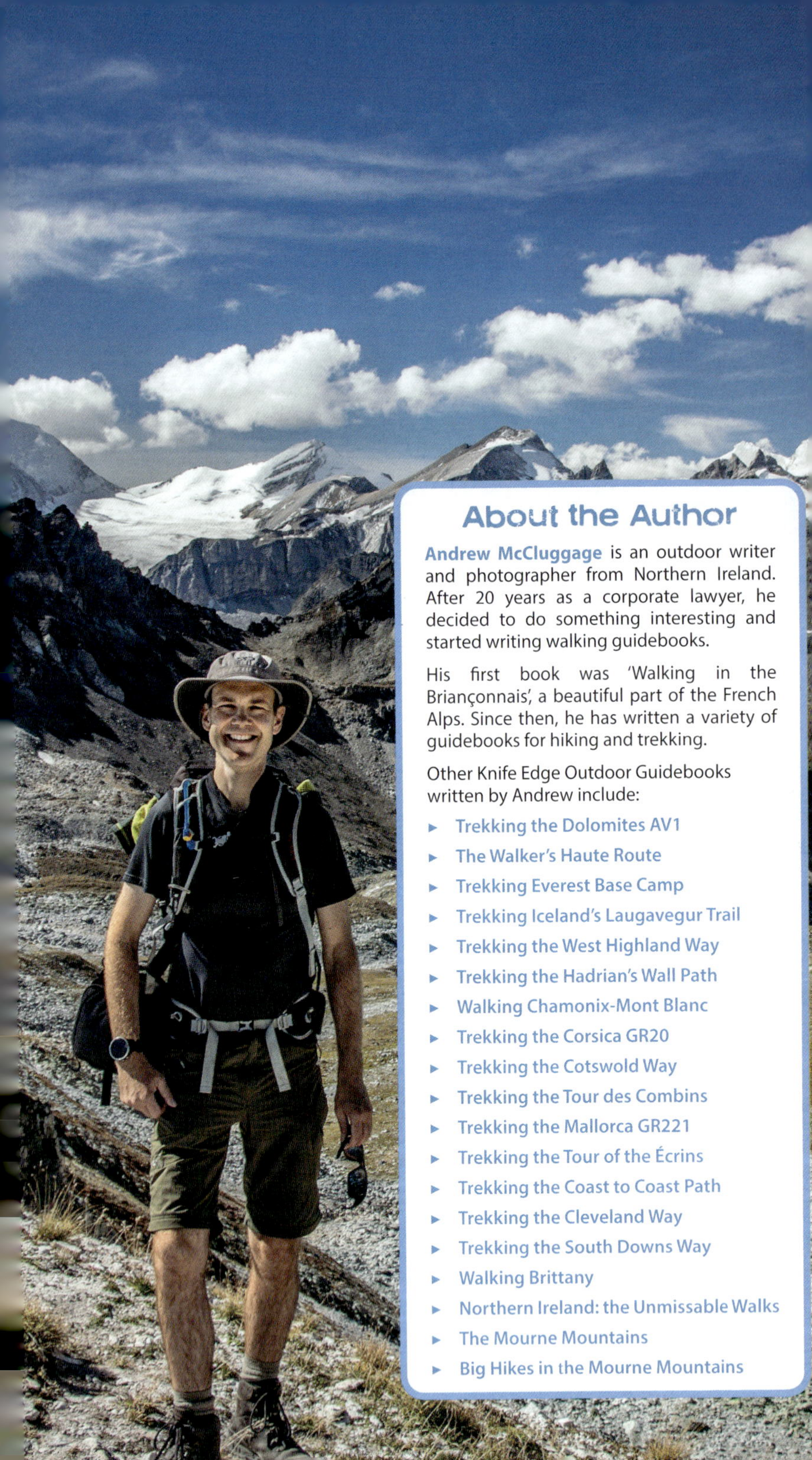

About the Author

Andrew McCluggage is an outdoor writer and photographer from Northern Ireland. After 20 years as a corporate lawyer, he decided to do something interesting and started writing walking guidebooks.

His first book was 'Walking in the Briançonnais', a beautiful part of the French Alps. Since then, he has written a variety of guidebooks for hiking and trekking.

Other Knife Edge Outdoor Guidebooks written by Andrew include:

- Trekking the Dolomites AV1
- The Walker's Haute Route
- Trekking Everest Base Camp
- Trekking Iceland's Laugavegur Trail
- Trekking the West Highland Way
- Trekking the Hadrian's Wall Path
- Walking Chamonix-Mont Blanc
- Trekking the Corsica GR20
- Trekking the Cotswold Way
- Trekking the Tour des Combins
- Trekking the Mallorca GR221
- Trekking the Tour of the Écrins
- Trekking the Coast to Coast Path
- Trekking the Cleveland Way
- Trekking the South Downs Way
- Walking Brittany
- Northern Ireland: the Unmissable Walks
- The Mourne Mountains
- Big Hikes in the Mourne Mountains

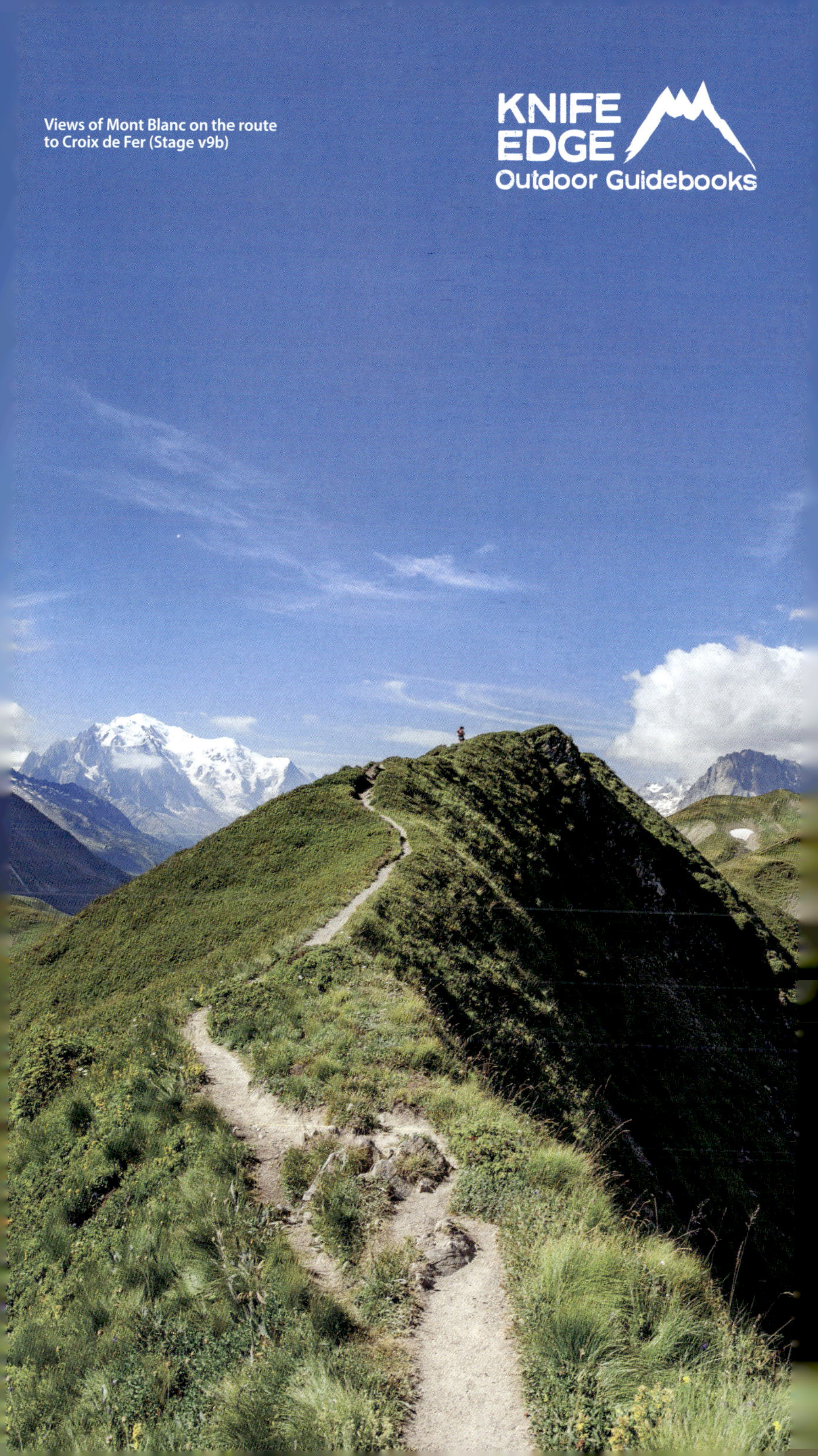

Views of Mont Blanc on the route to Croix de Fer (Stage v9b)

KNIFE EDGE
Outdoor Guidebooks

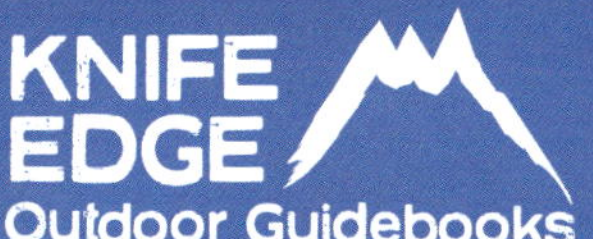

Publisher: Knife Edge Outdoor Limited (NI648568)
12 Torrent Business Centre, Donaghmore, County Tyrone, BT70 3BF, UK
www.knifeedgeoutdoor.com

Second edition 2026
ISBN: 978-1-912933-63-1

First edition 2019

A catalogue record for this book is available from the British Library.

Front cover: Descending from le Brévent (Stage 11a)

Back cover: An ibex overlooking Mont Blanc (Stage v10a; ladder-free route)

Title page: Refuge du Col de Balme (Stage v9a)

This page: Lac Blanc (Stage v10b/c)

All routes described in this book have been recently walked by the author and both the author and publisher have made all reasonable efforts to ensure that all information is as accurate as possible. However, while a printed book remains constant for the life of an edition, things in the wild often change. Trails are subject to forces outside our control. For example, landslides, avalanches, tree-falls or other matters can result in damage to paths or route changes; waymarks and signposts may fade or be destroyed by wind, snow or the passage of time; or trails may not be maintained by the relevant authorities. If you notice any discrepancies between the information in this guide and the facts on the ground, then please let us know by email (info@knifeedgeoutdoor.com).

Contents

Getting Help 1
Introduction 3
- The Mont Blanc Massif: basic facts 5
- Using this book 6
- When to go 7
- How hard is the trek? 9
- Direction and start/finish points 10
- Hiking shorter sections of the trek 13
- Skipping sections of the trek 13
- Guided tours, self-guided tours or independent walking? 14

Itinerary Planner: ACW 16
- Suggested Itineraries: ACW 17
- Variant Stages: ACW 21

Itinerary Planner: CW 22
- Suggested Itineraries: CW 23
- Variant Stages: CW 27

Accommodation 28
Camping 32
Accommodation Listings 35
Campsite Listings 41
Food 43
Travel to/from the trail-heads 45
On the Trail 52
- Costs & budgeting 52
- Weather 53
- Maps 53
- Paths and waymarking 54
- Snow bridges 55
- Water 55
- Storing bags 57
- Baggage transfer 57
- Fuel for camping stoves 58
- Outdoor shops 58
- Ticks 59
- Pastous 59

Equipment 60
- Recommended basic kit 61
- Additional gear for campers 64

Safety 66
General Information 67
Wildlife 69
Plants & Flowers 71
Mont Blanc Panorama 72
Route Descriptions
1 Les Houches/les Contamines 74
v1a/b Les Houches/les Contamines (via Col de Tricot) 82
v1c Les Houches/Col de Voza (via le Prarion) 86
2 Les Contamines/les Chapieux 88

v2a/b Les Contamines/Refuge de Nant-Borrant (via Refuge de Tré-la-Tête) 96
3 Les Chapieux/Rifugio Elisabetta Soldini 98
v3a Refuge de la Croix du Bonhomme/Refuge des Mottets (via Col des Fours) . . 104
4 Rifugio Elisabetta Soldini/Courmayeur 106
v4b Cabane du Combal/Courmayeur (via Val Veny) 114
v4c Rifugio Maison Vieille/Courmayeur (via Rifugio Monte Bianco) 116
5 Courmayeur/Rifugio Walter Bonatti 118
v5a Courmayeur/Chalet Val Ferret-Arnuova (via Italian Val Ferret) 122
v5b Rifugio Bertone/Rifugio Bonatti (via Mont de la Saxe) 126
6 Rifugio Walter Bonatti/la Fouly 128
7 La Fouly/Champex 134
8 Champex/Trient (via Bovine) 138
v8 Champex/Col de la Forclaz (via Fenêtre d'Arpette) 146
9 Trient/Tré-le-Champs 152
v9a Col de la Forclaz/Col de Balme (via Refuge les Grands) 158
v9b Le Peuty/Col de Balme (via Croix de Fer) 160
v9c Col de Balme/Tré-le-Champs (via le Tour) 162
10 Tré-le-Champs/Refuge de la Flégère 164
v10a Tré-le-Champs/la Tête aux Vents (Ladder-free Route) 170
v10b/c La Tête aux Vents/Refuge de la Flégère (via Lac Blanc) 174
11 Refuge de la Flégère/les Houches 176
Facilities along the route 182

Tour Noir viewed from la Fouly (Stage 6e/7)

Getting Help

Emergency services number: dial 112

Distress signal

The signal that you are in distress is 6 blasts on a whistle spaced over a minute, followed by a minute's silence; then repeat. The acknowledgment that your signal has been received is 3 blasts of a whistle over a minute followed by a minute's silence. At night, flashes of a torch can also be used in the same sequences. Always carry a torch and whistle.

Signalling to a helicopter from the ground

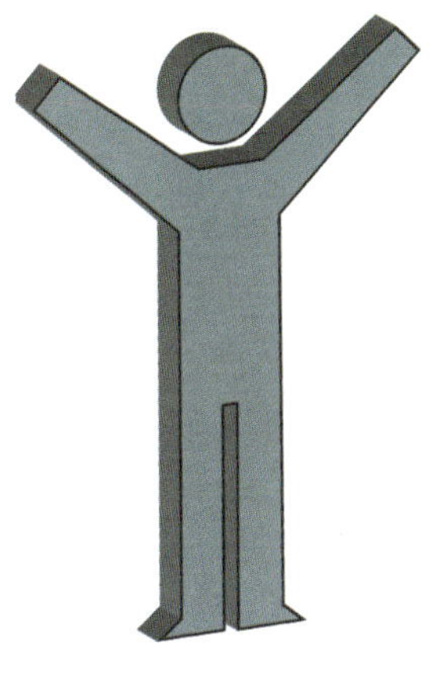

Help Required

Raise both arms in the shape of a 'Y'

Help Not Required

Raise one arm and extend the other arm down and outwards

WARNING

Hills, cliffs and mountains can be dangerous places and walking is a potentially dangerous activity. Some of the routes described in this guide cross potentially hazardous terrain. You walk entirely at your own risk. It is solely your responsibility to ensure that you and all members of your group have adequate experience, fitness and equipment. Neither the author nor the publisher accepts any responsibility or liability whatsoever for death, injury, loss, damage or inconvenience resulting from use of this book, participation in the activity of mountain walking or otherwise.

Some land may be privately owned and we cannot guarantee that there is a legal right of entry to the land. Occasionally, routes change as a result of land disputes.

Aiguille Verte & Grand Dru on the approach to Refuge de la Flégère (Stage 11a)

Introduction

The Tour du Mont Blanc (TMB) is the most famous trek in the Alps. In fact, it is possibly the most famous trek in the entire world and is at the top of most hikers' bucket lists. Its peerless reputation owes everything to the mountain after which it is named, the mighty Mont Blanc (MB): at 4806m, it is the highest peak in Western Europe. The TMB makes a complete circumnavigation of the entire Mont Blanc massif, passing through France, Italy and Switzerland. On the way, the trekker views MB (and a myriad of neighbouring peaks and glaciers) from every conceivable angle; and because the trek lasts for many days, there is plenty of time to savour the different views. By the end, you will be very well acquainted with this spectacular mountain range.

However, although MB is the focal point (frequently drawing the eye), the TMB has much more to offer: snow-frosted summits everywhere you look; lofty mountain passes (or cols) enabling passage from magnificent valley to magnificent valley; exquisite alpine pastures; sparkling azure lakes; carpets of wild-flowers; the soothing sound of cow bells; and an uninterrupted, easy to follow, path connecting all of these attractions. It is true 'Sound of Music' territory. Unforgettable. Unrivalled. Unsurpassed.

Aiguille de Tré-la-Tête (Stage 3b)

Because you need never leave the mountains, you will live and breathe these scenic delights day and night: fabulous accommodation is available in beautiful alpine villages and remote mountain huts, evenly spaced along the route; and for campers, there are spectacular campsites and remote zones for wild camping (where overnight bivouac has been authorised by the authorities). You will stay in places with views that most people dream of but few will ever see. Places that you will never forget. Places that will leave you with remarkable memories.

Whilst these are the tangible attractions of the TMB, there are also certain intangibles which give it an edge over many other treks. The trail, the accommodation and the scenery all coalesce to imbue the trekker with an intense sense of journey. And that is further amplified by the international nature of the trek: there is something exquisitely romantic about hiking across international borders from France to Italy to Switzerland and back to France again.

With such amazing experiences on offer, it is obvious that you will not be enjoying them alone. The TMB is a popular trek and rightly so. But such popularity is never oppressive. The MB massif and its surrounds are easily large enough to swallow the many walkers that descend upon them each summer. With a reasonably early start, you will find yourself largely alone for much of the day. You will occasionally pass, or be passed by, other trekkers but these meetings can be as fleeting as you wish. And at the end of the day, on arrival at your resting place, often high above the valleys, you will likely meet some of the people that you bumped into earlier: then bonds are formed over dinner or drinks and you will soon understand why the TMB has such a fine reputation as a sociable trek.

Most trekkers follow the main route of the TMB which is approximately 172km in length with 9700 metres of climbing and descent. However, the main route is not necessarily the best or most scenic option and there are many variants which you could choose instead: these alternative routes use different high passes, valleys and ridges to those travelled on the main route. In this book, we include all the official variants and (to give you even more choice) a range of unofficial variants: to be exact, we describe 17 variants in total, covering 141km; they are summarised in the tables on p21 and p27. Sometimes the variants are high altitude paths which are harder and more adventurous than the main route but, in other cases, they offer safer, low altitude alternatives (useful in periods of bad weather). Although many of the variants are widely known and well documented, for this second edition, we have developed some new alternatives which you are unlikely to find elsewhere. In fact, we have included so many different options that you could return for a second tour and, for the most part, hike different routes from those used first time around.

On paper, the length of the TMB may appear intimidating but it is reassuring to note that thousands of normal people complete the trail each year: with the right preparation, planning and approach, it is manageable for most people of reasonable fitness. Yes, it is a challenge but it is an achievable one. And that is where this book comes in: most of what you need to know to plan, and prepare for, the TMB is here within these pages and the entire route is described in detail (in both directions) to guide you on the trail itself. Furthermore, unlike some other books, this one contains real topographical maps: for each stage, there are 1:40,000 scale maps to go with the accurate and concise route descriptions. Because we were unable to find commercially available maps which suited our purposes, we commissioned our own maps and they are perfect for navigating the trail. As well as including those maps in this book, we have also produced a sheet map for the TMB which is extremely helpful for planning and navigation: ***Trekking Map: Tour du Mont Blanc*** (ISBN 9781912933556).

The first edition of this book (which was originally published in 2019) focused in most detail on trekkers staying in huts/hotels. However, since 2019, the popularity of the TMB has increased significantly and the demand for accommodation has become fierce. As a result, the number of people trekking with a tent has surged. Accordingly, for this second edition, our text has been completely rewritten and now focuses equally on 'hutters' and campers.

Wherever you choose to stay, we aim to ensure that you have the best chance possible of completing the trek. We place great importance on the correct preparation and we focus in detail on modern lightweight equipment (see p60). We also believe that it is crucial to match your itinerary to your experience, fitness and ability. Accordingly, we have included here an extraordinary level of detail on itinerary planning: our unique itinerary planner has 14 different itineraries to choose from. For each itinerary, we have completed for you all the difficult calculations of time, distance and altitude gain/loss. This makes it easy for you to design a manageable itinerary that suits your specific needs. Once on the trail, you will be able to relax and fully enjoy one of the world's great treks.

The Mont Blanc Massif: basic facts

- Mont Blanc is French for 'white mountain'. In Italy, it is known as Monte Bianco (which is Italian for 'white mountain').
- At 4806m above sea level, Mont Blanc is the highest peak in the Alps and Western Europe. It is also the highest mountain in the whole of Europe which is not in the Caucasus range: and even in the Caucasus mountains, only a handful of peaks are higher than MB (including the very highest peak in all of Europe, Mount Elbrus 5642m).
- The height of Mont Blanc can increase/decrease by a few metres, depending upon the thickness of the current snow-pack.
- The massif of which MB is part is known as the MB massif and it largely straddles France and Italy: the Franco-Italian border runs NE along the crest of the massif until it reaches Mont Dolent. At Mont Dolent (towards the N of the massif), the Franco-Italian border meets Switzerland: from there, the Franco-Swiss border continues along the crest of the massif.
- The ownership of MB's summit is disputed: the Italian Government claims that the Franco-Italian border crosses the very summit of MB and that the summit is partly French and partly Italian. However, the French Government argues that the summit is entirely within France.
- The MB massif is encircled by eight main valleys: the Chamonix valley (Vallée de l'Arve) runs along much of the French (W) side of the massif; Val Montjoie and Vallée des Glaciers run around the SW tip of the massif (still in France); Val Veny and Italian Val Ferret flank the Italian (E) side; Swiss Val Ferret, Val d'Arpette and Vallée du Trient wrap around the Swiss (N) tip of the massif.
- Geology: the core of the MB massif is coarse-grained granite (igneous rock) with an external shell of gneiss (metamorphic rock). The hard granite is easily recognisable by the jagged shape of the massif's crests and the steep sharp summits. In places where a gneiss shell covers the granite, the rock is more rounded and continuous. At the base of the granite and gneiss, there are various sedimentary rocks.
- The first recorded ascent of MB was on 8 August 1786 by Jacques Balmat and Michel Paccard. The first woman to summit was Marie Paradis in 1808. About 20,000 people now attempt the climb each year. It is thought that more people have died attempting to climb MB than any other mountain in the world: in 1994, a study estimated that there had been 6000-8000 fatalities.
- The MB tunnel runs for 11.6km through the MB massif, connecting Chamonix in France with Courmayeur in Italy. Construction started in 1959 and was completed in 1965. In 1999, a fire in the tunnel killed 39 people. See also p46.

Auberge du Truc (Stage v1b)

Using this book

This book is designed to be used by trekkers of differing abilities. Many guidebooks for long-distance treks rigidly divide the route into a fixed number of long day-stages, leaving it up to the hiker to break down those stages to design daily routes which suit his/her abilities. This book, however, has been laid out differently to give the trekker flexibility: it divides the route into 28 shorter stages which you can combine to design daily routes that meet your own specific needs.

Each stage (with two exceptions) covers the distance between one accommodation option and the subsequent one: the exceptions are Stages 10a and 10b which have at one end the important junction at la Tête aux Vents (where there is no accommodation). Most accommodation options along the route are the start/finish point of a stage. You can choose how many of these stages you wish to walk each day. Each stage has its own walk description, route map and elevation profile.

The labelling of the stages uses a combination of numbers and letters. It is a simple system but requires a little bit of explanation. Firstly, we have divided the route into 11 'Sections' (numbered from 1 to 11 starting at LH and working ACW): each Section represents one day of our standard 11-day itinerary. Within some Sections, the route is further broken down into two or more 'Stages': these Stages are also labelled with a number between 1 and 11, representing the relevant Section that the Stage is part of. Stages are also labelled with a letter: so, for example, the first stage in Section 6 is 'Stage 6a', the second stage is 'Stage 6b' and so on. Take a look at the detailed Itinerary Planner on p16 and all should become clear.

The Itinerary Planner includes a range of tables and graphs outlining 14 suggested itineraries of 5, 7, 8, 9, 10, 11 and 12 days. In each table, we have crunched the numbers for you so there is no need for you to waste time (and mental strength) working out daily distances, timings and altitude gain/loss.

Of course, the suggested itineraries are only suggestions. You can shorten or lengthen your day to suit yourself: just decide how many stages you want to walk that day. It is up to you. As there is accommodation at the end of nearly every stage, it is easy to design your own bespoke itinerary and adjust it on the ground as you go (subject to accommodation availability).

For example, day 5 of the standard 11-day ACW itinerary involves walking Stages 5a and 5b. However, you could decide to extend your day by walking Stages 5a, 5b and 6a, all on the same day. Or you might decide to shorten your day by walking only Stage 5a. With some other guidebooks, you would have to work out how to split stages yourself, involving some complicated maths to plan distances and times going forward. This guide, however, does all the hard mental work for you.

We also provide a comprehensive range of variants which you can choose instead of the main route. The labelling for variants is similar to that used for the main stages except variant stages also have the prefix 'v'. The variants are summarised in the tables on p21 and p27.

In this book:

Timings indicate the approximate time required by a reasonably fit walker to complete a stage (excluding stoppage time). Do not get frustrated if your own times do not match ours: everyone walks at different speeds. As you progress through the trek, you will soon learn how your own times compare with those given here and you will adjust your plans accordingly.

Walking distances are given in kilometres (km) to match maps and signposts in Europe. One mile equates to approximately 1.6km.

Place names in brackets in the route descriptions indicate the direction to be followed on signposts. For example, "('Trient')" would mean that you follow a sign for Trient.

Ascent/descent numbers are the aggregate of all the altitude gain or loss (measured in feet and metres) on the uphill or downhill sections of a stage. As a rule of thumb, a fit walker climbs 1000 to 1300 feet (300 to 400m) in an hour. The statistics tables in the route descriptions are based on ACW itineraries: CW trekkers should simply swap the ascent and descent figures.

Elevation profiles are provided for each Section, indicating where the climbs and descents fall on the route. The profiles are based on ACW itineraries: CW hikers should simply read them in reverse.

Real maps are provided. These are extracts from 1:40,000 scale maps produced by Knife Edge Outdoor Guidebooks. On the maps, we have marked the route of the trek (red for the main route; purple for variants), the start/finish points of stages (yellow markers), significant waypoints (red markers for the main route; purple for variants) and the accommodation/campsites along the TMB. On each map, N is at the top of the page. As well as printing these maps in this book, we have also published a sheet map for the TMB which is extremely helpful for planning and navigation: ***Trekking Map: Tour du Mont Blanc*** (ISBN 9781912933556).

Different colours are used to distinguish different parts of the text. **Blue** is used for ACW specific information; **pink** is used for CW information. Furthermore, in the accommodation listings and statistics tables, names of places are coloured **blue**, **green** or **red** depending upon which country they are located in: **France**, **Italy**, **Switzerland**.

The following terms are used:

BCE/CE	Before the Common Era/the Common Era (secular alternatives to BC/AD)
BSM	Bourg-St-Maurice
Hutters	those staying in huts/gîtes/hotels (as opposed to campers in tents)
LC	les Contamines
LH	les Houches
MB	Mont Blanc
MBE	Mont Blanc Express train (see p45)
OR	Off-route
Refuge de la CB	Refuge de la Croix du Bonhomme
SGLF	St-Gervais-le-Fayet
TMB	Tour du Mont Blanc
WW1/WW2	World War 1/World War 2

TL	Turn left	**N, S, E and W, etc.**	North, South, East and West, etc.
TR	Turn right	**ACW**	Anti-clockwise/counter-clockwise
SH	Straight ahead	**CW**	Clockwise

When to go

The weather window for hiking the TMB is quite short: the trekking season usually starts towards the end of June and finishes around the end of the third week of September. Even in this period, high winds, heavy rain, and low cloud (which reduces visibility), can occur: occasionally, it can even snow on the trail. You will probably hike in fine weather but you should prepare for the worst. Throughout the main trekking season, there is plenty of daylight. The relative merits of each season are discussed in detail below but, taking all the factors into consideration, we prefer to hike the TMB in the first two weeks of September.

Late June: this can be the most beautiful time for trekking. The weather is often sunny and warm. The peaks are frequently at their most photogenic, still fully frosted with snow. Summer haze has not yet arrived so visibility is generally excellent, with wide-ranging views. This is peak season for wild-flowers. Fewer visitors means that accommodation can be easier to find and significantly, the mountains are more peaceful. However, as with all Alpine treks, snow sometimes remains on the high passes until early July, making parts of the route difficult and/or dangerous: in such conditions, crampons/spikes and an ice axe might be helpful. There are now some very light, compact crampons available which weigh a mere 300g so carrying them just in case is not the burden it once was. For those planning an early season trek, the weeks prior to the start date can be stressful because it might not become clear until the very last minute whether the snow has cleared sufficiently to hike the route safely: changing bookings at the last minute can be challenging, time-consuming and costly (because you may not get all your money back).

July/August: this is the main summer season when the high cols are normally passable. During July/August, accommodation is harder to find and advance booking is recommended (unless you are camping). It can be hot, reaching more than 30°C. Mornings often start with clear, sunny skies and heat up as the sun gains height. If there is to be cloud or haze, often this will arrive in the afternoon when thunderstorms are more likely. Start walking early in the morning to complete the main climb while the temperature is cooler and before storms arrive. As July progresses, the trails gradually become busier. The busiest time is probably the first two weeks of August, when many of the Swiss, Italians and French will be taking annual vacations. Towards the end of August, the number of trekkers starts to decrease.

September: this is our favourite month for hiking as the weather is often more settled than in summer. Skies are usually clear and visibility excellent. Daytime temperatures are still warm but evenings get cooler and the days become shorter. As the month progresses, the risk of light snowfall on the cols increases but any snow usually clears quickly. Occasionally, there are more significant dumps of snow in September that adversely impact the safety of trekking for a few days or more: this occurred in both 2023 and 2024. During September, visitor numbers gradually reduce: the mountains are quieter and there is less demand for accommodation. However, towards the end of the month, some accommodation closes for the season.

October: this can be a very beautiful time, with spectacular autumn colours. However, careful planning is needed to undertake the route in October. The weather is less reliable, and can be much colder and nastier, than in summer: with shorter days, you have less time to seek help if something goes wrong on the trail. As the month progresses, the possibility of snowfall on the cols increases (which could make them impassable or dangerous). Check weather forecasts carefully along the way to avoid getting trapped by snow between cols. If fresh snow is forecast, do not set out. Some accommodation will be closed. You will need to be prepared to carry more food as there will be fewer places to eat or buy supplies. Trekking in October is for experienced and well-equipped hikers only.

Month	Pros	Cons
Late June	Pleasant temperatures **Frequent sunny skies** Good visibility **Wild-flower season** Fewer trekkers **Hut beds easier to find** Longest days	Snow on the high parts of the trail: cols and peaks occasionally inaccessible
July/August	Generally reliably fine weather **High cols normally passable** Long days	The hottest period **Sometimes hazy** Afternoon thunderstorms **Visitor numbers highest** Hut beds harder to find **Some snow remains in early July**
September	Pleasant temperatures **Frequent sunny skies** Excellent visibility **Fewer visitors** Hut beds become easier to find **Autumn colours** Still sufficient daylight	Accommodation closes as the month progresses **Cooler evenings** Increasing possibility of snow
October	Autumn colours **Frequent sunny skies** Excellent visibility **Fewer visitors**	Greater possibility of snow **Much accommodation closed** Short days **Cold mornings and evenings**

How hard is the trek?

The TMB is a multi-day trek with significant distances to travel each day. It crosses remote landscapes of mountains and valleys: each day, you will need to climb and descend significantly to negotiate the undulating terrain; for example, those on a 10-day itinerary will, on average, both climb and descend around 1000m/day. Sometimes, the climbs/descents are steep and challenging. As the days go by, such exertions take their toll on your body, both physically and mentally. Accordingly, a reasonable level of fitness is required and the fitter you are at the start of the trek, the better your chances of success and the more you will enjoy the experience.

The demand on your body is intensified by the requirement to carry a pack and the burden is greatest for campers who carry tents, sleeping bags, mats and cooking equipment. However, because there is plenty of accommodation along the route, you do not need to carry camping equipment or food (other than basic rations) and your pack can be kept light. Even so, it is fair to say that many trekkers set off carrying some equipment which is unnecessary or simply too heavy: this can contribute to injury and/or exhaustion, leading to abandonment. Accordingly, you should give equipment choice careful consideration (see p60): it will be crucial to your enjoyment of the trek and the likelihood of success. Anyone considering carrying camping gear should bear in mind that lugging many kilos of extra gear up the TMB's long climbs is very hard work.

On the main route, paths are largely clear and well maintained although they are sometimes rocky and challenging underfoot. Occasionally, you might have to climb up or down short sections of boulders but you will not require any technical scrambling/climbing skills. Often, the gradients are steep. Sometimes, the route is exposed with large, steep drops. High altitude variants tend to be more challenging than the main route. Mentally, the crux of the main route is perhaps Stage 10's famous metal ladders (see p165): if you can get past those, then you can conquer anything the route throws at you. However, these ladders can easily be bypassed using our Ladder-free Route (p170).

For the most part, the paths/tracks are clear, well-marked and simple to follow in good conditions. However, occasionally, the route is less obvious and more difficult to navigate: some short sections of the route have no paths and you will have to rely on cairns/waymarks. That said, most people have no major difficulties staying on course. However, take care in poor conditions or low visibility when navigation on the highest sections of the trail can be more tricky. Furthermore, on the high points of the route, snow can remain into July, covering paths and making progress/route-finding much more difficult and sometimes dangerous.

However, notwithstanding the challenges, thousands of hikers walk the TMB each year. It is therefore an achievable endeavour. To improve fitness, it is sensible to train in advance: there is no substitute for training hikes, carrying a pack. Although not absolutely necessary, previous experience of trekking will help. And, of course, the level of difficulty depends upon how quickly, and how far, you travel each day: faster itineraries are obviously more challenging than slower ones and the TMB will be more manageable if you choose an itinerary that matches your fitness and experience. Most people walk the TMB in 10-11 days. However, fit and experienced hikers can finish it faster. Others prefer to walk more slowly, adding more days to soak up all the delights on offer. Our Itinerary Planner will help you decide what is best for you: see p16.

Col des Fours (Stage v3a)

Direction and start/finish points

Because the TMB is a circuit, you will return to your starting point at the end of the trek (if you walk the full route). Traditionally, most trekkers start at les Houches (LH) and walk anti-clockwise (ACW). However, because you can hike in either direction, this book caters for both ACW and CW trekkers: full route descriptions and plenty of different itineraries are provided for each approach. Furthermore, the numbered waypoints on the real maps make the route easy to follow in either direction.

Popular consensus dictates that the trek is more difficult when hiked CW (due to the spacing of the accommodation and the climbs). However, in our opinion, there would be little of much significance to split the two approaches if it were not for one notable factor: over a mere 10km, the terrain rises without break from the valley floor at LH (one of the TMB's lowest points) to the summit of le Brévent (one of the TMB's highest points). When hiked CW, this is the TMB's biggest climb and, because there is only one place to stay mid-route (the small, hard to book, Refuge Bellachat), most CW trekkers have to complete it in one go. To make matters worse, there is nowhere to stay at le Brévent (the top of the climb): this means that, after reaching the top, CW trekkers then have to continue another 8km to Refuge de la Flégère before stopping for the night. This makes for a monster of a day which is especially challenging if tackled on the first day of the trek (starting from LH). If you are able to secure a booking at Refuge Bellachat or a bivouac site at Col de Bellachat/Lac du Brévent (see p33) then you can solve the problem by splitting the climb but otherwise, this may be too much for many trekkers to complete in one day. Fit and experienced hikers can usually manage it but, if you are not sure that you can do it, trekking ACW is a better idea.

It is also worth bearing in mind that, because most hikers travel ACW, that is probably the more sociable approach: you are more likely to bump into the same people each day, making it easier to develop trail friendships. However, some trekkers may prefer to walk CW (against the main flow) to avoid seeing the same hikers day after day.

LH (France) is the traditional starting point and it remains the most popular because it is the easiest place along the trek to access from Geneva Airport: furthermore, starting at LH and walking ACW allows you to begin the trek with a couple of easier days before the higher stages later on. However, because the CW climb from LH to le Brévent makes for a brutal first day, Champex (Switzerland) is a better starting point for CW trekkers. Courmayeur is the most easily accessible start/finish point in Italy: in either direction, you would start the trek with a long climb but CW trekkers could use a cable car to skip this.

Although it is not actually along the TMB's route, many trekkers prefer to start/finish at Chamonix because it is the most famous mountain town in the Alps, with a magnificent setting beneath MB: it is well served by public transport; and there are plenty of hotels, grocery stores and outdoor shops (where you can buy everything you could possibly need to hike the TMB). The TMB trail is easily accessed from Chamonix by taking the bus/train to LH or the cable car from Chamonix to Plan Praz/le Brévent (on Stage 11a) or the cable car from les Praz to Refuge de la Flégère (on Stage 10b/11a).

However, LH, Courmayeur, Champex and Chamonix are not the only possible staging points: you could also start from the other places along the route which can be accessed by public transport: we discuss the pros/cons of each in the table on p11. For public transport to each trail-head, see p45. Furthermore, if you travel to the region by car, you could start anywhere along the route which has road access and parking.

MB massif at sunset

Start/ finish point	Pros	Cons	Transport (further info on p48)
Les Houches	Easy access by public transport. **Shops and supermarkets.** Good selection of places to stay, including a campsite. **ACW trekkers can plan a few easier days before the harder stages later on.**	CW trekkers have a brutal first day. **Car parking difficult in summer.**	Bus **Train** Cable car
Col de Voza	In either direction, start the trek with a descent.	No shops or accommodation (except nearby Prarion 1860 Hotel). **No road access.** Transport is expensive.	Cable car from LH **Tramway du Mont Blanc from SGLF**
Les Contamines	Shops and supermarkets. **Good selection of places to stay, including a nearby campsite.** In either direction, start the trek with a relatively easy day.	More difficult to access than LH. **Long-term parking hard to find in summer.**	Bus from SGLF
Les Chapieux	Free long-term parking. **Free bivouac site.** Magnificent setting.	More difficult to access: only a few buses each day from/to BSM. **In either direction, the first day of the trek is tough.** No supermarket: small shop only. **Limited accommodation.**	Bus from BSM
La Visaille (2.8km hike from Combal)	Parking and campsites in Val Veny **Regular buses to la Visaille.**	2.8km hike from la Visaille to the TMB trail at Combal.	Bus (from Courmayeur) + hike
Courmayeur	Easy access by public transport. **Shops and supermarkets.** Excellent selection of places to stay. **Beautiful place for a post-trek celebration.** CW trekkers can use a cable car to skip the first climb.	In either direction, it is a steep start to the trek. **Car parking difficult in summer.**	Bus **Cable car from Chamonix**
La Fouly	Reasonable access by public transport. **Supermarket**. Reasonable selection of places to stay. **Beautiful place for a post-trek celebration.** ACW trekkers have an easy first day.	Harder to access than LH. **Car parking difficult in summer.** CW trekkers have a tough first day. **Only a few places to eat.**	Bus from Orsières/ Martigny

Start/ finish point	Pros	Cons	Transport (further info on p48)
Champex	Reasonable access by public transport. **Supermarket.** Good selection of places to stay. **Beautiful place for a post-trek celebration.** In either direction, start the trek with a relatively easy day. **For CW trekkers, Champex is an easier start point than LH.**	Harder to access than LH. **Car parking difficult in summer.**	Bus from Orsières
Trient	Reasonable access by public transport. **Free bivouac site.**	Harder to access than LH or Courmayeur. **Few places to stay.** Car parking hard in summer. **Both ACW and CW trekkers start with a long climb.**	Bus from Martigny
Col de Balme	Parking in le Tour (at bottom of Charamillon cable car). **In either direction, start the trek with a downhill stage.**	Access only by cable car. **Only one place to stay.** ACW trekkers will face the ladders at Aiguillette d'Argentière early in the trek before becoming 'trail hardened'.	Cable car (from le Tour) + 0.7km hike
Tré-le-Champs	Access by public transport. **Parking at car park just N of 84.** Supermarket in nearby Argentière.	Only one place to stay. **In either direction, it is a steep start to the trek.** ACW trekkers face the ladders at Aiguillette d'Argentière on day 1.	Bus from Argentière
Refuge de la Flégère	Easy access by cable car. **Shops/supermarkets in Chamonix.** Plenty of accommodation in Chamonix.	Long-term car parking difficult to find/expensive. **CW trekkers face the ladders at Aiguillette d'Argentière on day 1.**	Cable car from le Praz (near Chamonix)
Plan Praz	Easy access: cable car departs from Chamonix (well-served by trains/buses). **Shops/supermarkets in Chamonix.** Plenty of accommodation in Chamonix.	Long-term car parking difficult to find/expensive. **CW trekkers face the ladders at Aiguillette d'Argentière early in the trek.**	Cable car from Chamonix
Le Brévent	Easy access: the cable car departs from Chamonix (well-served by trains/buses). **Shops/supermarkets in Chamonix.** Plenty of accommodation in Chamonix.	Long-term car parking difficult to find/expensive. **CW trekkers face the ladders at Aiguillette d'Argentière early in the trek.**	Cable car from Chamonix

Hiking shorter sections of the trek

Hiking the TMB in one go is a wonderful experience but there are other ways to enjoy this incredible trail. It is also possible to walk shorter sections of the route because there are many access points along the way which have public transport: see p48. You could start at any of these places, walk a section or two and then use public transport to get away from your finishing point.

If you only want to walk some of the highlights of the trek then we would suggest the following hikes (all of which are served by public transport at both ends):

- **Les Houches to les Contamines (via Col de Tricot; Section v1; 1-2 days):** hike Stage v1a from LH to Refuge de Miage and spend the night there. The following morning, hike Stage v1b to LC. Fit hikers could walk this entire route in one day.
- **Les Chapieux to Courmayeur (Sections 3/4; 1-2 days):** take the bus from BSM to les Chapieux. Hike Section 3 from les Chapieux to Rifugio Elisabetta and spend the night there. The following morning, hike Section 4 to Courmayeur: from there, buses head E towards Turin or W into France; it would take a long time to return to BSM by public transport if you needed to collect bags. Fit hikers could walk this entire route in one day.
- **Courmayeur to la Fouly (Sections 5/6; 1-2 days):** hike Section 5 from Courmayeur to Rifugio Bonatti and spend the night there. The following morning, hike Section 6 to la Fouly: from there, buses head N towards Orsières and Martigny; it would take a long time to return to Courmayeur by public transport if you needed to collect bags.
- **Champex to Col de la Forclaz (Section 8 or v8; 1 day):** use public transport to travel from Martigny to Champex. Hike either Section 8 or Section v8 from Champex to Col de la Forclaz. Then take the bus back to Martigny.
- **Tré-le-Champs to LH (Sections 10/11; 1-2 days):** use public transport to travel from Chamonix to Tré-le-Champs. Hike Section 10 to Refuge de la Flégère and spend the night there. The following morning, hike Section 11 to LH. Very fit hikers could walk this entire route in one day. Alternatively, skip all or part of Section 11 by descending to Chamonix using one of the cable cars from la Flégère, Plan Praz or le Brévent.

Skipping sections of the trek

You could skip sections of the trek by leaving the route at one of the trail-heads and using public transport to resume at another point. You might do this if you become fatigued, the weather is bad or you are unable to find accommodation along certain parts of the route. Sections of the route which you can skip using public transport include the following:

- **Stage 1a:** cable cars travel between LH and Prarion/Bellevue (both of which are close to Col de Voza).
- **Section 1/v1:** train/bus between LH and LC (via SGLF).
- **Section 2:** taxi between LC and les Chapieux (see p50).
- **Stage 3a:** bus between les Chapieux and Ville des Glaciers/Parking des Mottets.
- **Stages 4b/4c:** bus between la Visaille (2.8km OR from Cabane de Combal) and Courmayeur.
- **Stage 4c:** cable cars between Rifugio Maison Vieille and Dolonne.
- **Section 5 and Stage 6a:** bus between Courmayeur and Chalet Val Ferret.
- **Stage 6e:** bus between Ferret and la Fouly.
- **Section 7:** buses between la Fouly and Champex (via Orsières).
- **Section 8/v8:** buses between Champex and Col de la Forclaz/Trient (via Martigny).
- **Stage 9c/v9c:** cable car (between Col de Balme and le Tour) + bus (between le Tour and Argentière) + bus (between Argentière and Tré-le-Champs).

- **Sections 10 and 11:** bus/train between Tré-le-Champs and LH (via Chamonix).
- **Section 10 only:** bus/train (between Tré-le-Champs and les Praz) + cable car (between les Praz and Refuge de la Flégère).
- **Section 11:** skip all or part of Section 11 by descending to Chamonix using one of the cable cars from la Flégère, Plan Praz or le Brévent.

For more information on public transport at trail-heads, see p48.

Guided tours, self-guided tours or independent walking?

Generally, there are two ways to organise a TMB trek: you can either book an organised tour with a trekking company or you can trek independently (not part of an organised tour). The choice is a personal one and depends upon your own particular circumstances and requirements.

Trekking independently

Independent trekkers plan and organise the trek themselves, making any required bookings without the help of a trekking company. They also hike the trail without the support or assistance of a trekking company: the independent trekker is therefore responsible for all daily decisions such as pacing, which way to go at junctions, when to stock up with food/water, and choice of route in bad weather. Navigating a trek independently is extremely satisfying and the sense of achievement on completion is to be savoured. If you have not done it before, the decision to walk independently can be almost life-changing, opening the door for other challenges in the future. It offers a greater sense of freedom and adventure and many prefer it to trekking in an organised group. However, for some, trekking independently would be too great a burden on top of the physical effort required simply to walk the route and a guided organised trek can therefore be preferable.

The main advantage of independent trekking is that costs are much lower because you do not have to pay the premium that trekking companies charge for their services. However, the principal disadvantage is that you get no help at all with the difficult process of booking TMB accommodation: for campers, this is rarely problematic because campsites do not usually need to be reserved far in advance. However, for hutters, the booking process is time consuming and complicated (see p29), although it is perfectly possible with timely planning, perseverance and a certain amount of luck. If you do not have the spare time and energy that the booking process requires, or you want to maximise your chances, then it may be better to use a trekking company and book an organised tour.

In times gone by, a major advantage of independent trekking was that you had the flexibility to change your plans during the trek to respond to adverse weather, fatigue or other factors. These days, however, only campers still enjoy this flexibility (because campsite bookings are usually unnecessary or can be amended at late notice): most huts/hotels are full to capacity throughout the season and the chances of being able to change a whole string of bookings on short notice is minuscule.

Organised treks

On an organised trek, you usually hike a fixed itinerary which you have selected in advance. A trekking company books all the accommodation along the route you have chosen, in the correct order, saving you a lot of stress and hassle. Finding beds on the TMB is their job and most are very good at it: the very best companies are wizards, seemingly conjuring available beds out of thin air and cleverly re-jigging schedules to make itineraries work. If you have absolutely set your heart on the TMB, these services are worth every penny of the fee. Although many tour companies offer different levels of accommodation at different prices, bear in mind that in some locations there may only be one basic mountain hut which is shared by everyone (irrespective of budget).

People choose an organised tour for many different reasons. It is a great solution for inexperienced trekkers and those who do not have the time or inclination to make their own arrangements. Others are attracted by the peace of mind that comes with having a trekking company make all the arrangements on their behalf. And those travelling alone frequently prefer the comfort and companionship of a guided organised trek.

In recent years, there has been a rise in the number of businesses offering organised tours. Consequently, some of the accommodation along the TMB is block-booked in advance by the tour companies. At peak times, this makes it harder for the independent trekker to secure accommodation unless booked well in advance. As a result, many confident trekkers (who would be perfectly capable of walking independently) book an organised trek simply to avail of the accommodation booking service. By booking a tour, much of the hassle of planning the trek is alleviated, albeit at a price.

However, selecting a trekking company can be a daunting prospect because there are dozens to choose from. By using a well-established and respected company, you can usually be confident that your tour will run smoothly and be of reasonable quality. These days, with a quick internet search, you will find numerous companies offering a variety of itineraries but it can be difficult to be sure that the companies are trustworthy. Common complaints include inexperienced guides, overly fast itineraries and hidden extras. Before choosing, read online reviews, talk to company staff over the phone and thoroughly check the terms and conditions on the company website: you can also seek advice on one of the TMB Facebook groups (see p68).

There are two types of organised treks:

Guided treks: generally, this is the most expensive option. For less experienced hikers and those who would not be confident enough to go it alone, a guided trek is a great solution. You could arrange a private tour for just you and your companion(s) or you could book spaces on a larger group: often those travelling alone prefer the companionship of a group. The trekking company typically organises food, accommodation and an experienced guide who looks after you on the trail (making all the trekking decisions and enabling the hiker to concentrate on the hiking). Tour companies can also usually organise transfer of luggage to your accommodation, however, the remoteness of a few of the huts on the TMB means that baggage transfer is not possible at every location: even guided trekkers need to carry their own gear for nights at the more remote huts (see p57). In fact, the trekker does not really have to think about anything except booking an international flight to Geneva, and some trekking companies can even do that as well. There are many tour companies operating a variety of different guided treks on the TMB: some treks include the full official route but others just cover some of the highlights.

Self-guided treks: these offer a sensible middle-ground between independent and guided treks and they have become very popular in recent years. Although they are usually cheaper than guided treks, the tour company still books all the accommodation. However, you will trek without a guide, navigating with the help of this guidebook and/or any instructions provided by the tour company. Normally, breakfast and evening meals will be provided and you can request packed lunches. As with guided tours, self-guided tour companies can also usually organise transfer of luggage to many accommodation locations. Unlike independent trekkers, you will have someone to contact if something goes wrong with your trip.

Grand Col Ferret (Stage 6c)

Itinerary Planner: ACW

All our ACW itineraries start/finish in LH. However, if you would prefer to begin your trek at one of the other trail-heads (see p10), then simply start reading from that location in the tables below.

Stage	Start	Finish	Time	Distance		Ascent		Descent		Max Alt	
			hr:m	km	miles	m	ft	m	ft	m	ft
1a	Les Houches	Refuge du Fioux	2:45	7.0	4.3	653	2142	158	518	1653	5423
1b	Refuge du Fioux	Les Contamines	3:00	10.5	6.5	350	1148	688	2257	1505	4938
2a	Les Contamines	Refuge de Nant-Borrant	1:55	5.6	3.5	310	1017	18	59	1459	4787
2b	Refuge de Nant-Borrant	Refuge de la Balme	1:00	2.5	1.6	247	810	0	0	1706	5597
2c	Refuge de la Balme	Refuge de la CB	2:30	5.6	3.5	790	2592	53	174	2479	8133
2d	Refuge de la CB	Les Chapieux	1:45	5.0	3.1	0	0	894	2933	2443	8015
3a	Les Chapieux	Refuge des Mottets	2:00	6.5	4.0	351	1152	30	98	1870	6135
3b	Refuge des Mottets	Rifugio Elisabetta	3:00	8.1	5.0	686	2251	361	1184	2516	8255
4a	Rifugio Elisabetta	Combal	0:50	3.3	2.1	15	49	235	771	2195	7201
4b	Combal	Rifugio Maison Vieille	3:00	7.5	4.7	460	1509	479	1572	2430	7972
4c	Rifugio Maison Vieille	Courmayeur	1:30	5.4	3.4	20	66	766	2513	1956	6417
5a	Courmayeur	Rifugio Bertone	2:30	5.3	3.3	781	2562	0	0	1991	6532
5b	Rifugio Bertone	Rifugio Bonatti	2:30	7.9	4.9	300	984	266	873	2025	6644
6a	Rifugio Bonatti	Chalet Val Ferret	1:20	5.1	3.2	60	197	323	1060	2025	6644
6b	Chalet Val Ferret	Rifugio Elena	0:55	2.2	1.4	293	961	0	0	2062	6765
6c	Rifugio Elena	Alpage de la Peule	2:30	6.5	4.0	475	1558	464	1522	2536	8320
6d	Alpage de la Peule	Ferret	1:15	4.6	2.9	30	98	401	1316	2071	6795
6e	Ferret	La Fouly	0:40	2.8	1.7	0	0	100	328	1700	5577
7	La Fouly	Champex	4:30	15.5	9.6	474	1555	607	1991	1600	5249
8a	Champex	Col de la Forclaz	4:50	14.6	9.1	790	2592	741	2431	2049	6722
8b	Col de la Forclaz	Trient	0:30	1.5	0.9	13	43	239	784	1526	5007
9a	Trient	Le Peuty	0:20	1.2	0.7	26	85	0	0	1326	4350
9b	Le Peuty	Refuge du Col de Balme	2:30	4.6	2.9	865	2838	0	0	2191	7188
9c	Refuge du Col de Balme	Tré-le-Champs	2:45	8.1	5.0	228	748	1002	3287	2191	7188
10a	Tré-le-Champs	La Tête aux Vents	2:10	3.4	2.1	716	2349	0	0	2135	7004
10b	La Tête aux Vents	Refuge de la Flégère	1:00	3.5	2.2	22	72	278	912	2135	7004
11a	Refuge de la Flégère	Refuge Bellachat	4:10	10.1	6.3	790	2592	531	1742	2525	8284
11b	Refuge Bellachat	Les Houches	2:45	7.9	4.9	36	118	1155	3789	2152	7060

Suggested Itineraries: ACW

12 Days: this is our most leisurely approach for trekkers with plenty of time. It is useful for those arriving in les Houches in the middle of the day as you can warm up with a half-day walk of 7km (to Refuge du Fioux) that same day. Days 7 and 12 are hard but your legs should be walked in by then. Otherwise, the lengths of the days are quite evenly balanced.

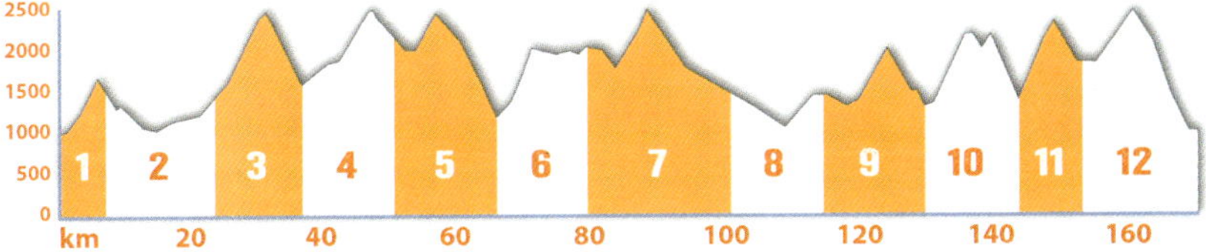

Day	Stages	Start	Finish	Time hr:m	Distance km	miles	Ascent m	ft	Descent m	ft
1	1a	Les Houches	Refuge du Fioux	2:45	7.0	4.3	653	2142	158	518
2	1b, 2a	Refuge du Fioux	Refuge Nant-Borrant	4:55	16.1	10.0	660	2165	706	2316
3	2b, 2c, 2d	Refuge Nant-Borrant	Les Chapieux	5:15	13.1	8.1	1037	3402	947	3107
4	3a, 3b	Les Chapieux	Rifugio Elisabetta	5:00	14.6	9.1	1037	3402	391	1283
5	4a, 4b, 4c	Rifugio Elisabetta	Courmayeur	5:20	16.2	10.1	495	1624	1480	4856
6	5a, 5b	Courmayeur	Rifugio Bonatti	5:00	13.2	8.2	1081	3547	266	873
7	6a, 6b, 6c, 6d, 6e	Rifugio Bonatti	La Fouly	6:40	21.2	13.2	858	2815	1288	4226
8	7	La Fouly	Champex	4:30	15.5	9.6	474	1555	607	1991
9	8a, 8b	Champex	Trient	5:20	16.1	10.0	803	2635	980	3215
10	9a, 9b, 9c	Trient	Tré-le-Champs	5:35	13.9	8.6	1119	3671	1002	3287
11	10a, 10b	Tré-le-Champs	Refuge de la Flégère	3:10	6.9	4.3	738	2421	278	912
12	11a, 11b	Refuge de la Flégère	Les Houches	6:55	18.0	11.2	826	2710	1686	5531

11 Days: our standard schedule is well balanced, successfully alternating harder and easier days. It is a tried and tested approach which will suit many trekkers. However, it may be too slow for fitter or more experienced hikers.

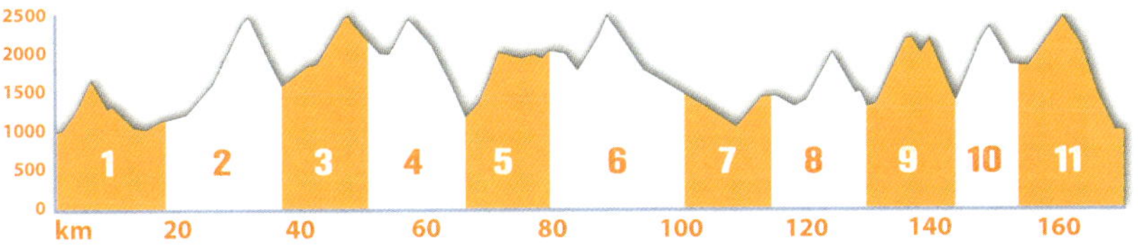

Day	Stages	Start	Finish	Time hr:m	Distance km	miles	Ascent m	ft	Descent m	ft
1	1a, 1b	Les Houches	Les Contamines	5:45	17.5	10.9	1003	3291	846	2776
2	2a, 2b, 2c, 2d	Les Contamines	Les Chapieux	7:10	18.7	11.6	1347	4419	965	3166
3	3a, 3b	Les Chapieux	Rifugio Elisabetta	5:00	14.6	9.1	1037	3402	391	1283
4	4a, 4b, 4c	Rifugio Elisabetta	Courmayeur	5:20	16.2	10.1	495	1624	1480	4856
5	5a, 5b	Courmayeur	Rifugio Bonatti	5:00	13.2	8.2	1081	3547	266	873
6	6a, 6b, 6c, 6d, 6e	Rifugio Bonatti	La Fouly	6:40	21.2	13.2	858	2815	1288	4226
7	7	La Fouly	Champex	4:30	15.5	9.6	474	1555	607	1991
8	8a, 8b	Champex	Trient	5:20	16.1	10.0	803	2635	980	3215
9	9a, 9b, 9c	Trient	Tré-le-Champs	5:35	13.9	8.6	1119	3671	1002	3287
10	10a, 10b	Tré-le-Champs	Refuge de la Flégère	3:10	6.9	4.3	738	2421	278	912
11	11a, 11b	Refuge de la Flégère	Les Houches	6:55	18.0	11.2	826	2710	1686	5531

10 Days: the level of difficulty ramps up a little. Similar to the standard 11-day itinerary except that Sections 1-5 are restructured to allow them to be completed in four days of similar length and difficulty (rather than five days). The first day is quite long and can be a shock to the system for those who are not in shape at the start of the trek.

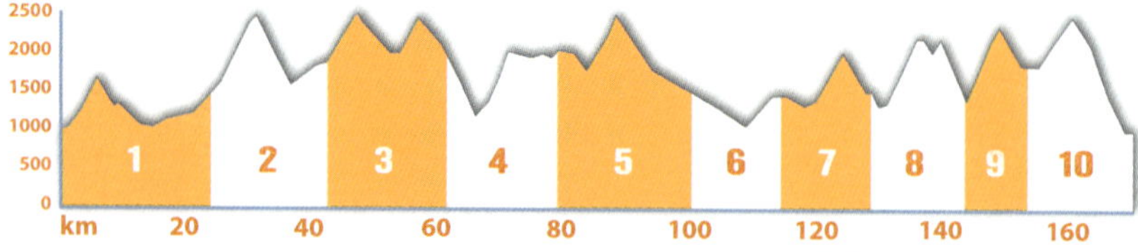

Day	Stages	Start	Finish	Time	Distance		Ascent		Descent	
				hr:m	km	miles	m	ft	m	ft
1	1a, 1b, 2a	Les Houches	Refuge Nant-Borrant	7:40	23.1	14.4	1313	4308	864	2835
2	2b, 2c, 2d, 3a	Refuge Nant-Borrant	Refuge des Mottets	7:15	19.6	12.2	1388	4554	977	3205
3	3b, 4a, 4b	Refuge des Mottets	Rifugio Maison Vieille	6:50	18.9	11.7	1161	3809	1075	3527
4	4c, 5a, 5b	Rifugio Maison Vieille	Rifugio Bonatti	6:30	18.6	11.6	1101	3612	1032	3386
5	6a, 6b, 6c, 6d, 6e	Rifugio Bonatti	La Fouly	6:40	21.2	13.2	858	2815	1288	4226
6	7	La Fouly	Champex	4:30	15.5	9.6	474	1555	607	1991
7	8a	Champex	Col de la Forclaz	4:50	14.6	9.1	790	2592	741	2431
8	8b, 9a, 9b, 9c	Col de la Forclaz	Tré-le-Champs	6:05	15.4	9.6	1132	3714	1241	4072
9	10a, 10b	Tré-le-Champs	Refuge de la Flégère	3:10	6.9	4.3	738	2421	278	912
10	11a, 11b	Refuge de la Flégère	Les Houches	6:55	18.0	11.2	826	2710	1686	5531

9 Days: similar to the 10-day itinerary except that Sections 8-10 are restructured to allow them to be completed in two days instead of three. Day seven is very tough.

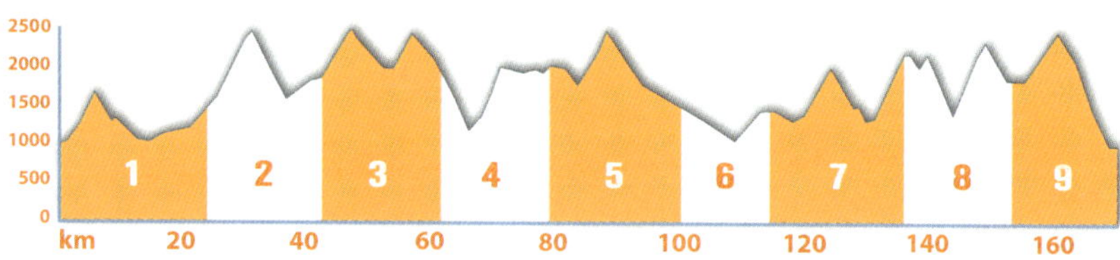

Day	Stages	Start	Finish	Time	Distance		Ascent		Descent	
				hr:m	km	miles	m	ft	m	ft
1	1a, 1b, 2a	Les Houches	Refuge Nant-Borrant	7:40	23.1	14.4	1313	4308	864	2835
2	2b, 2c, 2d, 3a	Refuge Nant-Borrant	Refuge des Mottets	7:15	19.6	12.2	1388	4554	977	3205
3	3b, 4a, 4b	Refuge des Mottets	Rifugio Maison Vieille	6:50	18.9	11.7	1161	3809	1075	3527
4	4c, 5a, 5b	Rifugio Maison Vieille	Rifugio Bonatti	6:30	18.6	11.6	1101	3612	1032	3386
5	6a, 6b, 6c, 6d, 6e	Rifugio Bonatti	La Fouly	6:40	21.2	13.2	858	2815	1288	4226
6	7	La Fouly	Champex	4:30	15.5	9.6	474	1555	607	1991
7	8a, 8b, 9a, 9b	Champex	Refuge du Col de Balme	8:10	21.9	13.6	1694	5558	980	3215
8	9c, 10a, 10b	Refuge du Col de Balme	Refuge de la Flégère	5:55	15.0	9.3	966	3169	1280	4199
9	11a, 11b	Refuge de la Flégère	Les Houches	6:55	18.0	11.2	826	2710	1686	5531

8 Days: for fit walkers used to trekking. Each of days 4, 5 and 6 are tough hikes and you will need to complete them back to back. The good news is that day 7 is comparatively easier.

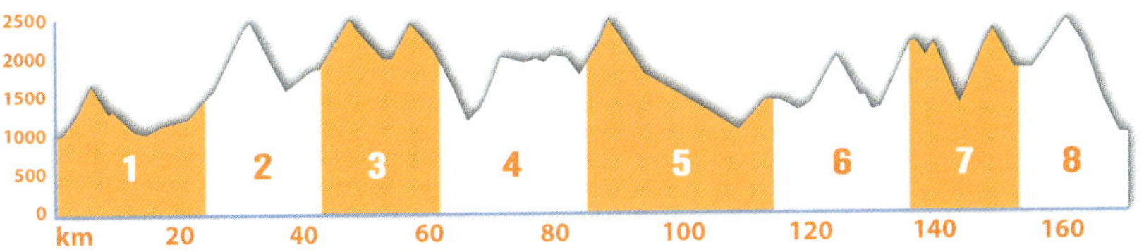

Day	Stages	Start	Finish	Time hr:m	Distance km	Distance miles	Ascent m	Ascent ft	Descent m	Descent ft
1	1a, 1b, 2a	Les Houches	Refuge Nant-Borrant	7:40	23.1	14.4	1313	4308	864	2835
2	2b, 2c, 2d, 3a	Refuge Nant-Borrant	Refuge des Mottets	7:15	19.6	12.2	1388	4554	977	3205
3	3b, 4a, 4b,	Refuge des Mottets	Rifugio Maison Vieille	6:50	18.9	11.7	1161	3809	1075	3527
4	4c, 5a, 5b, 6a, 6b	Rifugio Maison Vieille	Rifugio Elena	8:45	25.9	16.1	1454	4770	1355	4446
5	6c, 6d, 6e, 7	Rifugio Elena	Champex	8:55	29.4	18.3	979	3212	1572	5157
6	8a, 8b, 9a, 9b	Champex	Refuge du Col de Balme	8:10	21.9	13.6	1694	5558	980	3215
7	9c, 10a, 10b	Refuge du Col de Balme	Refuge de la Flégère	5:55	15.0	9.3	966	3169	1280	4199
8	11a, 11b	Refuge de la Flégère	Les Houches	6:55	18.0	11.2	826	2710	1686	5531

7 Days: these seven relentless and challenging days are for fit and experienced hikers. Each of the last four days is very long and hard.

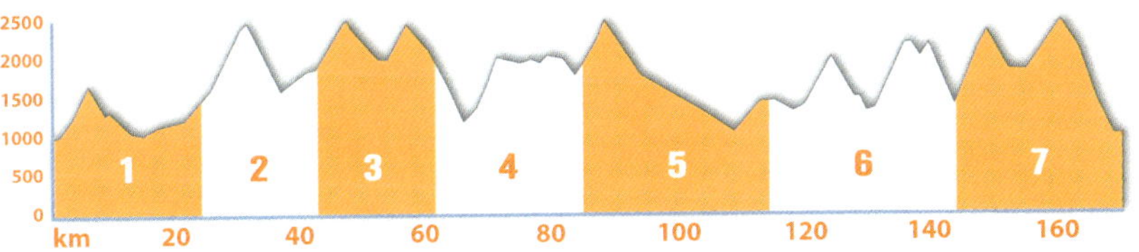

Day	Stages	Start	Finish	Time hr:m	Distance km	Distance miles	Ascent m	Ascent ft	Descent m	Descent ft
1	1a, 1b, 2a	Les Houches	Refuge Nant-Borrant	7:40	23.1	14.4	1313	4308	864	2835
2	2b, 2c, 2d, 3a	Refuge Nant-Borrant	Refuge des Mottets	7:15	19.6	12.2	1388	4554	977	3205
3	3b, 4a, 4b,	Refuge des Mottets	Rifugio Maison Vieille	6:50	18.9	11.7	1161	3809	1075	3527
4	4c, 5a, 5b, 6a, 6b	Rifugio Maison Vieille	Rifugio Elena	8:45	25.9	16.1	1454	4770	1355	4446
5	6c, 6d, 6e, 7	Rifugio Elena	Champex	8:55	29.4	18.3	979	3212	1572	5157
6	8a, 8b, 9a, 9b, 9c	Champex	Tré-le-Champs	10:55	30.0	18.6	1922	6306	1982	6503
7	10a, 10b, 11a, 11b	Tré-le-Champs	Les Houches	10:05	24.9	15.5	1564	5131	1964	6444

5 Days: a brutally hard itinerary for runners and trekkers who are fit and experienced and can cover very long distances day after day.

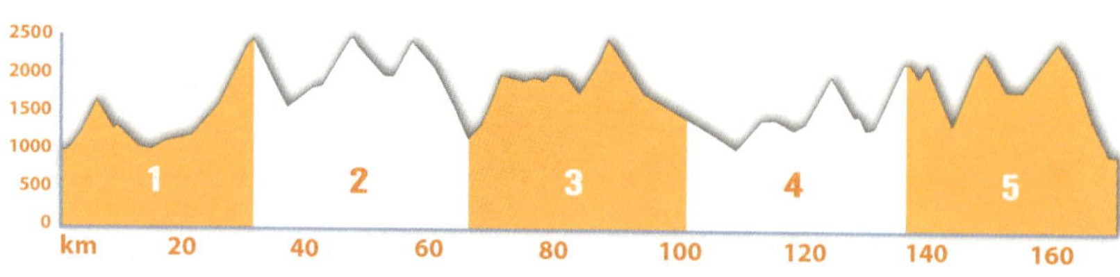

Day	Stages	Start	Finish	Time hr:m	Distance km	Distance miles	Ascent m	Ascent ft	Descent m	Descent ft
1	1a, 1b, 2a, 2b, 2c	Les Houches	Refuge de la Croix du Bonhomme	11:10	31.2	19.4	2350	7710	917	3009
2	2d, 3a, 3b, 4a, 4b, 4c	Refuge de la Croix du Bonhomme	Courmayeur	12:05	35.8	22.2	1532	5026	2765	9072
3	5a, 5b, 6a, 6b, 6c, 6d, 6e	Courmayeur	La Fouly	11:40	34.4	21.4	1939	6362	1554	5098
4	7, 8a, 8b, 9a, 9b	La Fouly	Refuge du Col de Balme	12:40	37.4	23.2	2168	7113	1587	5207
5	9c, 10a, 10b, 11a, 11b	Refuge du Col de Balme	Les Houches	12:50	33.0	20.5	1792	5879	2966	9731

Mont Blanc de Courmayeur & Aiguille Noire de Peuterey (Stage 4b)

Variant Stages: ACW

Stage	Start	Finish	Time	Distance		Ascent		Descent		Max Alt	
			hr:m	km	miles	m	ft	m	ft	m	ft
v1a	Les Houches	Refuge de Miage (via Col de Tricot)	5:30	14.3	8.9	1260	4134	711	2333	2120	6955
v1b	Refuge de Miage	Les Contamines	2:15	7.0	4.3	241	791	633	2077	1750	5741
v1c	Les Houches	Col de Voza (via le Prarion)	4:30	11.3	7.0	1003	3291	356	1168	1969	6460
v2a	Les Contamines	Refuge de Tré-la-Tête	2:40	5.6	3.5	817	2680	9	30	1969	6460
v2b	Refuge de Tré-la-Tête	Refuge de Nant-Borrant	0:45	2.7	1.7	29	95	538	1765	1969	6460
v3a	Refuge de la CB	Refuge des Mottets (via Col des Fours)	3:00	8.3	5.2	310	1017	889	2917	2665	8743
v4b	Cabane du Combal	Courmayeur (via Val Veny)	3:00	11.9	7.4	92	302	836	2743	1968	6457
v4c	Rifugio Maison Vieille	Courmayeur (via Rifugio Monte Bianco)	1:55	7.6	4.7	41	135	773	2536	1956	6417
v5a	Courmayeur	Chalet Val Ferret (via Italian Val Ferret)	4:25	13.8	8.6	591	1939	44	144	1771	5810
v5b	Rifugio Bertone	Rifugio Walter Bonatti (via Mont de la Saxe)	4:00	10.3	6.4	903	2963	869	2851	2584	8478
v8	Champex	Col de la Forclaz (via Fenêtre d'Arpette)	6:45	15.5	9.6	1208	3963	1149	3770	2665	8743
v9a	Col de la Forclaz	Col de Balme (via Refuge les Grands)	3:45	10.1	6.3	816	2677	151	495	2203	7228
v9b	Le Peuty	Col de Balme (via Croix de Fer)	3:30	6.6	4.1	1055	3461	190	623	2343	7687
v9c	Col de Balme	Tré-le-Champ (via le Tour)	1:40	6.5	4.0	52	171	826	2710	2191	7188
v10a	Tré-le-Champ	La Tête aux Vents (Ladder-free Route)	2:30	4.9	3.0	744	2441	28	92	2135	7004
v10b	La Tête aux Vents	Lac Blanc	0:50	1.6	1.0	230	755	11	36	2352	7717
v10c	Lac Blanc	Refuge de la Flégère	0:50	3.2	2.0	12	39	487	1598	2352	7717

Itinerary Planner: CW

All our CW itineraries start/finish in les Houches. However, if you would prefer to begin your trek at one of the other trail-heads (see p10), then simply start reading from that location in the tables below.

Stage	Start	Finish	Time hr:m	Distance km	Distance miles	Ascent m	Ascent ft	Descent m	Descent ft	Max Alt m	Max Alt ft
11b	Les Houches	Refuge Bellachat	4:00	7.9	4.9	1155	3789	36	118	2152	7060
11a	Refuge Bellachat	Refuge de la Flégère	3:30	10.1	6.3	531	1742	790	2592	2525	8284
10b	Refuge de la Flégère	La Tête aux Vents	1:20	3.5	2.2	278	912	22	72	2135	7004
10a	La Tête aux Vents	Tré-le-Champs	1:10	3.4	2.1	0	0	716	2349	2135	7004
9c	Tré-le-Champs	Refuge du Col de Balme	3:45	8.1	5.0	1002	3287	228	748	2191	7188
9b	Refuge du Col de Balme	Le Peuty	1:40	4.6	2.9	0	0	865	2838	2191	7188
9a	Le Peuty	Trient	0:20	1.2	0.7	0	0	26	85	1326	4350
8b	Trient	Col de la Forclaz	0:45	1.5	0.9	239	784	13	43	1526	5007
8a	Col de la Forclaz	Champex	4:45	14.6	9.1	741	2431	790	2592	2049	6722
7	Champex	La Fouly	5:00	15.5	9.6	607	1991	474	1555	1600	5249
6e	La Fouly	Ferret	0:50	2.8	1.7	100	328	0	0	1700	5577
6d	Ferret	Alpage de la Peule	1:50	4.6	2.9	401	1316	30	98	2071	6795
6c	Alpage de la Peule	Rifugio Elena	2:30	6.5	4.0	464	1522	475	1558	2536	8320
6b	Rifugio Elena	Chalet Val Ferret	0:35	2.2	1.4	0	0	293	961	2062	6765
6a	Chalet Val Ferret	Rifugio Bonatti	1:45	5.1	3.2	323	1060	60	197	2025	6644
5b	Rifugio Bonatti	Rifugio Bertone	2:25	7.9	4.9	266	873	300	984	2025	6644
5a	Rifugio Bertone	Courmayeur	1:30	5.3	3.3	0	0	781	2562	1991	6532
4c	Courmayeur	Rifugio Maison Vieille	2:45	5.4	3.4	766	2513	20	66	1956	6417
4b	Rifugio Maison Vieille	Combal	3:00	7.5	4.7	479	1572	460	1509	2430	7972
4a	Combal	Rifugio Elisabetta	1:10	3.3	2.1	235	771	15	49	2195	7201
3b	Rifugio Elisabetta	Refuge des Mottets	2:35	8.1	5.0	361	1184	686	2251	2516	8255
3a	Refuge des Mottets	Les Chapieux	1:25	6.5	4.0	30	98	351	1152	1870	6135
2d	Les Chapieux	Refuge de la CB	2:50	5.0	3.1	894	2933	0	0	2443	8015
2c	Refuge de la CB	Refuge de la Balme	1:30	5.6	3.5	53	174	790	2592	2479	8133
2b	Refuge de la Balme	Refuge de Nant-Borrant	0:35	2.5	1.6	0	0	247	810	1706	5597
2a	Refuge de Nant-Borrant	Les Contamines	1:25	5.6	3.5	18	59	310	1017	1459	4787
1b	Les Contamines	Refuge du Fioux	3:30	10.5	6.5	688	2257	350	1148	1505	4938
1a	Refuge du Fioux	Les Houches	2:00	7.0	4.3	158	518	653	2142	1653	5423

Suggested Itineraries: CW

12 Days: this is our most leisurely approach for those with plenty of time. The lengths of the days are quite evenly balanced. The itinerary splits up Section 11's brutal climb (which is too long and hard for many trekkers to complete in one day, especially on the first day of the trek). It is useful for those arriving in les Houches in the middle of the morning: because Refuge Bellachat is only about 4hrs away, you should be able to reach it that same day.

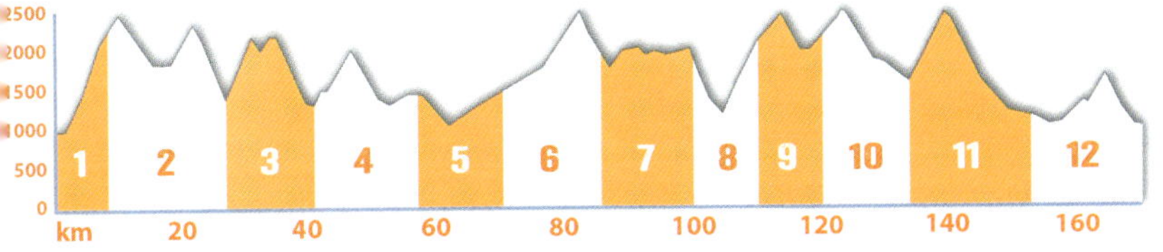

Day	Stages	Start	Finish	Time hr:m	Distance km	miles	Ascent m	ft	Descent m	ft
1	11b	Les Houches	Refuge de Bellachat	4:00	7.9	5.3	1155	3789	36	118
2	11a, 10b, 10a	Refuge de Bellachat	Tré-le-Champs	6:00	17.0	10.8	809	2654	1528	5013
3	9c, 9b, 9a	Tré-le-Champs	Trient	5:45	13.9	8.6	1002	3287	1119	3671
4	8b, 8a	Trient	Champex	5:30	16.1	10.0	980	3215	803	2635
5	7	Champex	La Fouly	5:00	15.5	9.6	607	1991	474	1555
6	6e, 6d, 6c	La Fouly	Rifugio Elena	5:10	13.9	8.6	965	3166	505	1657
7	6b, 6a, 5b	Rifugio Elena	Rifugio Bertone	4:45	15.2	9.4	589	1932	653	2142
8	5a, 4c	Rifugio Bertone	Rifugio Maison Vieille	4:15	10.7	6.6	766	2513	801	2628
9	4b, 4a	Rifugio Maison Vieille	Rifugio Elisabetta	4:10	10.8	6.7	714	2343	475	1558
10	3b, 3a	Rifugio Elisabetta	Les Chapieux	4:00	14.6	9.1	391	1283	1037	3402
11	2d, 2c, 2b, 2a	Les Chapieux	Les Contamines	6:20	18.7	11.6	965	3166	1347	4419
12	1b, 1a	Les Contamines	Les Houches	5:30	17.5	10.9	846	2776	1003	3291

Viewpoint near Col du Brévent (Stage 11a)

11 Days: our standard schedule is well balanced, successfully alternating harder and easier days. It is a tried and tested approach which will suit many trekkers. However, it may be too slow for fitter or more experienced trekkers. It splits up Section 11's brutal climb (which is too long and hard for many trekkers to complete in one day, especially on the first day of the trek). Section 6 is pretty tough in this direction.

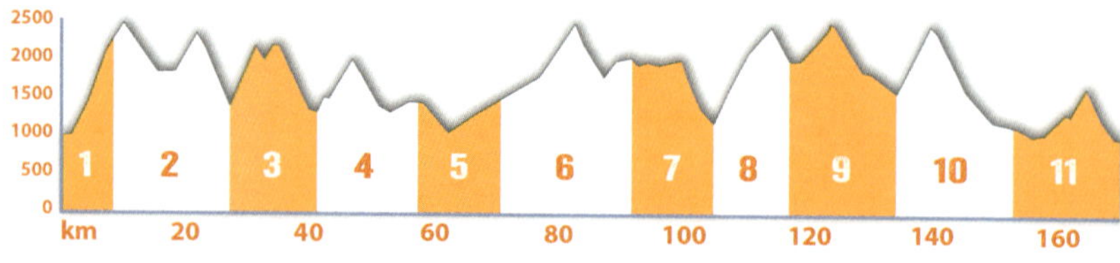

Day	Stages	Start	Finish	Time	Distance		Ascent		Descent	
				hr:m	km	miles	m	ft	m	ft
1	11b	Les Houches	Refuge de Bellachat	4:00	7.9	5.3	1155	3789	36	118
2	11a, 10b, 10a	Refuge de Bellachat	Tré-le-Champs	6:00	17.0	10.8	809	2654	1528	5013
3	9c, 9b, 9a	Tré-le-Champs	Trient	5:45	13.9	8.6	1002	3287	1119	3671
4	8b, 8a	Trient	Champex	5:30	16.1	10.0	980	3215	803	2635
5	7	Champex	La Fouly	5:00	15.5	9.6	607	1991	474	1555
6	6e, 6d, 6c, 6b, 6a	La Fouly	Rifugio Walter Bonatti	7:30	21.2	13.2	1288	4226	858	2815
7	5b, 5a	Rifugio Walter Bonatti	Courmayeur	3:55	13.2	8.2	266	873	1081	3547
8	4c, 4b	Courmayeur	Combal	5:45	12.9	8.0	1245	4085	480	1575
9	4a, 3b, 3a	Combal	Les Chapieux	5:10	17.9	11.1	626	2054	1052	3451
10	2d, 2c, 2b, 2a	Les Chapieux	Les Contamines	6:20	18.7	11.6	965	3166	1347	4419
11	1b, 1a	Les Contamines	Les Houches	5:30	17.5	10.9	846	2776	1003	3291

10 Days: the level of difficulty ramps up a little. Similar to the standard 11-day itinerary except that Sections 7 to 3 are restructured to allow them to be completed in four days rather than five. Days 5, 6 and 7 are long and hard.

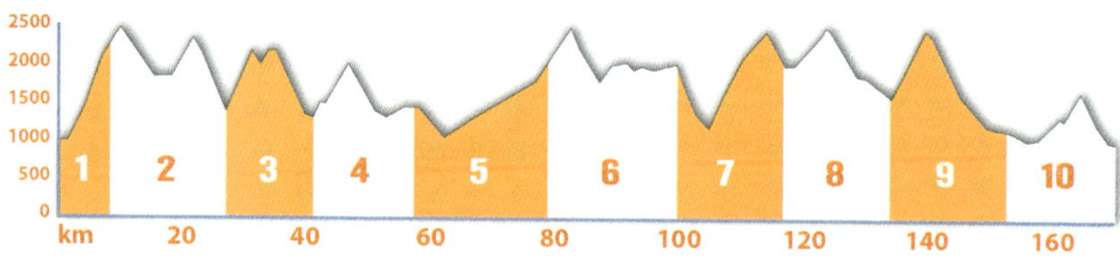

Day	Stages	Start	Finish	Time	Distance		Ascent		Descent	
				hr:m	km	miles	m	ft	m	ft
1	11b	Les Houches	Refuge de Bellachat	4:00	7.9	5.3	1155	3789	36	118
2	11a, 10b, 10a	Refuge de Bellachat	Tré-le-Champs	6:00	17.0	10.8	809	2654	1528	5013
3	9c, 9b, 9a	Tré-le-Champs	Trient	5:45	13.9	8.6	1002	3287	1119	3671
4	8b, 8a	Trient	Champex	5:30	16.1	10.0	980	3215	803	2635
5	7, 6e, 6d	Champex	Alpage de la Peule	7:40	22.9	14.2	1108	3635	504	1654
6	6c, 6b, 6a, 5b	Alpage de la Peule	Rifugio Bertone	7:15	21.7	13.5	1053	3455	1128	3701
7	5a, 4c, 4b	Rifugio Bertone	Combal	7:15	18.2	11.3	1245	4085	1261	4137
8	4a, 3b, 3a	Combal	Les Chapieux	5:10	17.9	11.1	626	2054	1052	3451
9	2d, 2c, 2b, 2a	Les Chapieux	Les Contamines	6:20	18.7	11.6	965	3166	1347	4419
10	1b, 1a	Les Contamines	Les Houches	5:30	17.5	10.9	846	2776	1003	3291

9 Days: similar to the 10-day itinerary except that Sections 11 to 8 are restructured to allow them to be completed in three days instead of four. You tackle Section 11's brutal climb all on the same day. Days 1, 3, 4, 5 and 6 are long and hard.

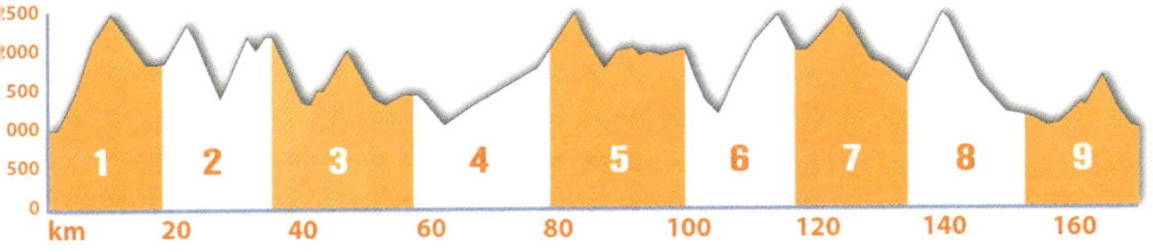

Day	Stages	Start	Finish	Time hr:m	Distance km	Distance miles	Ascent m	Ascent ft	Descent m	Descent ft
1	11b, 11a	Les Houches	Refuge de la Flégère	7:30	18.0	11.8	1686	5531	826	2710
2	10b, 10a, 9c	Refuge de la Flégère	Refuge du Col de Balme	6:15	15.0	9.3	1280	4199	966	3169
3	9b, 9a, 8b, 8a	Refuge du Col de Balme	Champex	7:30	21.9	13.6	980	3215	1694	5558
4	7, 6e, 6d	Champex	Alpage de la Peule	7:40	22.9	14.2	1108	3635	504	1654
5	6c, 6b, 6a, 5b	Alpage de la Peule	Rifugio Bertone	7:15	21.7	13.5	1053	3455	1128	3701
6	5a, 4c, 4b	Rifugio Bertone	Combal	7:15	18.2	11.3	1245	4085	1261	4137
7	4a, 3b, 3a	Combal	Les Chapieux	5:10	17.9	11.1	626	2054	1052	3451
8	2d, 2c, 2b, 2a	Les Chapieux	Les Contamines	6:20	18.7	11.6	965	3166	1347	4419
9	1b, 1a	Les Contamines	Les Houches	5:30	17.5	10.9	846	2776	1003	3291

8 Days: for fit walkers used to trekking. The first day is very hard because you tackle Section 11's brutal climb all on the same day. Comparatively, the second day is easier but after that, every day is long and challenging.

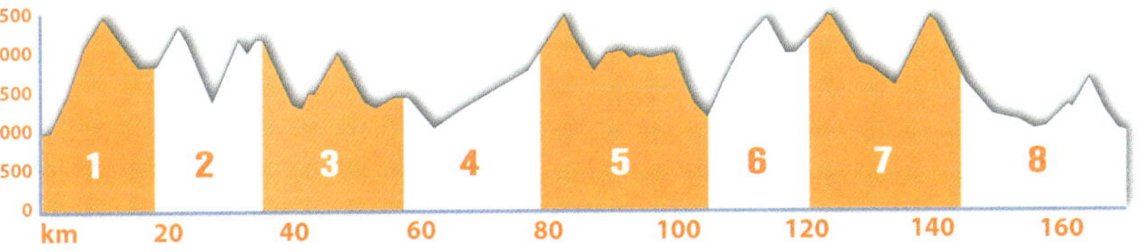

Day	Stages	Start	Finish	Time hr:m	Distance km	Distance miles	Ascent m	Ascent ft	Descent m	Descent ft
1	11b, 11a	Les Houches	Refuge de la Flégère	7:30	18.0	11.8	1686	5531	826	2710
2	10b, 10a, 9c	Refuge de la Flégère	Refuge du Col de Balme	6:15	15.0	9.3	1280	4199	966	3169
3	9b, 9a, 8b, 8a	Refuge du Col de Balme	Champex	7:30	21.9	13.6	980	3215	1694	5558
4	7, 6e, 6d	Champex	Alpage de la Peule	7:40	22.9	14.2	1108	3635	504	1654
5	6c, 6b, 6a, 5b, 5a	Alpage de la Peule	Courmayeur	8:45	27.0	16.8	1053	3455	1909	6263
6	4c, 4b, 4a	Courmayeur	Rifugio Elisabetta	6:55	16.2	10.1	1480	4856	495	1624
7	3b, 3a, 2d, 2c	Rifugio Elisabetta	Refuge de la Balme	8:20	25.2	15.7	1338	4390	1827	5994
8	2b, 2a, 1b, 1a	Refuge de la Balme	Les Houches	7:30	25.6	15.9	864	2835	1560	5118

7 Days: these seven relentless and challenging days are for fit and experienced hikers. The itinerary starts hard and does not relent until the end.

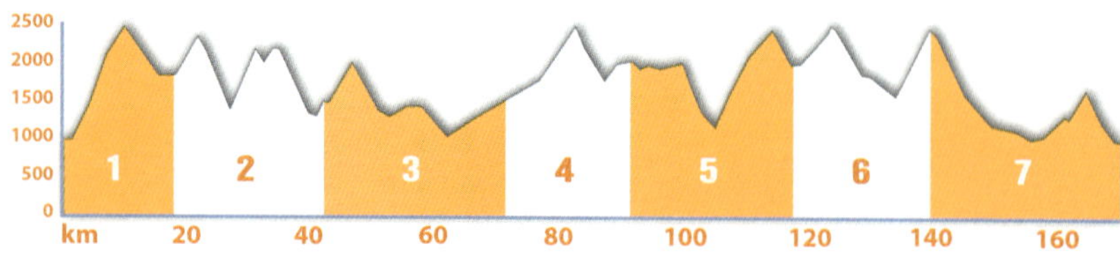

Day	Stages	Start	Finish	Time	Distance		Ascent		Descent	
				hr:m	km	miles	m	ft	m	ft
1	11b, 11a	Les Houches	Refuge de la Flégère	7:30	18.0	11.8	1686	5531	826	2710
2	10b, 10a, 9c, 9b, 9a, 8b	Refuge de la Flégère	Col de la Forclaz	9:00	22.3	13.9	1519	4984	1870	6135
3	8a, 7	Col de la Forclaz	La Fouly	9:45	30.1	18.7	1348	4423	1264	4147
4	6e, 6d, 6c, 6b, 6a	La Fouly	Rifugio Bonatti	7:30	21.2	13.2	1288	4226	858	2815
5	5b, 5a 4c, 4b	Rifugio Bonatti	Combal	9:40	26.1	16.2	1511	4957	1561	5121
6	4a, 3b, 3a, 2d	Combal	Refuge de la Croix du Bonhomme	8:00	22.9	14.2	1520	4987	1052	3451
7	2c, 2b, 2a, 1b, 1a	Refuge de la Croix du Bonhomme	Les Houches	9:00	31.2	19.4	917	3009	2350	7710

5 Days: a brutally hard itinerary for runners and trekkers who are fit and experienced and can cover very long distances day after day.

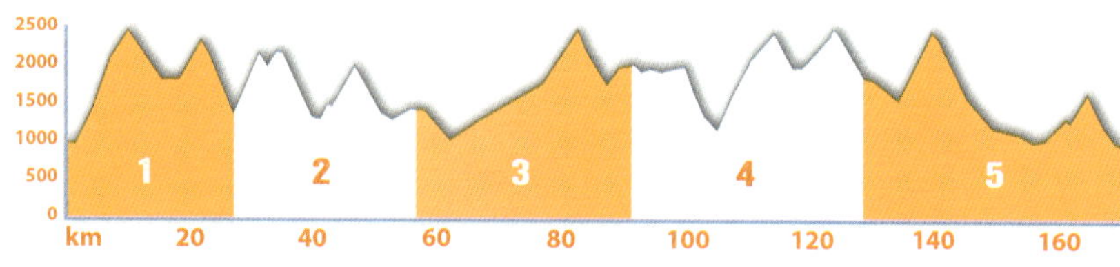

Day	Stages	Start	Finish	Time	Distance		Ascent		Descent	
				hr:m	km	miles	m	ft	m	ft
1	11b, 11a, 10b, 10a	Les Houches	Tré-le-Champs	10:00	24.9	16.1	1964	6444	1564	5131
2	9c, 9b, 9a, 8b, 8a	Tré-le-Champs	Champex	11:15	30.0	18.6	1982	6503	1922	6306
3	7, 6e, 6d, 6c, 6b, 6a	Champex	Rifugio Bonatti	12:30	36.7	22.8	1895	6217	1332	4370
4	5b, 5a, 4c, 4b, 4a, 3b	Rifugio Bonatti	Refuge des Mottets	13:25	37.5	23.3	2107	6913	2262	7421
5	3a, 2d, 2c, 2b, 2a, 1b, 1a	Refuge des Mottets	Les Houches	13:15	42.7	26.5	1841	6040	2701	8862

Pastures near Col de Voza (Stage 1a)

Variant Stages: CW

Stage	Start	Finish	Time hr:m	Distance km	Distance miles	Ascent m	Ascent ft	Descent m	Descent ft	Max Alt m	Max Alt ft
v10c	Refuge de la Flégère	Lac Blanc	1:40	3.2	2.0	487	1598	12	39	2352	7717
v10b	Lac Blanc	La Tête aux Vents	0:30	1.6	1.0	11	36	230	755	2352	7717
v10a	La Tête aux Vents	Tré-le-Champ (Ladder-free Route)	1:30	4.9	3.0	28	92	744	2441	2135	7004
v9c	Tré-le-Champ	Col de Balme (via le Tour)	3:00	6.5	4.0	826	2710	52	171	2191	7188
v9b	Col de Balme	Le Peuty (via Croix de Fer)	2:30	6.6	4.1	190	623	1055	3461	2343	7687
v9a	Col de Balme	Col de la Forclaz (via Refuge les Grands)	3:00	10.1	6.3	151	495	816	2677	2203	7228
v8	Col de la Forclaz	Champex (via Fenêtre d'Arpette)	6:40	15.5	9.6	1149	3770	1208	3963	2665	8743
v5b	Rifugio Walter Bonatti	Rifugio Bertone (via Mont de la Saxe)	4:00	10.3	6.4	869	2851	903	2963	2584	8478
v5a	Chalet Val Ferret	Courmayeur (via Italian Val Ferret)	3:20	13.8	8.6	44	144	591	1939	1771	5810
v4c	Courmayeur	Rifugio Maison Vieille (via Rifugio Monte Bianco)	3:15	7.6	4.7	773	2536	41	135	1956	6417
v4b	Courmayeur	Cabane du Combal (via Val Veny)	4:15	11.9	7.4	836	2743	92	302	1968	6457
v3a	Refuge des Mottets	Refuge de la CB (via Col des Fours)	3:45	8.3	5.2	889	2917	310	1017	2665	8743
v2b	Refuge de Nant-Borrant	Refuge de Tré-la-Tête	1:30	2.7	1.7	538	1765	29	95	1969	6460
v2a	Refuge de Tré-la-Tête	Les Contamines	1:25	5.6	3.5	9	30	817	2680	1969	6460
v1c	Col de Voza	Les Houches (via le Prarion)	3:30	11.3	7.0	356	1168	1003	3291	1969	6460
v1b	Les Contamines	Refuge de Miage	2:45	7.0	4.3	633	2077	241	791	1750	5741
v1a	Refuge de Miage	Les Houches (via Col de Tricot)	4:15	14.3	8.9	711	2333	1260	4134	2120	6955

Accommodation

Rifugio Bonatti (Stage 5b/6a)

The TMB is one of the most aspirational treks in the world and demand for accommodation is fierce. Furthermore, because the trek gets more popular each year, finding availability is becoming progressively more difficult and prices are rising. It is no surprise therefore that most people have their entire trip booked before they depart. In July/August, forward booking is essential: practically every bed along the trail is full every night. June and September used to be shoulder seasons when the TMB was much less busy but nowadays, they are only slightly less busy than July/August and advance booking is usually required (particularly at weekends and on stages where there is only one place to stay): occasionally, you may be able to cobble together last minute bookings for June/September (especially if you are travelling alone) but do not bet on it.

Traditionally, much of the accommodation outside of the larger towns was closed before mid-June and from late-September onwards. There was good reason for this: sometime around the middle of June, the winter snow usually clears sufficiently to allow for safe trekking; and after the third week in September, nights get pretty cold and snowfall at altitude becomes more likely. However, in recent years, many accommodation providers have responded to the increase in demand by opening a week or two earlier in the season and/or closing a week or two later: as a result, the TMB hiking season has expanded slightly. Nevertheless, you should exercise caution when arranging a TMB trek at the very fringes of the season: just because a gîte/hotel is selling beds does not mean that the trail is safe to hike. Although the weather in late September and October is often divine, it is less reliable and you are more likely to be turned back by snow on high passes. Furthermore, if you book your trek for June, you will probably not know until a few weeks (or even days) before your trek starts whether the trail is safe: this makes for a stressful run-up to what should be a relaxing experience.

Also, be aware that the Ultra Trail du Mont Blanc (UTMB), a long-distance trail-running race, takes place each year at the end of August/start of September: although it does not prevent you from hiking the trails (which are only slightly busier), accommodation around Chamonix can be scarce during the race.

Detailed accommodation listings are provided on p35. All accommodation is numbered and marked on the maps in this book. All contact details were correct at the date of press but this information frequently changes: please let us know about any changes you notice.

Accommodation types

One positive outcome of the TMB's increasing popularity is that the quality of accommodation has improved greatly over recent years: many huts, gîtes and hotels have been substantially refurbished and modernised. You will not find much five-star luxury but most places are comfortable.

Hotels: the majority of hotels are in the one to three star categories and quality varies. There are, however, some more luxurious options available in the larger villages/towns (such as Courmayeur, Champex and Chamonix). Most hotels offer 'half-board' (bed, breakfast and dinner) which can be good value. Most hotels have their own websites.

Chambres d'hôte/B&Bs: simple bed and breakfast accommodation. Normally, you will have a private room with an ensuite bathroom.

Gîtes d'étape: traditionally, a gîte would have been comparable to a youth hostel, offering beds in dormitories and evening meals. These days, gîtes are often more upmarket: private rooms are often available and they can be better than some hotels. Most gîtes have their own websites.

Refuge/Rifugio: these are mountain huts which offer dormitory accommodation, meals and drinks (including alcohol). Sometimes, it is also possible to book a private room. The huts are situated in the heart of the mountains where they are often accessible only to hikers: the settings are spectacular. A stay in a hut can be one of the highlights of a mountain adventure such as the TMB. Although prices have risen in recent years, the huts are still good value: see p52.

Dormitories are mixed-sex. Mattresses, pillows and duvets/blankets are provided but you will need your own sleeping sheet: this is a thin bag made of silk/cotton which can be purchased cheaply at most outdoor shops; in French, it is called a 'drap de couchage' or 'sac à viande'. Most of the huts on the TMB now offer showers free of charge. There are usually facilities for charging electronic devices but you may have to wait in line. Some huts have a winter room ('salle d'hiver') where you can stay in the off-season (when the hut is closed): winter room facilities vary but usually they will have blankets and a wood-burning stove for heat; you will have to bring your own food and sometimes cooking equipment.

The opening/closing dates for each hut are different and change from year to year: they are usually set out on the huts' websites. Usually, huts open sometime in June and close sometime in September/October. Most huts have English speaking staff these days. Huts which are affiliated to Club Alpin Français or Club Alpino Italiano offer a discount to members of other international alpine clubs: see also p52.

Mountain hut etiquette

- On arrival, check in at reception.
- Take off your boots and wet clothing at the front door and store them in the places provided near the entrance.
- Do not make noise after 10pm as most hikers go to bed early.
- If you change your plans, cancel your reservation as soon as possible to allow someone else to take your place.

How to book accommodation

The TMB threads its way through high mountain terrain, linking mountain huts, hamlets and villages which are often difficult to access by vehicle. To undertake the TMB, hutters need to arrange a chain of consecutive bookings covering their entire itinerary. Although it is perfectly possible to make accommodation bookings yourself, it requires timely planning, perseverance and a certain amount of luck: if you cannot secure a booking at any one location, then this could render your itinerary impractical or impossible and you may need to cancel bookings already made and start again from scratch (changing dates or adjusting your schedule). Some people enjoy the process of booking treks but others find it stressful. Plenty of people are successful but others fail because the reservations required have already been snapped up by others. If you do not have sufficient time and energy to give to the booking process, or you want to maximise your chances, then it may be better to use a trekking company (if you can afford it).

Most TMB accommodation is privately owned and each property manages its own bookings. Some properties have their own booking portals on their websites but others can only be booked by email/phone. However, a great many of the properties use the booking portal at **www.montourdumontblanc.com** where you can book a series of locations in one go: in the Accommodation Listings (p35), we highlight (in bold) properties which currently list on this website. Bear in mind though that you cannot modify bookings on this website: to cancel, change dates or request refunds, you need to contact each property individually. Furthermore, not all properties use montourdumontblanc.com and many key places (such as Rifugio Bonatti) still need to be booked independently.

These days, the TMB booking process for a particular season begins around the time the previous season finishes (end of September), although larger hotels may take bookings before that. The process is complicated by the fact that each property opens for bookings on different dates and many do not make the dates public: small family-run properties often open for booking with no prior notice. If you miss the opening date for a hut/gîte even by a few weeks/days, the dates you need could be sold out. This means that it pays to check websites regularly (including montourdumontblanc.com) and/or contact many properties individually by email. The most sought-after huts can sell almost every bed for the entire summer in a matter of days and you will be competing with trekking companies and a large number of other individuals (many of whom will be checking the websites daily). However, not every single bed in every single property for every single date sells out that quickly.

Hot spots

Competition is especially fierce for properties which are exceptionally beautiful or where there is only one or two places to stay. Notorious hot-spots include Refuge de Miage (v1a/v1b), Rifugio Bonatti (5b/6a), Alpage de la Peule (6c/6d), Col de la Forclaz (8a/8b), Tré-le-Champs (9c/10a), Refuge du Lac Blanc (v10b/v10c) and Refuge Bellachat (11a/11b). However, the most difficult part of the TMB to book is the entire section between les Chapieux and Courmayeur (Sections 3 & 4) where the terrain is remote and there are not enough beds: always try to book this part of the TMB first.

Increasing your chances of success

If you do wish to try to book the TMB yourself then the following steps will help you maximise your chances. The timings recommended below may change because the TMB becomes more popular each year.

- Plan your itinerary before booking opens: the TMB is a complicated trek to book and last-minute planners are less likely to be successful. Finish your research by the end of August in the year prior to your trek: finalise your proposed itinerary and become familiar with the different accommodation options along the route so that you can make itinerary adjustments quickly if any accommodation you require is unavailable. Reading this book, cover to cover, will help enormously.
- Familiarise yourself with booking processes: at the start of September, look at the websites of the properties you wish to book and montourdumontblanc.com. Diarise any booking opening dates listed on the websites. Take a note of the booking method required for each property. A spreadsheet is your friend! You will then be ready to pounce when bookings open.
- Email accommodation: at the start of September, email properties that do not use montourdumontblanc.com, requesting the bookings that you need. If you are lucky, they may confirm the booking or they may simply tell you when bookings will open and what you will need to do; others may not bother to reply at this stage. At the very least, there is a chance that early emails will sit at the top of the queue when they eventually start to process bookings. Although many accommodation providers speak English, it is a good idea to email in French (French/Swiss properties) or Italian (Italian properties): if you do not speak the relevant language, use Google Translate or similar.
- Check websites regularly: from early September onwards, frequently check montourdumontblanc.com and the websites of the other accommodation you need. Some properties start taking bookings without any prior notice. Even if booking opening dates have been previously advertised, they sometimes open earlier without notice. By checking regularly, you increase your chances of being one of the first to know that bookings have opened. Some people check websites daily.

- Pounce: when a property opens for booking on its website or montourdumontblanc.com, grab your dates immediately. You may need to pay the full price of the booking or at least a deposit (see p67). For properties that are booked by email, send another booking request as soon as booking opens (even if you sent emails previously).
- Keep following up: if you do not get a timely response from a property, do not be afraid to send chasing emails from time to time. However, try not to pester them too much.
- Be ready to adapt: unless you are very lucky, you may need to make a few changes to your itinerary before you have a full set of confirmed bookings. If you have researched the trek well, you will be better placed to make rapid adjustments to your itinerary in the event that any property you want is unavailable on your required date: to avoid having to change already successful bookings, if possible, try to book a different property around the same location as the unavailable property. If there is no other available property at the relevant location, try to adjust your itinerary slightly in a way that makes as few changes to confirmed bookings as possible: there is no guarantee that requests for changes to confirmed bookings will be successful. Although it is not optimal, you may need to change the lengths of some of your days, walking a little further than you would like some days and maybe stopping earlier than you would like on others. However, be careful not to bite off more than you can chew: attempting a hike that is well beyond your capabilities can end your trek (or worse). If you do need to change confirmed bookings, the quicker you make the request the better your chance of success. You cannot request changes on montourdumontblanc.com: you will need to email properties individually.
- Have a contingency plan (if possible): even the most persistent and 'sharp-elbowed' people can find themselves at a dead end. If you are beaten, act quickly to implement any contingency plan. For many people, this means contacting a trekking company to book an unguided trek: the quicker you do this, the more likely it is that the company will be able to find accommodation for you. It is a good idea to research trekking companies before bookings open so that you know exactly which one you will go to if you are unable to book the accommodation yourself.

Other booking tips

- If possible, try to book 'hot-spots' first (p30): once you have secured the accommodation which books up most quickly, you can normally slot in the rest more easily. If you leave hot-spots until last then you might have to unwind and rebook other reservations if any hot-spots that you desire are unavailable. It is particularly important to get accommodation on Sections 3 and 4 booked as quickly as possible.
- Start mid-week. A large number of trekkers start the trail at the weekend. Those who start mid-week are often 'out of sync' with the bulk of the other trekkers and may therefore find accommodation more easily.
- Weekends are often busier: if you can, plan your schedule to avoid hot-spots at weekends.
- Those who hike alone, or in pairs, find it easiest to find beds. For larger groups, it is more difficult.
- Some trekking companies block-book accommodation in advance: even if you cannot get bookings, they might have spaces.
- Occasionally, the last-minute booker can get lucky: people sometimes cancel at the last minute and trekking companies may release unsold beds a few weeks or months before the relevant dates. If you phone huts a few weeks before your trip, you may be lucky enough to bag some beds which have just been released.
- Towards the end of September, the trail is slightly less busy and recently, we have been able to find available beds at some properties at the last minute. At both Rifugio Maison Vieille and Rifugio Bonatti, for example, we called ahead and were told that there was no availability: however, when we turned up a few hours later, beds were available. Although difficult to explain, this clearly does happen. However, you would not be able to take the chance unless you were also carrying a tent just in case.

Camping

Camping near Lacs des Chéserys (Stage v10b)

The number of people trekking the TMB with a tent has surged in recent years and camping has a number of advantages. Firstly, it is significantly less expensive than staying in huts/gîtes/hotels: official campsites are cheap (see p52) and there are some wild camping sites which cost nothing; furthermore, campers tend to cook many of their own meals which saves a lot of money. Secondly, campsites do not usually need to be booked far in advance and often you cannot do so anyway: this means that campers do not need to run the gauntlet of the TMB's arduous accommodation booking process; furthermore, it gives campers the flexibility to change plans at the last minute to respond to factors such as bad weather and fatigue. However, the real joy of camping the TMB is the sense of adventure and freedom that it provides: campers are under no pressure to be anywhere or do anything at any particular time whereas hutters have fixed times for breakfast, dinner and checking in/out each day.

However, there are downsides to camping too. Most significantly, it makes the trek harder: campers need to carry much more gear: tent, sleeping bag, sleeping mat, cooker, food, etc; that extra weight makes a big difference to your legs over 172km (especially with so much daily climbing). Furthermore, official camping locations are fewer, and less evenly spaced, than the other accommodation options so days can be longer (unless you are prepared to spend the odd night in a refuge/gîte, head OR to find a campsite or wild camp).

Along much of the trail, it is not difficult to find somewhere to camp legally: there are campsites in all of the towns and villages along the route (except Courmayeur); and away from the villages, there are some authorised sites for overnight wild camping (known as 'bivouac' in France/Switzerland). However, there is one long section of the trail where there are no campsites or authorised bivouac sites along the main route: les Chapieux to la Fouly (Sections 3, 4, 5 & 6). Fortunately, there are a few solutions to this dilemma: there are campsites a short distance away in both Val Veny (Stage v4b) and Italian Val Ferret (Stage v5a); alternatively, you can bivouac above 2500m which is legal in Italy (p33), although it can be a hair-raising experience in bad weather; or you can try your luck at Rifugio Maison Vieille and/or Gîte Alpage de la Peule which sometimes allow camping. A list of current camping locations is set out on p41: bear in mind that some of the bivouac sites are tolerated but not officially authorised (which means that they are not technically legal); you pitch up there at your own risk.

Campsites are normally clean and well maintained with good facilities. Bivouac sites are simply basic grassy zones amongst the mountains which have been allocated for trekkers to wild camp in for a single night: usually there are no facilities, although a few have basic toilets.

Wild camping rules

Along the TMB, the rules on overnight wild camping (bivouac) are complicated. The trek enters three countries and different provisions apply in each: we set out below our understanding of the current rules in each country.

However, a few common principles apply in all three countries: firstly, emergency bivouac (where you have no choice due to injury, exhaustion, etc.) is usually tolerated and is unlikely to be penalised. Secondly, bivouac on private land is never permitted without landowner consent: accordingly, if you wish to camp near ski slopes, huts or 'alpages' (pastures used for grazing), then you should first ask for permission; that said, much of the land above the tree-line in France, Italy and Switzerland is communal land (not privately owned).

Rules/laws are subject to change so it is your responsibility to check them in advance. If you get caught breaking the rules, you may face a stiff fine: you bivouac at your own risk. Wherever you pitch up, leave no trace and follow the guidelines on p34.

France: around the Chamonix valley, local laws provide that bivouac is generally prohibited. However, outside of protected reserves, overnight bivouac (from 7pm to 9am) is permitted with the consent of the land-owner: above 1700m, that consent is deemed to have been given automatically (so you do not need to ask). Itinerant TMB trekkers are unlikely to be able to ask for prior consent so in practice, the rules mean that, in places that are outside protected reserves, you can only bivouac legally above 1700m.

Within the protected reserves of the Chamonix valley, different rules apply: for trekkers, bivouac is generally prohibited at any altitude. However, in the Réserve Naturelle des Aiguilles Rouges (which the TMB passes through on Sections 10/11), overnight bivouac (7pm to 9am) is permitted in certain specified areas including the following places close to the TMB:

- **Lacs des Chéserys:** Stage v10b; near la Tête aux Vents/Lac Blanc.
- **Lac du Brévent:** just N of Refuge Bellachat (Stage 11a).
- **Col de Bellachat:** just W of Refuge Bellachat (Stage 11a/11b).

You must book these bivouac sites in advance at **www.bivouac.nature-haute-savoie.fr** and numbers are limited: the website's map makes clear exactly where bivouac is permitted.

Different rules apply in Val Montjoie. Between Col de Voza and les Contamines (Sections 1/v1), bivouac is only permitted at the authorised sites at Refuge de Miage and Auberge du Truc. Furthermore, bivouac is not permitted in Réserve Naturelle des Contamines-Montjoie (Section 2) except at the authorised bivouac sites at la Rollaz and Refuge de la Balme (which must be booked in advance at **www.bivouac.nature-haute-savoie.fr**).

Italy: in the parts of Italy crossed by the TMB, camping is permitted above 2,500m from sunset to sunrise. This rule exists to facilitate climbers and mountaineers who often sleep out on long routes. If you bivouac discreetly above 2500m and leave no trace, then you are unlikely to have any issues.

Switzerland: Article 699 of the Swiss Civil Code contains a general access right: communal forests, pastures and meadows are generally accessible by everyone. The code does not prohibit wild camping, however, it does state that this general access right is subject to any specific restrictions imposed by a competent authority in the interests of conservation: accordingly, local authorities in the relevant canton/municipality can override Article 699. Putting it simply, the general rule is that wild camping is permitted unless it has been expressly prohibited/limited by another more specific law which has been implemented locally.

In the parts of Switzerland crossed by the TMB, specific laws have indeed been enacted which limit the general access right: wild camping is expressly prohibited in certain protected areas including hunting ban reserves, designated wildlife protection areas and nature reserves. This means that you are not permitted to wild camp in any parts of the TMB which lie within these types of areas. You can see the extent of these areas on a map at **www.map.geo.admin.ch**, however, the web page is difficult to use: you must select from various data sets so that the map displays only the information that you need. Fortunately, the Swiss Alpine Club has done the hard work for you and displays the map (with the correct filters applied) on its own website: **www.sac-cas.ch/de/umwelt/bergsport-und-umwelt/campieren-und-biwakieren**. The map shows that the reserves/protection areas along the TMB where wild camping is not permitted include the following:

- **Stages 6d, 6e & 7:** all land E of the river in Swiss Val Ferret between Ars Dessous and Issert.
- **Stages 9a/v9b:** the slopes W of le Peuty and Trient.

If you are intending to wild camp in Switzerland, you should check this map carefully to make sure that you will not be camping in a prohibited area.

Even outside of the prohibited areas, the situation is complicated. As usual, you are not permitted to bivouac on private land without permission: however, because it is difficult to determine exactly which land is private and which is communal, it is hard to be sure exactly when consent is required; furthermore, it is impractical for itinerant TMB trekkers to seek permission. To be safe, you should not bivouac near villages, huts, ski-slopes and lower level pastures (where it is more likely than not that you will be breaking the rules). However, away from these areas, bivouac at higher altitude (above the tree-line) is rarely a problem as long as you are discreet, pitching up after 7pm and breaking camp before 7am. Note that signs have recently been placed at Grand Col Ferret which ask you not to bivouac nearby.

Wild camping guidelines

- **Leave no trace:** you should leave the environment in exactly the same condition as you found it. Leave nothing behind and take nothing away with you. When you have packed up and are ready to leave, look back on your campsite and make sure that another person would not be able to tell that you have been there (except for the flattened grass where your tent was pitched).
- **Do not light open fires:** bush-fires are becoming more common. Parts of the trail are close to wooded areas so the lighting of open fires carries risk. Do not be that person who accidentally destroys acres of pristine countryside.
- **Perform toilet duties responsibly:** this means that you should use a trowel to dig a hole in which to 'do your business'. There are some incredibly lightweight backpacking trowels available these days. Your hole should be at least 30m from water-courses. Fill the hole in afterwards and carry away your used toilet paper in a bag that you have brought along specifically for that purpose. Defecating and placing a stone on top is not acceptable: animals can move stones and imagine how you would feel if you sat down next to such a place! Also carry out tampons and sanitary towels.
- **Be discreet and have respect for others:** try to camp where others cannot see you. Keep your group small: it is supposed to be a 'wild' experience. Do not make a lot of noise at night.
- **Stay for only one night** at a particular spot and then move on.
- **Pitch up late and break camp early:** it is good practice to pitch up after 7pm and break camp before 7am.

Refuge Bellachat (Stage 11a/11b)

Accommodation Listings

Key on back cover flap.

Any accommodation highlighted in bold is currently listed on **www.montourdumontblanc.com**

Stage		Name	Facilities	Contact Details
1a,11b les Houches	1	**Gîte Michel Fagot**		+33 (0)4 50 54 42 28/(0)6 75 31 27 41 info@gite-fagot.com www.gite-fagot.com
1a,11b les Houches	2	Rocky Pop Hotel		+33 (0)4 85 30 00 00 reservation@rockypop.com www.rockypop.com
1a,11b les Houches	3	Auberge du Montagny		+33 (0)4 50 54 57 37 contact@aubergedumontagny.com www.aubergedumontagny.com
1a,11b les Houches	4	Hotel Saint-Antoine		+33 (0)4 50 54 40 10 resa@hotelsaintantoine.com www.hotelsaintantoine.com
1a,11b les Houches	5	Hotel du Bois		+33 (0)4 50 54 50 35 www.hotel-du-bois.com
1a,11b les Houches	6	Ibis Styles		+33 (0)4 86 80 27 17 HB9P8@accor.com www.all.accor.com
1a,11b les Houches	7	Hotel les Campanules		+33 (0)4 50 54 40 71 hotel-campanules@wanadoo.fr www.hotel-campanules.com
1a,11b les Houches	8	**Chalet les Méandres**		+33 (0)4 50 54 56 66 emmanuel.ratouis@wanadoo.fr www.tupilak.com
v1c Prarion	8a	Prarion 1860 Hôtel		+33 (0)4 50 54 40 07 yves@prarion.com www.prarion.com At date of press, the hotel was temporarily closed: the restaurant remained open.
1a,1b	9	**Refuge du Fioux**		+33 (0)4 50 93 52 43
1b Bionnassay	10	Auberge de Bionnassay		+33 (0)4 50 93 45 23 contact@auberge-bionnassay.com www.auberge-bionnassay.com
1b, 2a les Contamines	11	Hôtel La Gelinotte		+33 (0)4 50 47 01 61/(0)6 07 96 47 31 lagelinotte@free.fr www.hotel-lagelinotte.net
1b, 2a les Contamines	12	Chalet-hotel Gai Soleil		+33 (0)4 50 47 02 94 contact@gaisoleil.com www.gaisoleil.com
1b, 2a les Contamines	13	Hotel le Christiania		+33 (0)4 50 47 02 72 www.lechristiania-hotel.com
1b, 2a les Contamines	14	Chalet CAF des Contamines		+33 (0)4 50 47 00 88 www.ffcam.fr

Stage		Name	Facilities	Contact Details
1b, 2a les Contamines	14a	La Ferme à Piron		+33 (0)7 45 08 43 49 lafermeapiron@gmail.com www.lafermeapiron.com
1b, 2a les Contamines	15	Gîte les Mélèzes		+33 (0)6 95 35 10 94/(0)9 80 89 22 18 bourdeu.eric@gmail.com
1b, 2a les Contamines	16	Chalet Hôtel La Chemenaz		+ 33 (0)4 50 47 02 44 info@chemenaz.com www.chemenaz.com
2a le Pontet	17	Camping et Gîtes le Pontet		+33 (0)4 50 47 04 04 www.campinglepontet.fr
v1a, v1b Miage	18	Refuge de Miage		+33 (0)4 50 93 22 91 refugedemiage@orange.fr www.refugemiage.com
v1b Truc	19	Auberge du Truc		+33 (0)6 79 23 64 00/(0)4 50 93 12 48 aubergedutruc@hotmail.fr
2a, 2b	20	Refuge de Nant-Borrant		+33 (0)4 50 47 03 57/(0)6 88 18 76 24 refugenantborrant@free.fr
v2a, v2b	20a	Refuge de Tré-la-Tête		+33 (0)4 50 47 01 68/(0)6 68 22 52 96 contact@trelatete.com www.trelatete.com
2b, 2c	21	Refuge de la Balme		+33 (0)4 50 47 03 54 refuge-labalme@outlook.fr www.refugedelabalme.com
2b, 2c (2km OR)	22	Refuge des Prés		+33 (0)6 61 86 50 43 www.lerefugedespres.com
2c, 2d/v3a	23	Refuge de la Croix du Bonhomme		+33 (0)4 79 07 05 28/(0)9 70 02 81 47 www.refugecroixdubonhomme.ffcam.fr
2d, 3a les Chapieux	24	Les Chambres de Soleil		+33 (0)4 79 31 30 22 lesoleildeschapieux@gmail.com www.leschambresdusoleil-montblanc.com
2d, 3a les Chapieux	25	Auberge de la Nova		+33 (0)9 82 12 64 35/(0)6 64 94 98 35 www.refugelanova.com
3a/v3a, 3b	26	Refuge des Mottets		+33 (0)4 79 07 01 70 refuge@lesmottets.com www.lesmottets.com/tour-du-mont-blanc
3b, 4a	27	Rifugio Elisabetta Soldini		+39 0165 844080 info@rifugioelisabetta.com www.rifugioelisabetta.com
4a, 4b Combal	28	Cabane du Combal		+39 0165 175 6421 cabaneducombal@gmail.com www.cabaneducombal.com
4b, 4c Col Chécrouit	29	Rifugio Maison Vieille		+39 337 230979/328 0584157 info@maisonvieille.com www.maisonvieille.com

Stage		Name	Facilities	Contact Details
4c Col Chécrouit	30	**Gîte le Randonneur**		+39 349 536 88 98/320 430 35 40 info@randonneurmb.com www.randonneurmb.com
v4b (0.5km OR)	31a	Camping Monte Bianco la Sorgente	Tent rental	+39 389 90 20 772 info@campinglasorgente.net www.campinglasorgente.net
v4c	31	**CAI Rifugio Monte Bianco**		+39 379 102 87 24/0165 86 90 97 info@rifugiomontebianco.eu www.rifugiomontebianco.eu
v4c (2km OR)	32a	Pré de Pascal		+39 0165 86 90 90/347 434 77 07 info@predepascal.com www.predepascal.com
4c Dolonne	32	Hotel Dolonne		+39 0165 846674 hoteldolonne@hoteldolonne.it www.hoteldolonne.it
4c/v4b, 5a Courmayeur	33	Le Vieux Pommier		+39 0165 842281 info@levieuxpommier.com www.levieuxpommier.com
4c/v4b, 5a Courmayeur	34	Hotel Edelweiss		+39 0165 841590 info@albergoedelweiss.it www.albergoedelweiss.it
4c/v4b, 5a Courmayeur	35	Hotel Centrale		+39 0165 846644 info@hotelcentralecourmayeur.com www.hotelcentralecourmayeur.com
4c/v4b, 5a Courmayeur	36	Grand Hotel		+39 0165 572653 info@ghcmontblanc.it www.grandhotelcourmayeurmontblanc.it
4c/v4b, 5a Courmayeur	37	Hotel Croux		+39 0165 846 735 info@hotelcroux.it www.hotelcroux.it
4c/v4b, 5a Courmayeur	38	Hotel Bouton d'Or		+39 0165 84 67 29 info@hotelboutondor.com www.hotelboutondor.com
4c/v4b, 5a Courmayeur	39	Maison la Saxe		+39 344 117 55 30 info@maisonlasaxe.it www.maisonlasaxe.it
4c/v4b, 5a Courmayeur	40	Le Massif		+39 0165 189 71 00 travel@lemassifcourmayeur.com www.lemassifcourmayeur.com
5a, 5b/v5b	41	**Rifugio Giorgio Bertone**		+39 347 032 57 85 info@rifugiobertone.it www.rifugiobertone.it
5b/v5b, 6a	42	Rifugio Walter Bonatti		+39 335 68 48 578 rifugiobonatti@gmail.com www.rifugiobonatti.it
v5a La Palud	43	Hotel Astoria		+39 0165 869730 info@hotelastoriacourmayeur.com www.hotelastoriacourmayeur.com
v5a Plampincieux	44	Hotel Miravalle		+39 0165 869777 marco@courmayeur-hotelmiravalle.it www.courmayeur-hotelmiravalle.it

Stage		Name	Facilities	Contact Details
v5a	45	Hotel Lavachey		+39 0165 869723 info@lavachey.com www.lavachey.com
6a/v5a, 6b Arnuova	46	Chalet Val Ferret		+39 0165 844959/333 827 36 62 info@chaletvalferret.com www.chaletvalferret.com
6b, 6c	47	Rifugio Elena		+39 328 919 79 41/0165 844688 info@rifugioelena.it www.rifugioelena.it
6c, 6d	48	Gîte Alpage de la Peule		+41 (0)79 290 34 93/(0)27 783 10 41 nicolas.lapeule@gmail.com
6d, 6e Ferret	49	Hotel du Col de Fenêtre		+41 (0)27 783 11 88 hotelducoldefenetre@gmail.com www.hotelducoldefenetre.ch
6e	50	Gîte de la Léchère		+41 (0)27 783 30 64 info@gitedelalechere.ch www.gitedelalechere.ch
6e, 7 la Fouly	51	Auberge des Glaciers		+41 (0)27 783 11 71 info@aubergedesglaciers.ch www.aubergedesglaciers.ch
6e, 7 la Fouly	52	Chalet le Dolent		+41 (0)79 220 39 91/(0)27 783 29 31 info@dolent.ch www.dolent.ch
6e, 7 la Fouly	53	Maya Joie Auberge		+41 (0)27 565 56 30 contact@mayajoie.ch
6e, 7 la Fouly	54	Gîte la Fouly		+41 (0)27 565 06 53/(0)79 293 37 13 info@gitedelafouly.ch www.gitedelafouly.ch
6e, 7 la Fouly	55	Hôtel Edelweiss		+41 (0)27 783 26 21 info@fouly.ch www.fouly.ch
7 les Arlaches	56	Croque Nature Chambres d'hôtes		+41 (0)79 509 14 24 www.croquenature.ch
7, 8a/v8a Champex	57	Au Club Alpin		+41 (0)27 780 14 14 contact@auclubalpin www.auclubalpin.ch
7, 8a/v8a Champex	58	Le Cabanon		+41 (0)27 783 11 72 info@le-cabanon.ch www.le-cabanon.ch
7, 8a/v8a Champex	59	Hôtel du Glacier		+41 (0)27 782 61 51 info@hotelglacier.ch www.hotelglacier.ch
7, 8a/v8a Champex	60	La Gentiana		+41 (0)27 783 12 58 leonlovey@netplus.ch
7, 8a/v8a Champex	61	Pension en Plein Air		+41 (0)79 858 78 54 contact@pensionenpleinair.com www.pensionenpleinair.ch
7, 8a/v8a Champex	62	Hotel Mont Lac		+41 (0)26 565 66 00 hotelmontlac@gmail.com www.hotel-montlac.com

Stage		Name	Facilities	Contact Details
7, 8a/v8a Champex	63	Le Belvédère		+41 (0)27 783 11 14 belvedere@dransnet.ch www.le-belvedere.ch
7, 8a/v8a Champex	64	Hôtel Splendide		+41 (0)27 783 11 45 hotel-splendide@bluemail.ch www.hotel-splendide.ch
7, 8a/v8a Champex	65	Hôtel Alpina		+41 (0)27 783 18 92 www.alpinachampex.ch
8a Champex d'en Haut	66	Gîte Bon Abri		+41 (0)27 783 14 23 contact@gite-bon-abri.com www.gite-bon-abri.com
8a Champex d'en Haut	66a	Chalet la Grange		+41 (0)79 916 49 33/(0)79 916 49 33 info@lagrangechampex.ch
v8a, v8b Arpette	67	Relais d'Arpette		+41 (0)27 783 12 21 info@arpette.ch www.arpette.ch
8a/v8b, 8b/v9a Col de la Forclaz	68	Hôtel du Col de la Forclaz		+41 (0)27 722 26 88 colforclazhotel@bluewin.ch www.coldelaforclaz.ch
8b, 9a Trient	69	Auberge du Mont Blanc		+41 (0)77 420 08 14 info@aubergemontblanc.com www.aubergemontblanc.com
8b, 9a Trient	70	Hôtel la Grande Ourse		+41 (0)27 722 17 54 contact@la-grande-ourse.ch www.la-grande-ourse.ch
9a, 9b/v9b le Peuty	71	Refuge le Peuty		+41 (0)78 719 29 83 info@refugelepeuty.ch www.refugelepeuty.ch
v9a	72	Refuge les Grands		+41 (0)79 928 65 38 nic@azymuthe.ch
9b/v9a/v9b, 9c/v9c Col de Balme	73	Refuge du Col de Balme		+33 (0)6 07 06 16 30 refugeducoldebalme@gmail.com www.refugeducoldebalme.com
9c/v9c, 10a/v10a Tré-le-Champs	74	Auberge la Boerne		+33 (0)4 50 54 05 14 www.la-boerne.fr
v9c Charamillon	75	Les Écuries de Charamillon	Tent rental	+33 (0)4 50 54 17 07 info@charamillon.fr www.charamillon.fr
v9c le Tour	76	Hotel l'Olympique		+33 (0)7 88 77 56 15 hotel.olympique@orange.fr www.hotel-olympique-chamonix.com
v9c le Tour	77	Chalet Alpin du Tour		+33 (0)4 50 54 04 16/(0)6 16 24 50 71 www.chaletdutour.ffcam.fr

Stage		Name	Facilities	Contact Details
v9c Montroc OR	78	**Gîte le Moulin**		+33 (0)6 82 33 34 54 contact@gite-chamonix.com www.gite-chamonix.com
Argentière OR	79	Hôtel de la Couronne		+33 (0)4 50 54 00 02 www.hotelcouronne.com
Argentière OR	80	Les Grands Montets Hotel		+33 (0)4 50 54 06 66 info@hotel-grands-montets.com www.hotel-grands-montets.com
10b/v10c, 11a la Flégère	81	Refuge de la Flégère		+33 (0)6 03 58 28 14 www.refuge-de-la-flegere.com
v10b, v10c	82	Refuge du Lac Blanc	Water not potable	+33 (0)7 67 56 74 14 contactrefugedulacblanc@gmail.com www.refuge-lac-blanc.fr
v11a, v11b	83	Refuge Bellachat		+33 (0)7 75 83 02 70 refuge.bellachat@gmail.com www.refuge-bellachat.com
Chamonix OR	84	Hotel Vallée Blanche		+33 (0)4 50 53 04 50 info@vallee-blanche.com www.vallee-blanche.com
Chamonix OR	85	Hotel le Chamonix		+33 (0)4 50 53 11 07 www.hotel-le-chamonix.com
Chamonix OR	86	La Folie Douce		+33 (0)4 50 55 10 00 infos@lafoliedoucehotels.com www.lafoliedoucehotels.com
Chamonix OR	87	Auberge du Manoir		+33 (0)4 50 53 10 77 contact@aubergedumanoir.com www.chalethotelchamonix.fr
Chamonix OR	88	Hotel le Morgane		+33(0)4 50 53 57 15 reservation@hotelmorganechamonix.com www.morgane-hotel-chamonix.com
Chamonix OR	89	Auberge de Jeunesse Chamonix		+33(0)4 50 53 14 52 chamonix@hifrance.org www.hifrance.org
les Praz OR	90	Hotel Eden		+33 (0)4 50 53 18 43 relax@hoteleden-chamonix.com www.edenchamonix.com
les Praz OR	91	Chalet Hotel le Castel		+33 (0)4 50 21 12 12 www.lecastel-chamonix.com
les Praz OR	92	Hotel les Lanchers		+33 (0)4 50 53 47 19 booking@lanchers.com www.lanchers.com
les Praz OR	93	Hotel le Labrador		+33 (0)4 50 55 90 09 info@hotel-labrador.com www.hotel-labrador.com

Campsite Listings

Key on back cover flap.

Stage		Name	Facilities	Contact Details/Information
1a, 11b les Houches	1	Camping Bellevue		+33 (0)6 33 50 34 12 campingbellevueleshouches@orange.fr www.camping-bellevue-leshouches.com
v1a, v1b Refuge de Miage	1a	Bivouac site: authorised		No booking required. First come, first served.
v1b Auberge du Truc	1b	Bivouac site: authorised		Ask at reception on arrival.
2a le Pontet	2	Camping et Gîtes le Pontet		+33 (0)4 50 47 04 04 www.campinglepontet.fr
2b la Rollaz	3	Bivouac site: authorised		Reservation required: see p33.
2b, 2c la Balme	4	Bivouac site: authorised		Reservation required: see p33.
2c, 2d/v3a Refuge de la CB	5	Bivouac site: authorised		Obtain permission from the hut warden upon arrival
2d, 3a les Chapieux	6	Bivouac site: authorised		No booking required. First come, first served.
3a, 3b les Mottets	7	Bivouac site: not officially sanctioned	No facilities	Not officially approved but seems to be tolerated.
4b, 4c Rifugio Maison Vieille	8	Bivouac site: unauthorised but may be tolerated		Trekkers often bivouac beside the refuge with permission from the manager. Ask upon arrival: if they are not too busy they may permit it if you buy dinner. They will remind you that it is not technically legal.
v4b Val Veny	9	Hobo Camping	Tent rental	+39 0165 86 90 73 info@campinghobo.com www.campinghobo.com
v4b Val Veny	10	Camping Aiguille Noire	Tent rental	+39 351 804 88 46/392 196 61 70 info@aiguillenoire.com www.aiguillenoire.com
v4b Val Veny (0.5km OR)	11	Camping Monte Bianco la Sorgente	Tent rental	+39 389 90 20 772 info@campinglasorgente.net www.campinglasorgente.net
v5a Italian Val Ferret	12	Camping Grandes Jorasses	Chalet rental	+39 347 700 82 25 www.grandesjorasses.com

Stage		Name	Facilities	Contact Details/Information
v5a Italian Val Ferret	13	Camping Tronchey		+39 0165 869707/347 135 16 90 info@tronchey.com www.tronchey.com
6c, 6d Gîte Alpage de la Peule	14	Bivouac site: only permitted with consent of manager		Trekkers sometimes bivouac beside the gîte with permission from the manager. Ask upon arrival: if they are not too busy they may permit it if you buy dinner.
6d	15	Bivouac site: not officially sanctioned	No facilities	Not officially approved but seems to be tolerated
6e, 7 la Fouly	16	Camping des Glaciers	Tent rental	+41 (0)27 783 18 26 info@camping-glaciers.ch www.camping-glaciers.ch
7, 8a/v8a Champex	17	Camping les Rocailles		+41 (0)27 783 19 79
v8a, v8b Arpette	18	Relais d'Arpette		+41 (0)27 783 12 21 info@arpette.ch www.arpette.ch
8a, 8b/v8b Col de la Forclaz	19	Hôtel du Col de la Forclaz		+41 (0)27 722 26 88 colforclazhotel@bluewin.ch www.coldelaforclaz.ch
8b, 9a Trient	20	Bivouac site		Managed by Commune de Trient (+41 (0)27 722 21 05); small fee; first come, first served; covered eating area.
9a, 9b/v9b le Peuty	21	Bivouac site		Managed by Commune de Trient (+41 (0)27 722 21 05); small fee; first come, first served; covered eating area.
9c/v9c, 10a/v10a Tré-le-Champs	22	Auberge la Boerne		+33 (0)4 50 54 05 14 www.la-boerne.fr
Argentière OR	23	Camping du Glacier d'Argentière		+33 (0)4 50 54 17 36 camping.glacier.argentiere@gmail.com www.campingchamonix.com
10b/v10c, 11a la Flégère	24	Refuge de la Flégère: bivouac permitted at nearby lake		+33 (0)6 03 58 28 14 www.refuge-de-la-flegere.com Meals available at refuge: book in advance
v10b Lac des Chéserys	25	Bivouac site: authorised	No facilities	Reservation required: see p33.
Lac du Brévent/Col de Bellachat	26	Bivouac site: authorised	No facilities	Reservation required: see p33.
Chamonix OR	27	Camping les Arolles		+33 (0)6 75 02 26 44/47 60 92 21 infocamping@lesarolles.com www.lesarolles.com
Les Praz OR	28	Camping de la Mer de Glace		www.chamonix-camping.com

Food

Auberge la Boerne (Stage 9c/10a)

Generally, the food on the TMB is pretty good. Hikers are hungry people and most accommodation caters for this, providing breakfast, dinner and packed lunches for the following day.

Breakfast: most accommodation (including mountain huts) will provide breakfast. In hotels, there is usually a breakfast buffet with a wide selection of foods: cereals, bread, fruit, cheese, cold meats, jams and boiled eggs are common. In mountain huts, the choice is more limited and quality varies widely. In some huts, there is little more than a continental breakfast of cereal, bread and jam but in others, this may be supplemented with cold meats and cheese. Coffee and tea are provided: in huts, breakfast coffee may be instant/granulated.

Lunch: on many stages, there are villages, towns or mountain huts along the route which have restaurants serving local cuisine at lunchtime (normally 12-2pm). However, on some more remote sections of the trek, there is nowhere to buy a meal mid-route and you will need to bring a picnic lunch. Fortunately, excellent bread, cheeses and cold meats are available in bakeries, grocery shops and supermarkets in the villages: however, a little forward planning is required as there are some stages where there are no shops. Furthermore, shop opening hours can be a little irregular: usually, they open in the morning around 8-9am; often they close for a long lunch (12-3pm) and then re-open for a few hours in the late afternoon/evening. If you arrive in a town/village late then the shops may be closed.

Alternatively, you can buy picnic lunches from most hotels and huts along the route: order these the night before. In mountain huts, it is not generally acceptable to make up a sandwich for lunch using the breakfast food.

Rösti

Evening meals: most accommodation (including mountain huts) will provide evening meals which are usually hearty three-course affairs suitable for weary hikers. A starter (often soup) is normally followed by a main course of meat with vegetables, rice, pasta or salad. This will be rounded off with dessert or cheese. Vegetarian/vegan options are normally available: request these when you book and remind them when you arrive. Closer to civilisation, quality tends to improve. Local specialities are often rich and filling (and cheese based!): for example, fondues (melted cheese mixed with wine that you dip bread into) and tartiflette (a tasty concoction of potatoes, cream, ham and Reblochon cheese).

Self-catering: because huts and hotels rarely have communal kitchen facilities, self-catering is only a practical option if you are camping. Food is heavy and therefore it is not wise to attempt to start the trek carrying all the food that you will require for the full distance. Fortunately, on many stages, there are villages/towns along the route which have grocery shops/supermarkets. However, there are some stages where there are no shops so you will need to plan ahead. For shop opening hours, see p43.

It is sensible to carry dried food (such as pasta/rice): water is food's heaviest component. Pre-packed freeze-dried meals for backpackers are an excellent choice because they are light and are prepared simply by adding boiling water: you can eat them directly out of the bag so there is no washing-up. These days, there are some very tasty meals available from companies like Real Turmat and Firepot. Canned food is not a good choice as it usually has a high water content and is therefore heavy.

How much food do I need?

According to the National Health Service (NHS) in the UK, the recommended daily calorie intake is 2,000 calories for women and 2,500 for men. As you will be expending a lot of energy, it seems sensible to increase this slightly: perhaps a minimum of 2,500 calories for women and 3,000 for men. Of course, every person has a different metabolism and will have different requirements but this is a good starting point. Also bear in mind that your daily requirement will depend on how far you are planning to hike each day: the further you hike, the more energy you will use and the more food you will need. Remember also to bring a little extra food (over and above your estimated daily requirements) for emergencies.

Suggested daily menu for campers

Breakfast: instant porridge is a good option because it is light and packed with calories. You can get a variety of different flavours. It is also cheap and, in many countries, it is available in supermarkets. You prepare it simply by adding hot water. You can also buy pre-packed freeze-dried breakfast meals: although they are convenient, they are more expensive.

Lunch & snacks during the day: nuts are hard to beat as they are light and packed with energy. Peanuts, for example, have more calories per gram than most other foods. Dried fruit is also good and will help keep your bodily functions regular. Energy bars and candy can help to provide some variety (and boost moral in tough moments).

Dinner: freeze-dried meals are a good choice. Although they can be expensive, the good quality brands make dinner on the trail something to look forward to. Dried pasta and rice are good too: you can eat these with packet sauces (prepared by adding water).

Travel to/from the trail-heads

The Tramway du Mont Blanc (Stage 1a/v1a)

Getting to/from les Houches/Chamonix (France)

Chamonix is the Chamonix valley's main town: more buses/trains travel to Chamonix than LH. From Chamonix, there are regular buses and trains to LH (15-20min).

By train: the Mont Blanc Express (MBE) travels between St-Gervais-le-Fayet in France and Martigny in Switzerland, stopping at both LH and Chamonix along the way. From SGLF, the train takes 30/45min to get to LH/Chamonix; from Martigny, it takes 1.5/2hr to reach Chamonix/LH (including a change at Vallorcine). Both SGLF and Martigny are connected to the wider European rail network so you can travel there from numerous other European cities (including London, using the Eurostar train).

Alternatively, if you are travelling to the TMB from the E, you could take a train to Aosta in Italy. From there, buses travel to Chamonix (via Courmayeur): see p46.

By bus: Flixbus travels to Chamonix from Lyon (3-4hr), Milan (3.5 to 4 hr), Turin (3hr) and many other places; for further information, see p46. Both Arriva and Flixbus run daily buses between Chamonix and Courmayeur.

By air: the closest international airport to LH/Chamonix is Geneva in Switzerland. Geneva Airport has flights to/from many cities in Europe, North America and other parts of the world. There are a few different ways to travel to Chamonix from Geneva Airport/Geneva city centre:

- **Shuttle bus:** this is usually the fastest way of getting to LH/Chamonix. Many businesses offer shared and private transfers throughout the day which are scheduled to depart shortly after flights land. They must be booked in advance and take 75-90min. Cheaper shared services drop-off at fixed points in Chamonix/LH but other shared services can drop you at your hotel. Private transfers are the most expensive. Popular businesses include Mountain Drop-offs (**www.mountaindropoffs.com**) and AlpyTransfers (**www.alpytransfers.com**).
- **Scheduled bus:** there are plenty of scheduled buses between Geneva Airport and Chamonix. Advance booking is recommended. Popular services include Flixbus, easyBus (every 75min; **www.easybus.com**) and AlpyTransfers (**www.alpytransfers.com**). These services are useful for Chamonix, however, they usually pass LH without stopping: frequent buses/trains run from Chamonix back to LH.
- **Train:** both French and Swiss rail operators provide trains between Geneva Airport/ city centre and Chamonix/LH. The French service uses the Léman Express to SGLF: from there, you change to the MBE (see above) to travel to Chamonix/LH; the entire trip takes 3-4hr and you have to change three times. The Swiss service runs from Geneva Airport/ city centre to Martigny; from there, change onto the MBE to Chamonix/LH; the entire trip takes about 4hr (with two changes). Neither option is particularly fast or cost effective when compared to the shuttles or scheduled buses.

However, Geneva Airport is not the only option. You could also fly to another European airport and then take a train/bus to Chamonix. The following are good choices:

- **Turin Airport:** take a train/bus/taxi from the airport to one of the two main stations in Turin city centre: Torino Porta Susa or Torino Porta Nuova. From the city centre, Flixbus travels to Chamonix (3hr; departs from Corso Vittorio Emanuele II, 1km from Torino Porta Susa).
- **Milan Bergamo Orio al Serio Airport:** direct buses to Chamonix from the airport (5hr; www.flixbus.com). See also p47.
- **Milan Linate Airport:** take a taxi/Metro from Linate Airport to Milan Lampugnano bus station; Flixbus operates buses from Lampugnano to Chamonix (3.5 to 4hr).
- **Milan Malpensa Airport:** Flixbus operates buses to Chamonix from the airport (3.5 to 5hr). See also p47.
- **Zurich Airport:** 5-6hr by train from the airport station to Chamonix/LH.
- **Lyon Airport:** 5-6hr by train from the airport station to Chamonix/LH; Flixbus operates direct buses to Chamonix from Lyon Airport (3hr).
- **Paris Charles de Gaulle Airport:** 8-10hr by train from the airport to Chamonix/LH.

By cable car: you can travel between Courmayeur and Chamonix using a series of five cable cars (see p47).

By car: because the TMB is circular, you could leave a car in Chamonix/LH and return to it at the end of the trek. However, there are few parking spaces in Chamonix which are free of charge and long-term parking can be hard to find at a reasonable price. Free parking is easier to find at LH: you can park free of charge for up to 15 days at the Prarion ski-lift car park; however, spaces are in high demand and occasionally, there are reports of break-ins.

The Mont Blanc Tunnel

Courmayeur and Chamonix lie on opposite sides of the MB massif and the road connecting them uses the MB Tunnel (which travels through the massif). All buses travelling between Courmayeur and Chamonix use the tunnel: this includes buses from Turin/Milan to Chamonix (all of which travel via Courmayeur). Sometimes the tunnel closes for maintenance (often in September) and this can throw TMB travel plans into disarray because, without the tunnel, it is a long taxi ride around the massif (taking hours and costing hundreds of euros): 150km around the N side of the massif (via Grand-Saint-Bernard Tunnel) or 160km around the S side of the massif (via Col du Petit-Saint-Bernard); a more pleasant option would be to use the cable cars between Courmayeur and Chamonix (see p47).You can check for planned tunnel closures at **www.tunnelmb.net**.

Getting to/from Courmayeur (Italy)

By train: the closest train station to Courmayeur is Aosta (which is at the end of the line from Turin): you can travel there from numerous other European cities. From Aosta, Arriva runs regular buses to Courmayeur (1hr). Alternatively, take a taxi directly from Aosta to Courmayeur (45min).

By bus: Arriva runs daily buses between Turin and Courmayeur (3-4hr; via Aosta). Flixbus runs buses to Courmayeur from Turin (2.5hr), Milan (3hr) and Milan Bergamo Orio al Serio Airport (4hr): they all travel via Aosta. Arriva and Flixbus also run daily buses between Chamonix and Courmayeur. Courmayeur's main bus stop is at the tourist office in Piazza Monte Bianco.

By air: the closest international airport to Courmayeur is Turin. Trains travel from Turin to Aosta, however, you first have to travel by train/bus/taxi from the airport to one of the two main stations in Turin city centre: Torino Porta Susa or Torino Porta Nuova. After reaching Aosta, take Arriva's bus or a taxi to Courmayeur (see above). There are also buses between Turin city centre and Aosta/Courmayeur (see above).

Turin Airport is not the only option. The following are also good choices:

- **Milan Bergamo Orio al Serio Airport:** Flixbus runs direct buses to Courmayeur from the airport (4-5hr). Alternatively, take the train from Bergamo city centre to Aosta and a bus from Aosta to Courmayeur (see p46). Or take a bus from the airport to Milan Centrale station, then the train from Milan Centrale to Aosta and a bus from Aosta to Courmayeur.
- **Milan Linate Airport:** Flixbus runs buses to Courmayeur from Milan Lampugnano bus station (3 to 3.5hr). Alternatively, take the train from Milan Centrale to Aosta and a bus from Aosta to Courmayeur (see p46). Use a taxi/Metro to travel from Linate Airport to Lampugnano/Centrale.
- **Milan Malpensa Airport:** Flixbus runs a few direct buses to Courmayeur from the airport (3.5 to 5hr). Alternatively, take a bus/train from the airport to Milan Centrale, then the train from Milan Centrale to Aosta and a bus from Aosta to Courmayeur (see p46).

By cable car: you can travel from Courmayeur to Chamonix using a series of five cable cars. The first two (Skyway Monte Bianco) take you from Entrèves (just N of Courmayeur) to Punta Helbronner; then the Panoramic Mont Blanc Gondola travels from Helbronner to the Aiguille du Midi in France; from there, the two cable cars of the Aiguille du Midi take you down to Chamonix. You can buy tickets for Skyway Monte Bianco at **www.montebianco.com** and Aiguille du Midi tickets at **www.montblancnaturalresort.com**: alternatively, the latter sells a Mont Blanc Multi-pass which includes the two Helbronner lifts and the two Aiguille du Midi lifts plus many other lifts in the area. Annoyingly, buying tickets in advance for the Panoramic Mont Blanc Gondola (the middle lift) is not so easy: you have to go to the lift ticket offices in person and either buy a single ticket or an extension to the Multi-pass. The whole trip is unforgettable but it is not cheap and it is weather dependent.

By car: you could leave a car in Courmayeur and return to it at the end of the trek. However, there are few parking spaces in Courmayeur which are free of charge and long-term parking can be hard to find at a reasonable price. Some trekkers use Parcheggio della Val Sapin which is currently free of charge: it is a small parking area along the TMB route just N of Courmayeur (near 42).

Getting to/from Champex (Switzerland)

To reach Champex, you must first travel to Orsières (which is at the end of a train line from Martigny): from Orsières, bus 271 travels to Champex (20-30min). You can travel by rail to Orsières from Geneva Airport (3 to 3.5hr), Zurich Airport (4.5 to 5.5hr) and numerous other European cities. You can buy Swiss train and bus tickets together (in a single transaction) at the airports or online at **www.sbb.ch** or using SBB's efficient smart-phone app. For timetables and route maps, see **www.sbb.ch**, **www.postauto.ch** or **www.tmrsa.ch**.

Getting to/from other trail-heads

In addition to the main trail-heads at LH, Courmayeur, Champex and Chamonix, there are other places along the TMB which you can access by public transport. You could start/finish the trek at any of these places. Or you could skip sections of the trek by leaving the route at one of these trail-heads and using public transport to resume at another point: this can be a good option in the event of fatigue or bad weather. See the table below.

Shuttle bus at les Chapieux (Stage 2d/3a)

Trail-head	Public transport to/from trail-head
Les Houches Start/finish	**Train:** MBE towards Chamonix/Martigny (N) or SGLF (W). **Bus:** frequent buses run daily along the Chamonix valley between le Tour, Argentière, Chamonix and LH; www.chamonix.net. **Cable cars:** see *Col de Voza* below. For further information , see p45.
Col de Voza 4 1a/v1a	**Prarion cable car:** between LH and Prarion (1.5km from Col de Voza); early June to mid-Sept; continuously all day; **www.chamonix.net**. **Bellevue cable car:** between LH and Bellevue (1.6km from Col de Voza; 0.2km from 7 on Stage v1a); late June to early Sept; continuously all day; **www.chamonix.net**. **Tramway du Mont Blanc:** runs between SGLF and le Nid d'Aigle via St-Gervais-les-Bains, Col de Voza 4 and Bellevue (0.1km from 7 on Stage v1a); mid-June to late Aug; **www.tramwaydumontblanc.montblancnaturalresort.com**.
Tresse 1b: between 9 and 10	**LC shuttle bus:** see *les Contamines* below.
Les Hoches 10 1b	**LC shuttle bus:** see *les Contamines* below.
Plan du Moulin-la Chapelle 1b: near 10	**LC shuttle bus:** see *les Contamines* below.
La Frasse v1b	**LC shuttle bus:** see *les Contamines* below.
Les Contamines 11 1b,v1b/2a,v2a	**Les Contamines shuttle bus:** circulates throughout the day calling at Tresse (less frequently), LC, la Frasse (less frequently), Notre-Dame-de-la-Gorge, le Pontet, les Hoches (less frequently) and Plan du Moulin/la Chapelle; free of charge; **www.lescontamines.com**. **Bus:** buses run daily between LC, SGLF station and Sallanches (**www.sat-montblanc.com**). From SGLF, trains go to LH, Chamonix and Geneva/Geneva Airport. AlpyTransfers also runs buses between SGLF and Chamonix/Sallanches/Geneva Airport.
Le Pontet 13 2a	**LC shuttle bus:** see *les Contamines* above.
Notre-Dame-de-la-Gorge 14 2a	**LC shuttle bus:** see *les Contamines* above.
Les Chapieux 25 2d/3a	**Bourg-St-Maurice shuttle bus:** circulates throughout the day, calling at les Chapieux, Ville des Glaciers and Parking des Mottets (near Refuge des Mottets 28); mid-June to mid-Sept; **www.lesarcs.com**. In high season, this bus also travels 3-4 times/day between les Chapieux and BSM (where there is more accommodation); at the start/end of the season, it only travels once each day to/from BSM.
Ville des Glaciers 27 3a,v3a	**BSM shuttle bus:** see *les Chapieux* above.
Parking des Mottets 3a,v3a/3b: near Refuge des Mottets 28	**BSM shuttle bus:** see *les Chapieux* above.
La Visaille 27 v4b: 2.8km from 32	**Val Veny shuttle bus:** runs regularly throughout the day to/from Courmayeur (along Val Veny); also stops at Val Veny's campsites; free of charge; early June to end Sept; **www.arriva.it**.

Trail-head	Public transport to/from trail-head
Rifugio Maison Vieille (35) 4b/4c,v4c	**Cable car:** Maison Vieille ski-lift between Col Chécrouit (35) and Plan Chécrouit (37). A second ski-lift runs between Plan Chécrouit (37) and Dolonne (near Courmayeur). Both July/August only; **www.courmayeur-montblanc.com**.
Courmayeur (41) 4c,v4b/ 5a,v5a	**Val Veny shuttle bus:** see *la Visaille* above. **Italian Val Ferret shuttle bus:** see *Chalet Val Ferret* below. **Buses to Chamonix:** Arriva and Flixbus; daily. **Cable car to Chamonix:** see p47. For detailed information on getting to Courmayeur, see p46.
(39) v5a: 1.5km from Rifugio Bonatti	**Italian Val Ferret shuttle bus:** see *Chalet Val Ferret* below.
Chalet Val Ferret-Arnouva/Arp Nouvaz (49) 6a,v5a/6b	**Italian Val Ferret shuttle bus:** runs regularly throughout the day between Courmayeur and Chalet Val Ferret; also stops at Entrèves, Val Ferret's hotels/campsites and (39) (for access to Rifugio Bonatti; see p121); free of charge; end June to end Sept; **www.arriva.it**.
Ferret (55) 6d/6e	**Bus 272:** runs throughout the day between Ferret and Orsières, calling at la Fouly, Praz-de-Fort (Stage 7) and Issert (Stage 7). From Orsières, bus 271 runs to Champex. **www.tmrsa.ch**.
La Fouly (60) 6e/7	**Bus 272:** see *Ferret* above.
Praz-de-Fort 7	**Bus 272:** see *Ferret* above.
Issert 7	**Bus 272:** see *Ferret* above.
Champex (68) 7/8a,v8a	**Bus 271:** heads to Orsières; see p47.
Col de la Forclaz (75) 8a,v8b/8b,v9a	**Bus 213:** heads E to Martigny; W to Trient (77) and le Châtelard (where you can catch the MBE either N to Martigny or S towards Chamonix/SGLF).
Trient (77) 8b/9a	**Bus 213:** heads E to Col de la Forclaz (75) and Martigny; W to le Châtelard (where you can catch the MBE either N to Martigny or S towards Chamonix/SGLF).
Col de Balme (80) 9b,v9a,v9b/ 9c,v9c	**Cable car:** Autannes ski-lift runs between Autannes (0.7km from Col de Balme) and Charamillon. Then the Charamillon ski-lift runs between Charamillon and le Tour (60). Early June to early Sept; continuously all day; **www.chamonix.net**.
Col des Posettes (82) 9c	**Cable car:** Vallorcine ski-lift between Vallorcine and 1950m (0.6km from Col des Posettes); late June to end of Aug; continuously all day (except closes for lunch); **www.chamonix.net**. The MBE stops at Vallorcine (enabling transport to Martigny or Chamonix).
Le Tour (60) v9c	**Bus:** frequent buses run daily along the Chamonix valley between le Tour, Argentière, Chamonix and LH; **www.chamonix.net**. **Cable car:** see *Col de Balme* above.
Tré-le-Champs (85) 9c,v9c/ 10a,v10a	**Bus:** buses run daily between Tré-le-Champs and Argentière (**www.chamonix.net**). From Argentière, trains/buses run to Chamonix/LH.

Trail-head	Public transport to/from trail-head
Argentière 63; OR	**Train:** MBE towards Martigny (N) or Chamonix/SGLF (S). **Bus:** buses to le Tour, Tré-le-Champs and Chamonix.
Refuge de la Flégère 89; 10b,v10c/11a	**Cable car:** la Flégère ski-lift between les Praz (near Chamonix) and Refuge de la Flégère; early June to late Sept; continuously all day; **www.chamonix.net**
Plan Praz 92;11a	**Cable car:** see *Le Brévent* below.
Le Brévent 96 11a	**Cable car:** Brévent ski-lift runs between le Brévent and Plan Praz; Then the Plan Praz ski-lift runs between Plan Praz and Chamonix; mid-June to mid-Sept; every 15min; **www.chamonix.net**.

Taxis

A number of taxi businesses operate from towns/villages near the TMB. They can often pick you up from the TMB, drive you to nearby accommodation and leave you back to the TMB the next morning. Or they can help you to skip stages of the trek by picking you up at one trail-head and dropping you off at another. Some of them operate surprisingly far from their hubs. Taxis are expensive but can be cost effective for groups of three or more people: some of the vehicles carry up to eight passengers.

- **Besson Transports/Taxi Mont Blanc (Chamonix valley):** serves Geneva Airport, Lyon Airport and the entire Chamonix valley (including LH, Chamonix and Argentière); they can also take you between LC and les Chapieux; **www.taxi-montblanc.com**; contact@taxi-montblanc.com; +33 (0)4 50 93 62 07.
- **Go Prime Transfer (Chamonix):** serves Geneva Airport, Lyon Airport, Courmayeur and the entire Chamonix valley (including LH, Chamonix and Argentière); **www.goprimetransfer.com**; +33 (0)6 41 80 89 34.
- **Taxi AArthur Transport (Bourg-St-Maurice):** taxis between BSM and les Chapieux/Ville des Glaciers/Parking des Mottets; Geneva Airport transfers; **www.taxibourgsaintmaurice.com**; aarthur.transport@gmail.com; +33 (0)6 14 18 26 11.
- **Taxil'Vie (Bourg-St-Maurice):** taxis between BSM and les Chapieux/Ville des Glaciers/ Parking des Mottets; Geneva Airport transfers; **www.taxi-bourg-st-maurice.net**; +33 (0)6 47 47 18 86.
- **Transfer Courmayeur:** transfers between Courmayeur and Aosta/Turin Airport/ Milan Malpensa Airport/Chamonix/Geneva; also serves Val Veny and Italian Val Ferret; **www.transfercourmayeur.com**; +39 347 49 00 051.
- **Courmayeur Centrale Taxi:** +39 0165 842 960.
- **Taxi Fen'yx (Orsières):** serves la Fouly, Champex, Relais d'Arpette, Col de la Forclaz and Trient; also provides Geneva Airport transfers and taxis to Courmayeur/Chamonix; **www.taxiorsieres.ch**; info@taxifenyx.ch; +41(0)79 773 77 40.

Further information, timetables and route maps:

Chamonix valley buses/ski-lifts: www.chamonix.net

Flixbus: www.flixbus.com

French trains: www.sncf-connect.com

Italian buses: www.arriva.it

Italian trains: www.trenitalia.com

Mont Blanc Express: www.mont-blanc-express.ch

Swiss trains: www.sbb.ch

Swiss buses: www.sbb.ch; www.postauto.ch; www.tmrsa.ch

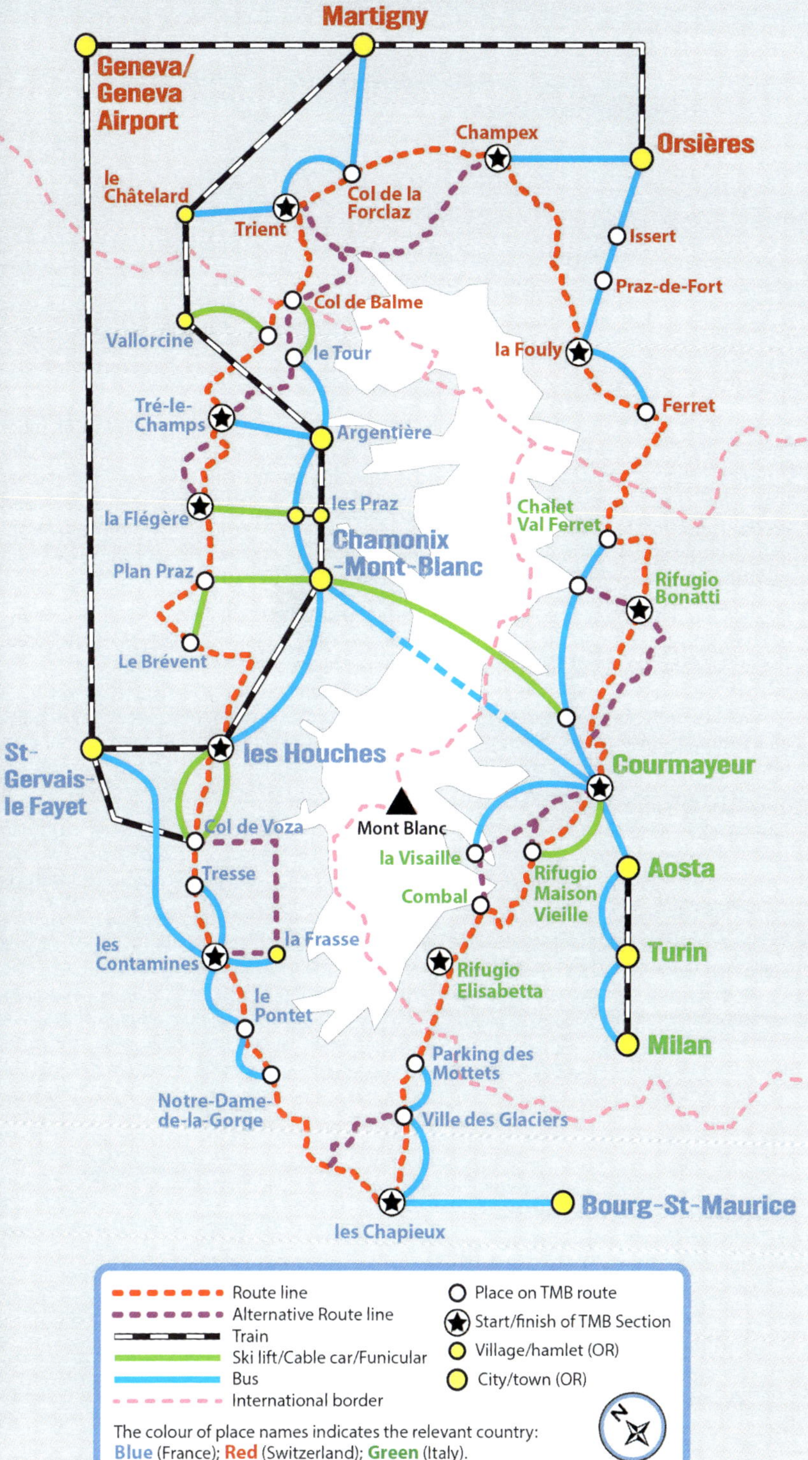
Martigny
Geneva/
Geneva
Airport
Orsières
Champex
le
Châtelard
Col de la
Forclaz
Trient
Issert
Praz-de-Fort
Col de Balme
Vallorcine
le Tour
la Fouly
Ferret
Tré-le-
Champs
Argentière
les Praz
la Flégère
Chalet
Val Ferret
Chamonix
-Mont-Blanc
Plan Praz
Rifugio
Bonatti
Le Brévent
St-
Gervais-
le Fayet
les Houches
Courmayeur
Mont Blanc
Col de Voza
la Visaille
Rifugio
Maison
Vieille
Aosta
Tresse
Combal
les
Contamines
la Frasse
Turin
Rifugio
Elisabetta
le
Pontet
Milan
Parking des
Mottets
Notre-Dame-
de-la-Gorge
Ville des Glaciers
Bourg-St-Maurice
les Chapieux
Route line
Alternative Route line
Train
Ski lift/Cable car/Funicular
Bus
International border
Place on TMB route
Start/finish of TMB Section
Village/hamlet (OR)
City/town (OR)
The colour of place names indicates the relevant country:
Blue (France); Red (Switzerland); Green (Italy).
N

Pastures above les Chapieux (Stage 2d)

Costs & budgeting

Although no permits are required to hike the TMB, its popularity means that it is more expensive than most other Alpine treks. In particular, Switzerland tends to be slightly more expensive than other parts of the Alps: food is especially costly there, however, what you get is normally good quality. Generally, both France and Italy are a little cheaper than Switzerland: food and alcohol are best value in Italy. Buses/trains are fairly expensive in Switzerland but are less costly in France/Italy. Some of the local shuttle buses along the TMB are free of charge: in particular, those serving Courmayeur. Cable cars are expensive everywhere.

Prices in mountain huts have risen greatly over the last decade but we think that they still offer good value when you consider the high cost of getting supplies to the remote locations. In the huts, the cost of half-board (breakfast, dinner and a dormitory bed) varies widely: the price range in each country is set out below; rates are higher for private rooms. Huts which are affiliated to Club Alpin Français or Club Alpino Italiano offer a discount to members of other international alpine clubs: Chalet CAF des Contamines, Refuge de la CB, Rifugio Elisabetta, Rifugio Monte Bianco and Chalet Alpin du Tour.

In hotels along the TMB, double/twin rooms (for 2 people including breakfast) start from around CHF150/€110 in total. However, some hotels are significantly more expensive than that, particularly in the larger settlements (Chamonix, LH, Courmayeur and Champex). Solo travellers will usually pay a single supplement, making hotels relatively expensive for those travelling alone.

Trekkers booking independently should budget for approximately €85-100/day on the trail if staying in huts/gîtes. If you add nights in hotels, you will need to spend a bit more than this. By camping, you can save a lot of money, perhaps spending as little as €25-30/day if you stay in campsites and cook your own meals; €15-20/day if you use free bivouac sites and cook your own meals. All of these estimations exclude baggage transfer costs, alcoholic drinks and travel costs (flights, buses, trains, taxis and cable cars).

	Approximate Cost (subject to change) Switzerland/France/Italy
Half-board in mountain hut/gîte (dormitory bed, breakfast & dinner)	**CHF68-95**/**€60-80**/**€60-80** per person
Double room in hotel (including breakfast)	From **CHF150**/**€110**/**€110** upwards (for 2 people sharing a double/twin room)
Campsite	**CHF16-22**/**€10-20**/**€10-20** per person
Main course in restaurant	**CHF20-40**/**€12-25**/**€11-25**
Beer (0.5L)	**CHF6-8**/**€6-9**/**€5-8**

Weather

The Alps have a relatively dry and predictable climate compared, for example, to mountain ranges in the UK: clear and sunny skies are common during the hiking season. However, conditions can still change quickly so be prepared for high winds, rain, low cloud and poor visibility. Furthermore, snow is always possible on high passes and summits, even in summer. Sometimes you might experience a mixture of conditions during the day: perhaps some sun and clear skies for a while with cloud and/or rain during other parts of the day. Always remember that mountains can be dangerous so treat them with respect and caution, even if the weather forecast is favourable.

The region has many micro-climates with the weather often differing from valley to valley. It is possible therefore to find blazing sunshine on one side of a ridge and cloud/rain over the other side.

If you can, obtain a weather forecast on your smartphone before setting out each day. MeteoSwiss (the Swiss meteorological office) provides national, regional and local forecasts at **www.meteoswiss.admin.ch**. It also has an excellent smartphone app which provides regularly updated local forecasts. For the French parts of the TMB, Météo-France (the French meteorological office) provides national, regional and local forecasts at **www.meteofrance.com**. It also has an excellent smartphone app which provides regularly updated local forecasts. For the Italian parts of the TMB, the smartphone app **Meteo.it** is useful.

Many other internet sites and apps also provide forecasts, with a varying degree of reliability. If you are unable to obtain a forecast on your smartphone then it is sensible to speak to the hut managers: their understanding of local weather conditions can be invaluable and you should follow their advice if they tell you it is not safe to hike. Local forecasts are also displayed at tourist information offices and huts.

Maps

In this book, we have included maps for the entire TMB (and all the variants): each stage has 1:40,000 scale maps produced by Knife Edge Outdoor Guidebooks. Because we were unable to find commercially available maps that suited our purposes, we commissioned our own topographical maps: they are great for both planning and navigation while on the trek. However, we also recommend obtaining our sheet map for the TMB, **Trekking Map: Tour du Mont Blanc** (ISBN 9781912933556). It covers the entire trek and clearly shows the TMB route (and its variants) and the facilities at all relevant locations; it is printed on ultra-lightweight, waterproof, tear-proof paper and can be used seamlessly with this book; the scale is 1:40,000 (with a larger-scale 1:10,000 inset for Fenêtre d'Arpette which is particularly difficult to navigate in poor conditions). With so many variants, the TMB is a complicated trek to plan: being able to view the entire route on a single sheet map will save you a lot of time and effort. A sheet map also makes it easier to navigate in poor conditions and identify peaks along the trail. Our map is available from **www.knifeedgeoutdoor.com**, online retailers and many shops. It is best to buy this map before leaving home, because there are few book shops along the route.

IGN (the French mapping agency) also produces 1:25,000 sheet maps that cover the TMB; however, the paper used is comparatively heavy and two sheets are required, adding weight to your pack: 3531ET St-Gervais-les-Bains and 3630OT Chamonix-Mont-Blanc. IGN also produce a 1:50,000 map which has the whole route on one sheet: Tour du Mont Blanc 89025. Various other maps are available but we do not think that they are as good as IGN's.

Both IGN and Swisstopo also have useful smart-phone apps. The Swisstopo app covers the N half of the TMB including some French and Italian sections. The Cartes IGN app covers almost the entire TMB (except a small Italian section). Both apps use GPS to show your location on the map: they are free of charge but you will need mobile data to use them. There are also heaps of other smartphone navigation apps: some of them charge for their services but others are free.

Paths and waymarking

Paths and tracks are generally well-maintained, straightforward to walk upon and simple to follow but there are rocky, challenging sections too: occasionally, you will need to climb over rocks/boulders. The terrain undulates regularly and some sections are steep and/or exposed: sometimes drops are sheer and occasionally, ropes/chains have been fixed to the rocks for safety. Some paths can be muddy and slippery after rain.

Generally, the route is well marked and navigation is usually straightforward in good conditions: there are often waymarks (painted on trees and rocks) and signs to assist. However, occasionally paths are less easy to follow and navigation is more difficult (particularly in bad conditions): for example, where the trail crosses rocky zones, it can be faint or disappear completely.

Swiss waymark

Swiss waymark

French waymark

Italian waymark

Signposts are often adorned with the 'TMB' logo (see image on p55) and display times/distances to specific destinations: the timings are not always reliable. In France, waymarks are usually red/white stripes; in Italy, there are yellow arrows or yellow/black diamonds (with 'TMB' written on them); in Switzerland, there are either red/white stripes or yellow/black diamonds. Waymarks tend to be placed sparingly to avoid sullying the natural environment with man-made marks: often they are found only at junctions or where absolutely necessary to prevent deviation from the route. A red/white cross on a rock or tree indicates that you are off the route (see image on p55).

In the route descriptions, we do not highlight every junction because the waymarking is usually good: generally, we only mention junctions if they are particularly significant or if there are no waymarks. As a rule of thumb, remain on the main path unless instructed otherwise by signs/waymarks on the ground or the maps/route descriptions in this book: however, keep your wits about you because there will, of course, be the occasional exception to this rule! Also, bear in mind that waymarking is at the mercy of the environment: for example, signs and waymarks are sometimes destroyed or concealed by rockfall or snow.

On the high points of the TMB, snow can remain into July, covering paths and making progress/route-finding more difficult: follow waymarks carefully because they can be hard to spot in the snow. Normally, early in the season, the trail will become quickly tracked by others ahead of you but always be wary of following someone else's footprints: there is a good chance that they are on the correct path but it is obviously possible that they may have strayed from the route. Also, remember that any fresh snow will obscure footprints.

Wrong way
TMB waymark
Italian Signpost
Swiss Signpost

Take care if you see mountain biking signs, usually indicated by the letters 'VTT' (Vélo Tout Terrain): mountain bikes are fast and often quiet and a collision between a walker and a mountain bike could be serious.

Snow bridges

On the high parts of the TMB, winter snow melts gradually throughout spring and early summer. Snow bridges commonly form over streams and they often remain well into June (and sometimes until early July). A snow bridge occurs when snow melts under the surface, forming a gap underneath (which is often not visible from above). Sometimes you will be able to see underneath the bridge or spot holes in the snow showing the gap below. However, at other times, there may be no visible signs that the snow has weakened below. If a snow bridge on which you are walking collapses, you could be seriously injured and, if the stream's flow is strong, pulled under the snow bridge by the current. In recent years, at least one TMB hiker has been killed by a collapsing snow bridge.

If you are crossing a snow-covered stream, then always be aware that there could be a cavity beneath the surface. When there is snow on the ground, check maps so that you know roughly where the streams are located (although smaller streams may not be shown on maps). Listen out for the sound of running water which could alert you to the presence of a stream beneath the snow that you cannot see. Sometimes a long linear groove in the snow's surface can indicate a stream's location.

Always be wary of following someone else's footprints across snow bridges: they tend to weaken over time and, just because the bridge successfully supported the party ahead of you, does not necessarily mean that it will support you. Test the ground ahead with a walking pole. If you are concerned, look for a better place to cross. If you do decide to cross, move as quickly as safety allows and do not stop on the bridge. If there is no safe way across/around then turn back.

Parts of the TMB where snow bridges are common in early season include the following:

- **Stage v3a:** E of Col des Fours, snow bridges form over steep torrents. A TMB trekker was killed there a few years ago.
- **Stage 4b:** the trail contours around steep slopes, crossing torrents where snow bridges form.
- **Stage 5b:** snow bridges seem to last a long time in this area.

Water

Drinking water should be one of your primary considerations each day. The sun in the mountains is extremely strong: dehydration and sunstroke are possibilities and you will need more water than usual. Tap water is drinkable and you should fill up your bottles each morning before you depart: it is good practice to start the day with at least 1.5 litres. Along the trail, you can top up water supplies at fountains, bars and shops in villages/towns or from the many streams/rivers: plan carefully so that you know where the next water point is and always check your water levels when you pass a water point.

Remember that the volume of water in streams may vary depending upon the season and the amount of rainfall over previous weeks and months: at the start of the season (June), the rivers are usually in full flow but by the end of the season (September), many of the smaller ones may be dry. Although some do it, we do not recommend drinking water from a river, stream or lake, without first dealing with possible contaminants including visible particulates, bacteria, viruses, protozoa (for example, giardia) and parasites.

It is possible to deal with most contaminants using one or more of the methods described below but you should research thoroughly the specific product you are planning to use to understand its effectiveness and any possible risks:

- **Boiling** is the traditional method. A rolling boil of 1min should kill everything in the water. However, it does not remove visible particulates so the boiled water will remain the same colour as when you found it, which can be off-putting. It also uses up a lot of fuel and takes time so is impractical.
- **Filtering** usually removes visible particulates, working miracles by turning coloured water clear. It also normally removes around 99.9% of bacteria, protozoa and parasites. Filters are often cheap and light. It is the quickest method of treatment so it is useful for long-distance routes. However, most filters cannot remove viruses (although these are unlikely to be an issue on this trek): if you are concerned about viruses then you will need to invest in one of the more expensive (and heavier) filters that remove them or combine filtering with another method (boiling, UV or chemical treatment).
- **Chemical treatment** can remove bacteria, protozoa, viruses and parasites: each product is different so read the labels carefully. However, there are many disadvantages to chemicals: they do not remove visible particulates so the water will remain the same colour as when you found it; water treated with chemicals often has a taste (although you can usually buy additional chemicals to deal with that); the water usually cannot be drunk immediately as chemicals take time to kill pathogens; and from a health perspective, consuming chemicals may not be good for you.
- **UV treatment** kills bacteria, protozoa, viruses and parasites. However, it does not remove visible particulates so the water will remain the same colour as when you found it: coloured water can be off-putting and the UV treatment is less effective if the water is not completely clear. That said, coloured water is not usually a problem on this trek. The most common products are Steripens which are very light.

Perhaps the most practical single method for this trek is filtering: because virus contamination is unlikely, many hikers drink water which has only been filtered with a standard filter, running a small risk of virus contamination. However, if you prefer to be more cautious, you could buy one of the heavy and expensive filters that deal with viruses: alternatively, combine filtration with UV treatment (using a Steripen) which removes or kills practically everything.

The actual effectiveness of individual products varies and is beyond the scope of this book so do your research beforehand. However, it is worth noting that many products claim to be 99.9% effective indicating that drinking water from wild sources can never be said to be 100% risk free. You will have to weigh up the risks and make up your own mind. You drink the water at your own risk!

If, like many, you do decide to drink from natural sources then, as well as treating the water, there are a few rules that you should follow to reduce further any risk:

- Avoid water where there is evidence nearby of animals, especially cows or sheep: carcasses (of dead animals) or faeces can cause contamination.
- Do not collect water downstream from buildings or grazing areas.
- Preferably drink from moving water. The faster the better.
- The bigger the river/stream the better.
- Generally the higher the altitude the better.

	Visible Particulates	Bacteria	Virus	Protozoa	Parasites
Boiling	✗	✓	✓	✓	✓
Filter	✓	✓	Only top of the range filters remove viruses	✓	✓
Chemical Treatment	✗	✓	✓	✓	✓
UV Treatment (such as Steripen)	✗	✓	✓	✓	✓

Storing bags

Many trekkers travel to the TMB carrying only the gear that they will actually take on the trek. However, those who want to spend time elsewhere afterwards will probably have additional baggage which they need to store while trekking. Normally, a hotel that you have stayed at (before the trek) in Geneva, LH, Chamonix, Courmayeur or Champex will let you store bags until your return: some may charge extra for this so check when booking. Because the TMB is a circuit, it is easy to pick up your bags at the end of the trek. Baggage transfer companies may also store surplus bags (see below). Camping les Arolles in Chamonix also offers baggage storage for a fee.

You could also use official luggage storage facilities. At Geneva Airport, Geneva Cornavin and Zurich Airport train stations, there are manned baggage counters (near the SBB travel centres) where you can leave luggage for CHF12/day. However, you can only deposit/reclaim baggage during the travel centres' opening hours. There are also unmanned luggage lockers at many large Swiss train stations (including Geneva Airport station, Geneva Cornavin and Zurich): however, the maximum storage time is 96 hours which will be insufficient for most trekkers.

Bounce provides luggage storage facilities in LH, Chamonix and Courmayeur: **www.usebounce.com**; €4-6/day. Stasher (**www.stasher.com**), Radical Storage (**www.radicalstorage.com**) and Luggage Hero (**www.luggagehero.com**) also offer bag storage in Courmayeur.

Baggage transfer

Businesses offering baggage transfer services can transport your bags to your accommodation each night so that you only need to carry a small day-pack on the trail. This spares you from the burden of having to carry a heavy backpack and enables you to pack more clean clothes and some luxuries. However, although they can facilitate baggage transfer at most towns/villages along the route, they can only service mountain huts which are accessible using road vehicles: they cannot reach more remote huts (including Refuge de la CB, Rifugio Elisabetta, Cabane Combal, Rifugio Bertone, Rifugio Bonatti, Alpage de la Peule, les Ecuries de Charamillon, Refuge du Lac Blanc, Refuge de la Flégère and Refuge Bellachat). Usually, they can also store surplus baggage while you are on the trail.

Most of the companies offering guided/unguided tours will offer baggage transfers as part of the package. A few businesses also offer baggage transfer services for independent trekkers: you do not need to book a tour to use them. However, prices are not cheap and it can cost more than €300 in total for solo trekkers: however, the more people in your group, the cheaper it gets.

The maximum bag weight is normally 15kg. Always use a waterproof pack-liner inside the bag to make sure your gear stays dry.

Businesses offering luggage transfer to independent trekkers include:

- **Besson Transports:** long-established and reliable; you can check prices and book online; www.taxi-montblanc.com; contact@taxi-montblanc.com; +33 (0)4 50 93 62 07.
- **Chamonix Valley Transfers (CVT):** www.chamonix-valley-transfers.co.uk; info@chamonix-valley-transfers.com; +33 (0)4 85 80 01 32.

Fuel for camping stoves

Airlines will not permit the transport of fuel so campers will need to source it upon arrival, before setting out on the trek. Generic screw-in gas canisters (which are now pretty much the universal standard) are readily available in France, Italy and Switzerland; Campingaz canisters (pierceable and twist-on) which are popular in France are readily available there but slightly less common in Switzerland and Italy. Outdoor shops normally stock canisters (see below) and you may find them in supermarkets/grocery shops and at campsites. If you need petrol/diesel for a multi-fuel stove, the closest gas stations to the TMB are at LH and Courmayeur; there are also gas stations at Chamonix, St-Gervais-les-Bains (near LC) and Orsières (near Champex). White gas/Coleman fuel is harder to find but it is sometimes stocked in outdoor shops.

Outdoor shops

Along the TMB route, there are outdoor shops at LH, LC, Courmayeur, la Fouly and Champex. Off the route, there are outdoor shops at Argentière (near Tré-le-Champs) and Orsières (near Champex). There are also countless outdoor shops in Chamonix where many trekkers stay before and after the trek: they sell everything that you could possibly need and Chamonix is therefore the best place to stock up before the trek.

However, those travelling from Geneva could also visit one of the outdoor shops in Geneva city centre: many trains from Geneva Airport to Chamonix stop at Geneva Cornavin which is close to the following stores:

- **Decathlon:** Rue de Lausanne 16-20, 1201 Geneva; +41 (0)22 900 0404; www.decathlon.ch.
- **Univers Sports:** Rue de la Servette 52, 1202 Geneva; +41 (0)22 733 3358; www.univers-sports.ch.
- **Ochsner Sport:** Rue du Marché 9/11, 1204 Geneva; +41 (0)22 310 8968; www.ochsnersport.ch.

There are also a few outdoor shops in Martigny:

- **Look Montagne:** Rue du Léman 19, 1920 Martigny; +41 (0)27 722 9155; www.lookmontagne.ch.
- **Sport X:** Av. de Fully 63, 1920 Martigny; +41 (0)27 720 6882; www.sportx.ch.

Flying with trekking poles

Some overseas trekkers fly with only hand luggage and do not check in additional bags. Because most airlines do not permit trekking poles to be carried onto the plane as hand luggage, they source them upon arrival, before setting out on the trek; at the end of the trek, the poles are gifted to other trekkers or discarded. Most outdoor shops stock poles but the budget poles at Decathlon in Chamonix are amongst the cheapest: although they are slightly heavier than upmarket carbon poles, they are perfectly adequate for the TMB and cost less than €20 each; we have successfully completed thousands of miles of trekking with them.

Ticks

As is often the case in Europe, ticks are present in the Alps. They can carry Lyme disease or tick-borne encephalitis so check yourself regularly. Remove ticks with a tick removal tool (making sure that you get all of it out) and then disinfect the area.

Pastous

A Pastou keeping watch over its flock

The trail enters rural areas and sheep are grazed in the high mountains in summer. Often, the shepherd will live at high altitude in a tiny cabin throughout the grazing season. To protect the sheep from wolves (which are now prevalent again), flocks are often accompanied by dogs. Frequently, the dog is a Pastou (or Patou) which is very large, white and long-haired: it is related to an old Pyrenean breed. They are usually raised with the flock so form a close bond with the sheep. Often they growl or bark if you approach the flock. Although uncommon, occasionally visitors to the Alps are bitten by a Pastou which thought that there was a threat to its sheep. Accordingly, the best advice is to give them a wide berth and assume that there may be a Pastou with any flock you encounter. Remember that from afar, the colour and texture of Pastous' coats makes them hard to spot amongst the sheep.

Stage 5b's balcony path

Equipment

The underrated Stage 11b

The trekker has no influence over challenges like weather and terrain but can control the contents of a pack carried on the trail. Nevertheless, many trekkers set off carrying equipment which is unnecessary or simply too heavy. The more your pack weighs, the harder the trek will be: lugging a heavy pack can lead to exhaustion, injury and/or abandonment. Accordingly, you should give equipment choice careful consideration: it will be crucial to your enjoyment of the trek and the likelihood of success.

Of course, it is easy to understand why a pack should be light, however, it is much more difficult to put this into practice when there are so many things you 'need' in daily life. With experience, it becomes easier to sift between essentials and luxuries but, if you have not been on a multi-day trek before, this can be an unfathomable dilemma. However, if you follow the advice here and limit yourself to the items on our checklist then you should not go far wrong.

A trekker's base weight is the weight of his/her pack, excluding food and water. If you are not carrying camping gear and cooking equipment, it is perfectly possible to get by with a base weight of 5-6kg (13lb) or less. If you intend to carry camping equipment then, by investing in some modern lightweight gear, you could start the trek with a base weight of 8-9kg (17lb) or less. Many people are quick to tell you that the lighter the gear, the greater the price but that is not always the case. While it is true that lightweight gear can be expensive, there are also some excellent lightweight products which are great value. Tents, sleeping bags and backpacks are the three heaviest items that you will carry so they offer the biggest opportunities for weight-saving. But do not ignore the smaller items either as the weight can quickly add up. Accordingly, if you can afford it, it is sensible to invest some money in gear before you leave home. The lighter your gear, the more you will enjoy the trek and the better your chance of success. Be ruthless as every ounce counts.

Recommended basic kit

When undertaking any long-distance route, you should be properly equipped for the worst terrain and the worst weather conditions which you could encounter. In the Alps, this means that you should carry clothing to combat cold, heat, sun, and rain. Becoming cold and wet in the mountains is unpleasant and can be dangerous. Furthermore, if you are lucky and the sun does shine, you will not want to get sunburn (which can put an end to your trek). Also remember that, even in summer, you could experience snow at altitude.

Layering of clothing is the key to managing body temperature. In cool weather, layers can be added: warm air becomes trapped between the layers, acting as insulation. In warmer weather, you simply remove layers and carry them in your pack. Merino wool or man-made materials are preferable: they are lightweight and warm and they wick moisture away from the skin. Do not wear cotton: it is heavy and it does not dry quickly (making you cold).

Hiking Boots/Shoes	Good quality, properly fitting and worn in. Robust soles (such as Vibram) are advisable. Some use trail-running shoes but many prefer boots with ankle support. Shoes/boots with a waterproof membrane (such as Gore-Tex) are good, particularly if there is snow on the ground.
Socks	Two pairs of good quality, quick-drying walking socks.
Camp shoes	It is nice to have spare footwear for the evenings. Flip-flops or Crocs are a common choice as they are light. However, if you have comfortable hiking boots/shoes then you might consider not bringing camp shoes to save weight.
Waterproof jacket and trousers	They should be waterproof and breathable. A mid-weight jacket is fine: the heaviest material is unnecessary but the lightest fabrics may not give adequate protection at altitude.
Base layers	Two T-shirts and underpants of man-made fabrics or merino wool, which wick moisture away from your body.
Fleece	A warm middle layer. Man-made fabrics are best.
Trousers/shorts	1 pair of lightweight walking trousers and 1 pair of shorts. Alternatively, some prefer 2 pairs of trousers. Convertible trousers are practical as you can remove the legs on warm days.
Gloves	Lightweight gloves are usually sufficient. However, it is sensible to choose waterproof ones.
Warm hat & buff	Even in summer, it can be cold at altitude, particularly on windy days.
Down jacket	Even in summer, prepare for low temperatures, especially in the evening and early morning.
Sunglasses, sun hat, sunscreen and lip salve	The sun is strong at altitude: do not set out without these items.
Sleeping sheet	A thin liner/bag made of silk or cotton. Required to sleep in mountain huts: see p29.
Head-light with spare batteries	A flashlight is useful (in both huts and tents) if you need to go to the bathroom in the night. Furthermore, it is good practice to carry one for emergencies: it can assist if you get caught out late and enables you to signal to rescuers.

Backpack	Your backpack is one of the heaviest items that you will carry. The difference in the weights of various packs can be surprisingly large. 35-40 litres should be sufficient if you are not carrying camping gear. 45-60 litres should be adequate for campers. If you need a pack bigger than these then you are probably carrying too much. Look for well-padded shoulder straps and waist band. Much of the weight of the pack should sit on your hips rather than your shoulders.
Waterproof pack-liner	Most backpacks are not very waterproof. An internal liner will keep your gear dry if it rains. Many trekkers use external pack covers but we do not find them to be very useful: they flap in the wind and, in heavy rain, water still leaks into the pack around the straps (so you need an internal liner anyway).
Basic first-aid kit	Including plasters, a bandage, antiseptic wipes and painkillers. Blister plasters, moleskin padding or tape (such as Leukotape) can be useful to prevent or combat blisters. A tick removal tool/card is also recommended.
Map, compass & GPS device	For maps, see p53. A GPS unit or a smart-phone mapping app is a useful addition but they are no substitute for a map and compass: after all, batteries can run out and electronics can fail.
Walking poles	These transfer weight from your legs onto your arms, keeping you fresher. They also save your knees (particularly on descents) and can reduce the likelihood of falling or twisting an ankle. Poles are invaluable in snowy conditions.
Phone and charging cable	A smart-phone is a very useful tool on a trek. It can be used for emergencies. Furthermore, apps for weather, mapping and hotel booking are invaluable. It can also serve as your camera, saving weight.
Ziplock plastic bag	A lightweight way of keeping money and passports dry.
Ear plugs	Useful if staying in hut dormitories: you will thank us if someone snores!
Emergency food	Carry some emergency food over and above your planned daily rations. Energy bars, nuts and dried fruit are all good.
Toilet paper and trowel	Bring a lightweight backpacking trowel in case nature calls on the trail: bury toilet waste and carry out used toilet paper.
Whistle	For emergencies. Many rucksacks have one incorporated into the sternum strap.
Knife	A Swiss Army knife for cutting cheese and for emergencies.
Portable battery pack	Although huts have charging points for electronic devices, they will be in high demand. Accordingly, many people carry portable battery packs: Anker make good ones.
Toiletries	If you wish to take showers at campsites and huts, a small hotel-size bottle of shower gel should be enough to last the trek, saving weight. An almost empty toothpaste tube will also save weight. Leave that make-up behind!
Towel	If you wish to take showers at campsites or huts, you will need a towel: light trekking towels save a lot of weight.

Dolonne (Stage 4c)

Additional gear for campers

Tent: this is one of the heaviest things that you will carry so it provides a big opportunity for weight saving. Some 2-person tents weigh more than 3kg while others weigh less than 0.6kg. The heaviest ones are normally built for extreme winter conditions and are overkill for the normal Alpine trekking season. Some of the lightest ones, however, are not particularly robust and the thin material can be prone to damage on rocky ground.

Although a few premium brands charge a lot for their products and there are some very expensive tents at the lightest end of the scale, these days there are plenty of mid-weight tents available at reasonable prices. Tents weighing 1 to 1.6kg often strike a good balance between price, longevity and weight. Consider money spent here as an investment in your well-being and enjoyment of one of the world's great trails. Believe us when we say that a few kgs can be the difference between success and failure.

Your tent should be waterproof to ensure that you stay dry during rainy nights. A footprint is a good idea to protect its base: 'footprint' is a trendy, modern word for what used to be known as a groundsheet. Sometimes you can buy footprints specific to your tent model but we prefer to use a sheet of Tyvek which can be cut to size: Tyvek is extremely tough and is cheaper, and normally lighter, than most branded footprints.

Tent pegs: tent weights provided by manufacturers normally exclude the weight of the pegs. The pegs actually provided with tents can be quite heavy and many trekkers buy replacement ones which are lighter. Six heavy pegs can weigh as much as 240g while 6 light pegs can weigh as little as 6g. There are many different types available these days and it is important to match the peg with the type of ground they will be used in. You will usually find grassy pitches on this trek, and therefore pegs do not need to be overly strong: titanium ones (which are very light) are a good choice although they can be expensive.

Sleeping bag: every sleeping bag has a 'comfort rating': this is the lowest temperature at which the standard woman should enjoy a comfortable night's sleep. There is also a 'lower comfort limit' which is for men. That may sound simple but it is not. Although all reputable sleeping bag manufacturers use the same independent standard, the bags are not tested in the same place so there is a lack of consistency amongst ratings. Also, the ratings are designed with an average man and woman in mind, however, every person is different: some people get colder than others and need a warmer bag. The ratings should therefore be used as a guide only and it is wise to choose a bag with a comfort rating which is at least 5°C lower than the night temperatures that you are likely to encounter.

Between the start of July and the middle of August, a bag with a comfort rating between -5°C and 5°C (depending on whether you sleep hot or cold) is normally sufficient to cope with the likely night temperatures. Outside of this period, it can be prudent to go with something a little warmer in case the weather throws a cold spell at you: perhaps a bag with a comfort rating between -10°C and 0°C. It is quite a difficult decision because although you want to be warm at night, you do not want to bring a bag that is much too warm as that would add unnecessary weight to your pack.

Unfortunately, with sleeping bags, price tends to be inversely proportional to weight. This is largely because the lightest bags are filled with goose/duck down which is expensive. Synthetic bags are also available but they are much heavier so down is a better choice for trekking. The disadvantage of down bags is that they can lose their warmth if they get wet but that is less likely if you have a good tent and pack liner. Our advice is first to decide what comfort rating you will require. Then choose the lightest bag (with that rating) which you can afford.

Sleeping mat: this makes it comfortable for you to sleep on the hard ground and insulates you from the ground's cold surface. There are three types: air, self-inflating and closed-cell foam. The advantages and disadvantages of each are set out below. All factors considered, we prefer air mats although the very lightest ones may not be sufficiently warm for some trekkers. Thermarest's NeoAir Xlite and NeoAir Xtherm are good choices.

Sleeping mat type	Pros	Cons
Air mats: need to be blown up	Lightest **Very comfortable** Most compact when packed **Thicker: good for side sleepers**	Most expensive **Hard work to inflate** Can be punctured **Less warm than self-inflating**
Self-inflating mats: a combination of air and closed-cell foam. The mat partially inflates itself when the valve is opened	Warmest **Very comfortable** Quite compact **More durable than air mats** Firmness is adjustable by adding air	Heavier **More expensive than closed-cell foam** Can be punctured
Closed-cell foam mats	Light **Least expensive** Most durable **Cannot be punctured**	Not compact: needs to be strapped to the outside of your pack **Least warm** Least comfortable

Pillow: some use rolled-up clothing but we prefer inflatable trekking pillows which only weigh around 50g.

Stove: you should choose a stove that uses a type of fuel which is readily available in the Alps. Airlines do not permit you to carry fuel on planes so, if you are flying, you will need to source fuel on arrival (see p58). Although white gas/Coleman fuel is sometimes stocked in outdoor shops, these days gas is more widely available. Most gas stoves are designed to fit generic screw-on canisters which are readily available in Europe. Canisters for Campinggaz stoves (which are popular in France) are available too. Multi-fuel stoves that burn petrol/diesel are useful but they tend to be heavier, dirtier and more complicated than many gas stoves: the locations of service stations along the route are listed on p58

Hundreds of different stoves are available, some more complicated than others. Often the lightest ones are the most simple and often the most simple ones are relatively inexpensive. If, like most campers, you will eat dried food such as pasta and rice then your stove will need to do little more than boil water. A basic stove which mounts on top of a gas canister will therefore be adequate: such a stove should also be cheap and lightweight (less than 100g).

Aiguille Verte & Grand Dru (Stage v10a)

Safety

Col de la Seigne (Stage 3b)

On a calm summer's day, the Alps are paradise. But a sudden weather shift or an injury can alter your circumstances dramatically so treat the mountains with respect and be conscious of your experience levels and physical capabilities. The following is a non-exhaustive list of recommendations:

- The fitter you are at the start of your trip, the more you will enjoy the hiking.
- Start early to avoid ascending during the hottest part of the day and to allow more surplus time in case something goes wrong.
- Do not stray from the waymarked paths so as to avoid getting lost and to help prevent erosion of the landscape.
- Before you set out each day, study the route and make plans based upon the abilities of the weakest member of your party.
- Obtain a weather forecast (daily if possible) and reassess your plans in light of it. Avoid exposed routes if the weather is uncertain.
- Never be too proud to turn back if you find the going too tough or if the weather deteriorates.
- Bring a map and compass and know how to use them. GPS devices are useful too.
- It can be sensible to call ahead to your accommodation and tell them what time you will arrive. If you do not turn up then they can raise the alarm.
- Carry surplus food and clothing for emergencies.
- Avoid exposed high ground in a thunderstorm. If you get caught out in one then drop your walking poles and stay away from trees, overhanging rocks, metal structures and caves. Generally accepted advice is to squat on your pack and keep as low as possible.
- In snowy conditions, follow waymarks carefully and do not leave the route. Be wary of following someone else's footprints: there is always a chance that they have strayed from the trail.
- In the event of an accident, move an injured person into a safe place and administer any necessary first-aid. Keep the victim warm. If possible, use your cell-phone to call for help: for emergency numbers, see p67. If you have no signal then send someone to the nearest mountain hut or settlement for help.
- Mountain biking is very popular in the Alps so take care. A collision with a bike would not be pleasant.
- When cooking on a camping stove, place the stove on the ground. Avoid using it on a picnic table. We have witnessed a trekker knocking over his stove and spilling boiling water on his legs: this is a sure-fire way to end your trek.

General Information

Language: French is the first language in both France and the parts of Switzerland which the TMB travels (the Swiss canton of Valais). German and Italian are also official languages in Switzerland and are widely spoken in the Valais. In the parts of Italy which the TMB travels (the Aosta Valley), Italian is the first language but many locals also speak French. In most places, locals will have at least some basic English: along the trail, it seems that English has largely been adopted as the TMB's lingua franca.

Charging electronic devices: almost all accommodation provides charging facilities. In mountain huts, you sometimes have to queue to use communal power points and therefore many trekkers also bring their own portable battery packs. In France/Italy, continental two-pin plugs are used. In Switzerland, these days, most tourist accommodation also provides continental two-pin sockets: older properties may still have the traditional Swiss three-pin sockets but these are becoming more rare. Travellers from outside the EU should get by in all three countries with a Type-C Europlug adapter.

Money: France/Italy uses the Euro (€). Switzerland has the Swiss Franc (CHF) but Euros are normally accepted too (although you may not get a great exchange rate). Hotels and most huts accept credit cards, however, it is a good idea to carry some cash in case credit card machines in remote locations are out of order. Along the route, there are ATMs in, LH, LC, Courmayeur, la Fouly and Champex: however, it is wise to carry surplus cash in case an ATM is out of order. A short distance OR, there are ATMs in Chamonix, BSM, Argentière and Orsières.

Paying accommodation deposits: to secure a booking, you may be required to pay a deposit in euros or Swiss francs by transferring funds to the accommodation provider's bank account. One of the easiest ways of doing this (if you do not already have a euro/CHF account) is to open an online account with Wise at **www.wise.com**. Wise enables you to hold funds in numerous different currencies (including euros and Swiss francs), exchange funds from your home currency to euros/CHF and make low-cost transfers in euros/CHF to the accommodation provider's account: exchange rates are reasonable.

Visas: France, Italy and Switzerland are all in the Schengen zone. Citizens of the UK, EU, Australia, New Zealand, Canada or the US do not need a visa for short tourist trips to Schengen countries. Schengen entry requirements for non-EU nationals (including British nationals) are scheduled to change in late 2025 with the introduction of a new Entry/Exit System (EES) which will require travellers to provide biometric data before entry: this will apply to both travellers requiring visas and those who do not need one; you will not need to do anything in advance but clearing immigration may take longer. Furthermore, a new travel authorisation scheme (ETIAS) is scheduled to commence in late 2026, which will apply to visa-exempt travellers (including UK, Australia, New Zealand, Canada and US nationals): travellers who do not need a visa to enter Schengen countries will nevertheless need to apply for an ETIAS travel authorisation before starting their trip; the ETIAS authorisation will be valid for three years and will allow multiple entries of up to 90 days within any 180 day period.

Cell-phones: these days, there is cell network along much of the trail (particularly in towns and villages). However, in some remote valleys, network coverage is poor: in particular, there is little network along the stretch of the TMB between Refuge de Nant-Borrant (2a/2b) and Col de la Seigne (3b). When network is available, it is likely to be a 4G/5G service, enabling access to the internet from smart-phones.

International dialling codes: the country codes for France, Italy and Switzerland are +33, +39 and +41 respectively. If dialling from overseas, the first 0 in both French and Swiss area codes is omitted. However, the 0 in Italian area codes is not omitted.

WiFi: most hotels/gîtes have WiFi. Some huts have WiFi but some do not.

Emergencies and rescue: the emergency number is 144 in Switzerland, 112 in France and 118 in Italy. However, in fact, **112** is the universal European emergency number and it works in Italy and Switzerland as well as France. Generally, rescue services in France are free of charge. However, rescue services in Switzerland and Italy's Aosta Valley are not always free: in particular, helicopter evacuation could cost you a lot of money. Accordingly, it is wise to buy rescue insurance. A good option is membership of the British section of the Austrian Alpine Club (which is open to everyone and not just British trekkers): see **www.alpenverein.at/britannia**. Membership costs around £62 and includes worldwide rescue insurance: it also gives you a discount on the price of a bed at huts which are affiliated to Club Alpin Français or Club Alpino Italiano (see p52).

Medical insurance: depending upon your nationality, any required medical treatment in France/Italy/Switzerland may not be provided free of charge so it is wise to purchase travel/medical insurance which covers hiking. Medical insurance is not the same as rescue insurance: rescue insurance usually covers only the cost of the rescue itself but not any required medical treatment.

Further information: the following websites are useful:

- **www.autourdumontblanc.com:** information on the TMB
- **www.chamonix.com:** tourist information for the **Chamonix Valley**
- **www.chamonix.net:** tourist information for the **Chamonix Valley**
- **www.myswitzerland.com:** the official tourism website for **Switzerland**
- **www.lovevda.it:** the official tourism website for Italy's **Aosta Valley**
- **www.sac-cas.ch:** the official website for **Club Alpin Suisse** (the Swiss Alpine Club)
- **www.ffcam.fr:** the official website for **Club Alpin Français** (the French Alpine Club).

Facebook groups are also an excellent source of information and enable you to draw on the experience of others: questions posted on the groups are answered by numerous people who have already completed the trail. The best Facebook groups for the TMB are:

- **Tour du Mont Blanc Q&A:** www.facebook.com/groups/tourdumontblancforum
- **Tour du Mont Blanc:** www.facebook.com/groups/MontBlancTour

Aiguillette d'Argentière (Stage 10a)

Wildlife

Ibex near Lac Blanc (Stage v10c)

The extremely varied ecosystems mean that there are plenty of vertebrates in the Alps. Generally, early morning is the best time for sightings: often the first party on the trail spots many chamois or ibex but following groups do not see any.

Bouquetin (ibex): a member of the goat family with long scimitar shaped horns (which have deep ridges). It was saved from extinction by the Savoy kings who banned most hunting in 1821 and created a royal reserve in 1856 (which finally became Italy's Gran Paradiso National Park). After a series of reintroductions in the 20th century, they are now fairly widespread throughout the Alps.

Chamois: another type of mountain goat which is smaller than the ibex and is widespread in the Alps. It has shorter horns which do not have deep ridges. Chamois are frequently spotted in herds. They are much more wary of humans than ibex.

Deer: various species are common below the tree line. Chevreuil (roe deer) are reddish or grey-brown and daim (fallow deer) tend to be brown with white spots. Look out for them when climbing through forests early in the morning.

Marmots: everyone loves these fat rodents which are easily spotted in summer when they graze relentlessly to put on layers of fat to last the long winter hibernation. They live in colonies in grassy parts of the mountains, often standing upright on their hind legs like a meerkat. They whistle as you approach to warn their colony of an intruder.

Marmot

Sanglier (wild boar): a member of the pig family with small tusks. They are common in forests. In the unlikely event that you spot one, keep your distance because they can be dangerous.

Wolves: they were hunted almost to extinction in the Alps in the 20th century. In recent decades, conservation efforts in Italy increased numbers and many have crossed the border into neighbouring countries through the mountains. They are protected but their presence is controversial and particularly unpopular with shepherds who lose sheep to them. They are rarely spotted by hikers.

Other mammals: squirrels, foxes, badgers, weasels and mice are fairly common below the tree line.

Fish: species of trout are found in many rivers, streams and lakes. Some high alpine lakes also contain Arctic char.

Lagopède (or ptarmigan): a grouse-like bird. Its plumage is white in the winter and largely brown in the summer.

Golden eagle: during the hot parts of the day, they can sometimes be seen circling in the thermals to gain altitude as they scan the ground for prey.

Gypaète barbu (bearded vulture): a vulture with a wingspan of up to 3m. In Germany it was given the name 'Lammergeier' (lamb-hawk) because it was believed (probably incorrectly) that it attacked lambs. It is the largest bird in the Alps. Although rare, numbers have increased in recent years.

Golden eagle

La Fouly (Stage 6e/7)

Plants & Flowers

A flower-filled alpine meadow in June

The Alps are home to thousands of species of plants including the incredible wild-flowers. June is a fabulous month for flowers, which wait patiently throughout the winter for the snow to clear and then rapidly spring to life. At this time, carpets of different colours cover the slopes and pastures. Although spring is the peak time for flowers, there are still plenty throughout the summer. Watch out for the following:

Alpenrose: a bright pink member of the rhododendron family which coats the slopes at altitude in June/July.

Viola: a small flower in a variety of colours including yellow, white and blue (or a combination of those colours). It is often found in grassy areas.

Edelweiss: it is the most famous alpine plant, perhaps because it has a song named after it. This rare white flower is striking and hard to spot because it only grows at high altitude (1800–3300m). It prefers limestone's calcareous soils.

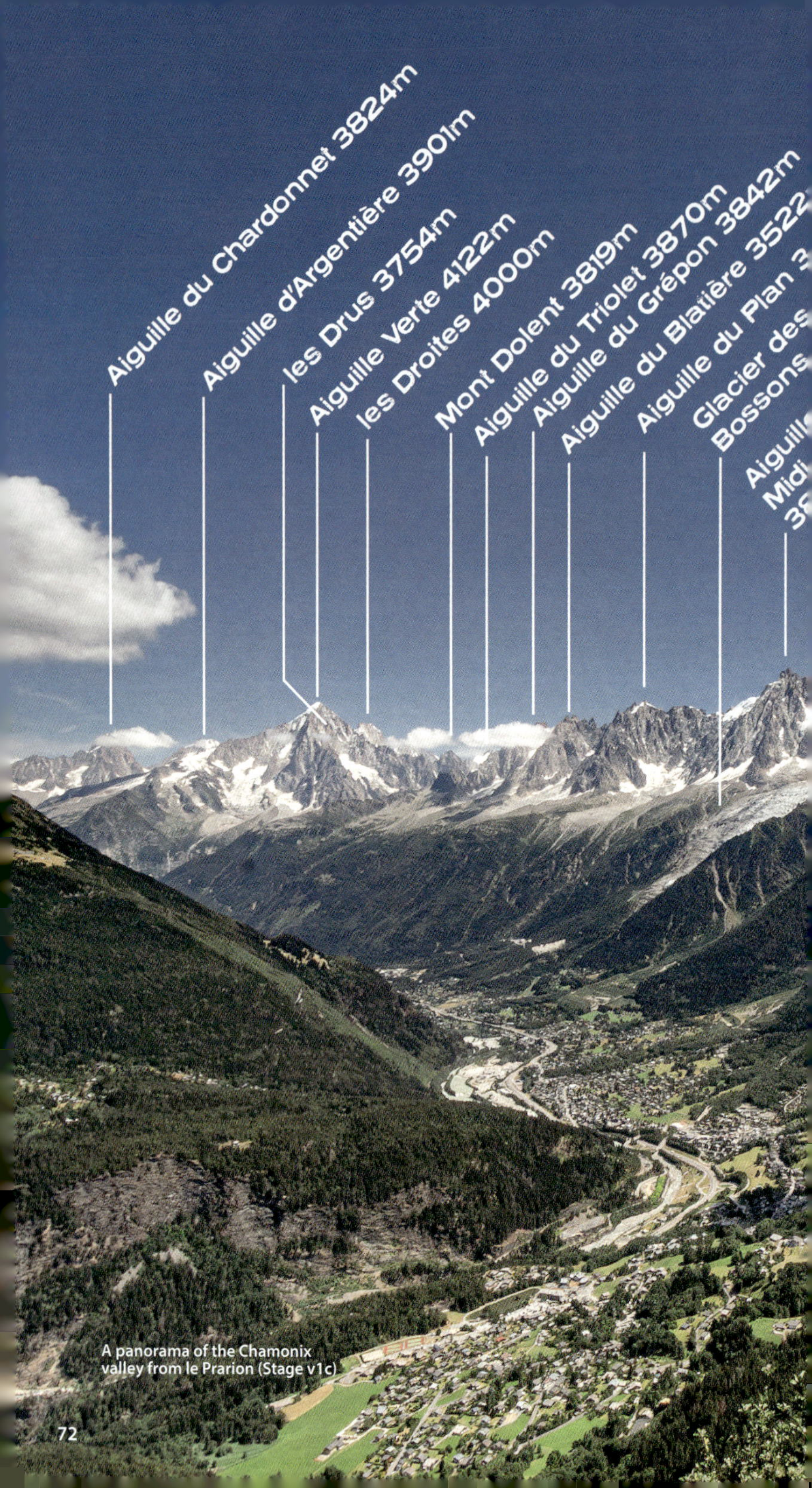

Aiguille du Chardonnet 3824m
Aiguille d'Argentière 3901m
les Drus 3754m
Aiguille Verte 4122m
les Droites 4000m
Mont Dolent 3819m
Aiguille du Triolet 3870m
Aiguille du Grépon 3842m
Aiguille du Blatière 3522
Aiguille du Plan
Glacier des Bossons
Aiguille du Midi

A panorama of the Chamonix valley from le Prarion (Stage v1c)

Glacier de Taconnaz
Mont Blanc du Tacul 4248m
Mont Maudit 4465m
Mont Blanc 4812m
Glacier de Bionnassay
Aiguille de Bionnassay 4052m

1 Les Houches/les Contamines

Stage 1a (Les Houches/Refuge du Fioux): for ACW trekkers, this is a fine introduction to the TMB. The steady climb to Col de Voza is a good warm-up for the bigger challenges ahead: long enough to walk your legs in but not too long; and the terrain is not exposed or particularly steep. Once over Col de Voza, the views of Aiguille de Bionnassay (and its amazing glacier) will take your breath away. Then a short descent on an easy path leads to the wonderful Refuge du Fioux. For CW trekkers finishing in LH, the hard work lies behind and only a short climb and a straightforward descent stand in the way of completion of one of the world's great treks.

Stage 1b (Refuge du Fioux/les Contamines): for ACW trekkers, this is an enjoyable, and mostly gentle, descent (interspersed with a few short climbs). Pass through a series of lovely villages and hamlets to Tresse (near the valley floor). Then, a gentle climb alongside the River Bon Nant leads to the small town of LC. Although there is a bit of road walking, this is no imposition as the views are magnificent. For CW trekkers, this stage incorporates the final long climb of the TMB and your legs may be ready to stop: however, the end of the trek is not far away so be sure to soak up all the sights and sounds on offer.

	Start	Finish	Time	Distance	Ascent (ACW)	Descent (ACW)	Max Alt
1a	Les Houches	Refuge du Fioux	2:45 2:00	7.0km 4.3miles	653m 2142ft	158m 518ft	1653m 5423ft
1b	Refuge du Fioux	Les Contamines	3:00 3:30	10.5km 6.5miles	350m 1148ft	688m 2257ft	1505m 4938ft

Aiguille de Bionnassay overlooks Col de Voza

Itinerary options: Stage v1c is an alternative route between LH and Col de Voza (4); although longer and steeper than Stage 1a, it is more beautiful (see p86).

Between Col de Voza and LC, there are two options: Section 1's valley route (described in this chapter) or the high variant via Col de Tricot (Stages v1a/v1b; p82).

Terrain	Good paths/tracks which are simple to follow. Some short sections along minor roads.
Route-finding	Generally straightforward. However, follow signs carefully through villages (where there are plenty of different paths/tracks/roads).
Camping	Camping Bellevue at LH. Otherwise, there are no campsites or places to bivouac legally. Bivouac is possible along Section v1 (p82).
Trail notes	At the time of writing, the snack bar at Col de Voza was closed and it is unclear if it will reopen.
Transport	You can use the Prarion/Bellevue cable cars to shorten Stage 1a (p48). **LH:** buses/MBE run daily along the Chamonix valley between LH, Chamonix and Argentière; Bellevue/Prarion cable cars. See also p45. **Col de Voza:** Bellevue/Prarion cable cars to/from LH; Tramway du Mont Blanc to SGLF (where there is a mainline train station). **Tresse:** LC shuttle bus. **Les Hoches:** LC shuttle bus. **Plan du Moulin-la Chapelle:** LC shuttle bus. **Les Contamines:** LC shuttle bus; buses to SGLF.

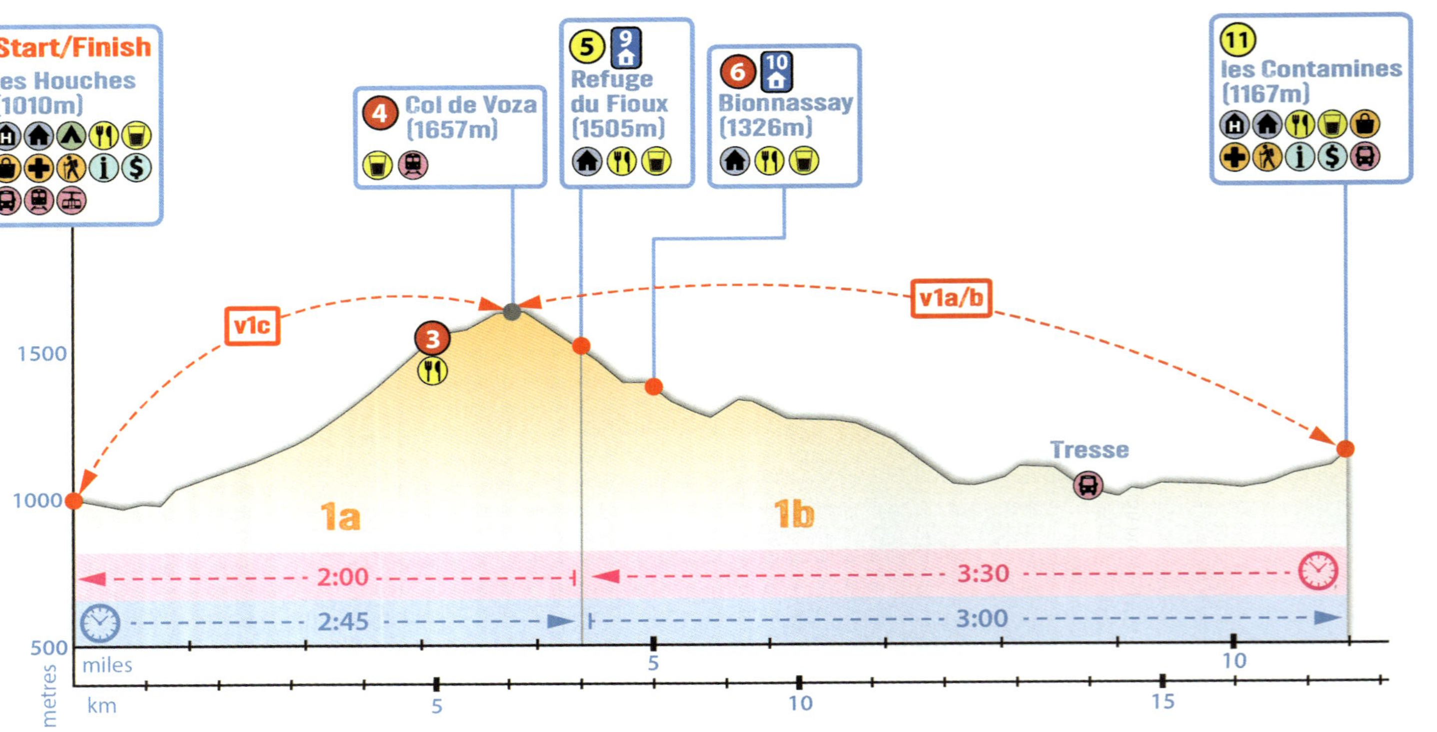

Start/Finish
les Houches
(1010m)
4
Col de Voza
(1657m)
5 9
Refuge
du Fioux
(1505m)
6 10
Bionnassay
(1326m)
11
les Contamines
(1167m)
v1c
v1a/b
3
Tresse
1a
1b
1500
1000
500
metres
2:00
3:30
2:45
3:00
miles
km
5
10
15

Stage 1a: les Houches to Refuge du Fioux

See map on p79. From the **TMB arch**, walk W through **les Houches**. Pass the **Bellevue lift station**. Go through a tunnel.

1 0:20: TL at a building called '**le Grand Balcon**' and climb grassy steps; alternatively, keep SH along the road for the **Prarion lift station**. Then follow a path uphill. Keep SH at a track, still climbing. TL at a junction.

2a 5min later, TL onto a road. TR at a road junction. After 10min, TR onto a path. Shortly afterwards, cross a road and continue uphill on a path.

2 0:55: TL on the road again and continue climbing through the hamlet of **la Maison Neuve**. At the foot of a ski-lift, TR onto a track, **Chemin de la Carbotte**.

3 1:50: Keep heading uphill through a small ski station. There is a restaurant (la Frémi).

4 2:30: Arrive at **Col de Voza (1657m)**. Keep SH at a junction, still on the track. Soon, at the **Tramway du Mont Blanc station**, there is a water tap. Cross the tram tracks. Just afterwards, reach a junction: TR to continue on Stage 1a and descend on a track; alternatively, TL for Stage v1a ('Col de Tricot').

5 2:45: Arrive at **Refuge du Fioux (1505m)** which has a magnificent setting.

Stage 1a: Refuge du Fioux to les Houches

5 **See map on p78.** From **Refuge du Fioux**, climb N on a track: ignore offshoots.

4 0:25: At **Col de Voza (1657m)**, cross the tracks of the **Tramway du Mont Blanc**. Immediately afterwards, TL along a track. Just afterwards, at the tram station, there is a water tap. Shortly afterwards, TR at a junction on another track (which soon descends).

3 0:45: Descend through a small ski station. There is a restaurant (la Frémi).

2 1:10: Keep SH past the bottom of another ski station. Then bear right around the back of a grassy bank. Shortly afterwards, TL down a road. Soon, TR down a path. Shortly, cross a road and descend on a path. Shortly afterwards, TL down the road.

2a 5-10min later, TR down a path (easy to miss). A few minutes later, TR onto a track. A few minutes after that, keep SH down a path.

1 1:40: At a building called '**le Grand Balcon**', TR along the road. Pass the **Bellevue lift station**. Go through a tunnel.

2:00: Walk under the **TMB arch** in **les Houches (1010m)**. Congratulations, you have completed the trek!

The TMB arch in LH

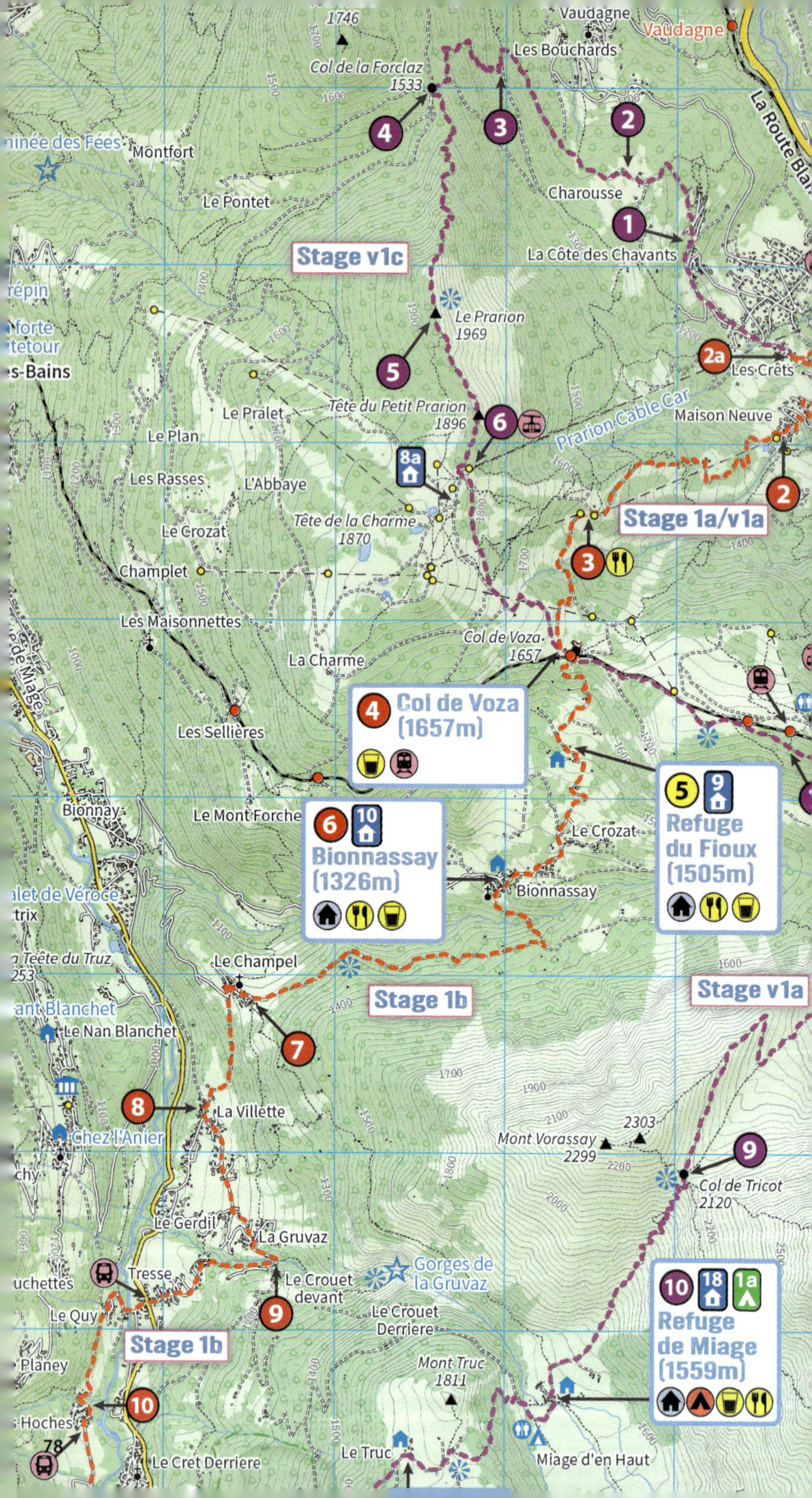

Stage v1c
Stage 1a/v1a
Stage 1b
Stage v1a
Col de la Forclaz 1533
Les Bouchards
Vaudagne
Charousse
La Côte des Chavants
Le Prarion 1969
Tête du Petit Prarion 1896
Les Crêts
Maison Neuve
Prarion Cable Car
Tête de la Charme 1870
Col de Voza 1657
Col de Voza (1657m)
Refuge du Fioux (1505m)
Bionnassay (1326m)
Bionnassay
Le Crozat
Montfort
Le Pontet
Le Pralet
Le Plan
Les Rasses
L'Abbaye
Champlet
Les Maisonnettes
La Charme
Les Sellières
Le Mont Forche
Bionnay
Le Champel
Le Nan Blanchet
La Villette
Chez l'Anier
Le Gerdil
La Gruvaz
Tresse
Le Crouet devant
Le Crouet Derriere
Gorges de la Gruvaz
Le Quy
Mont Vorassay 2299
2303
Col de Tricot 2120
Refuge de Miage (1559m)
Mont Truc 1811
Le Truc
Miage d'en Haut
Le Cret Derriere
La Route Blanche

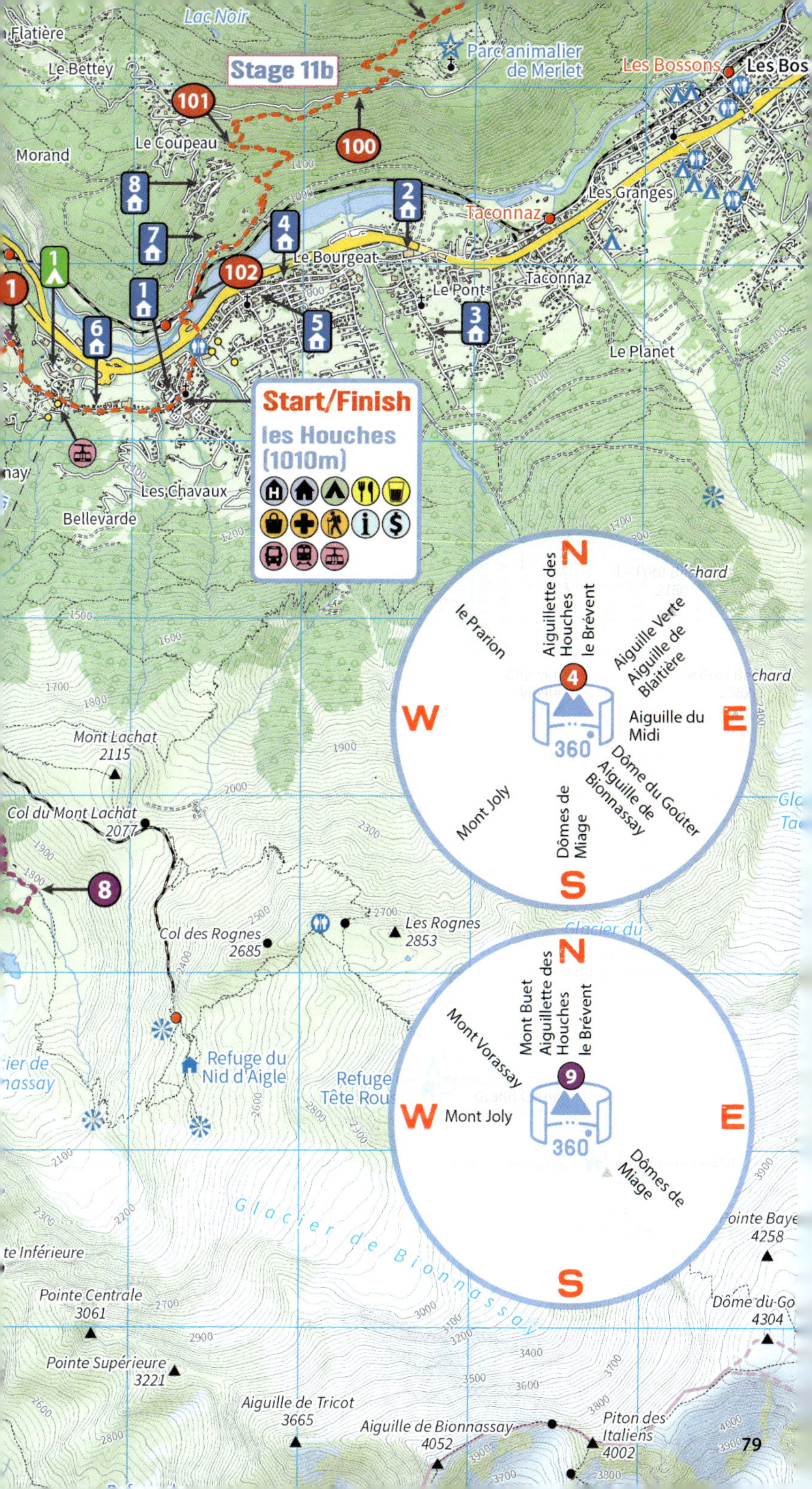
Stage 11b
Lac Noir
Flatière
Le Bettey
Parc animalier de Merlet
Les Bossons
Les Bos
Le Coupeau
Morand
Les Granges
Taconnaz
Le Bourgeat
Le Pont
Le Planet
Start/Finish
les Houches (1010m)
Les Chavaux
Bellevarde
Le Petit Béchard
le Prarion
Aiguillette des Houches
le Brévent
Aiguille Verte
Aiguille de Blaitière
Aiguille du Midi
Dôme du Goûter
Aiguille de Bionnassay
Dômes de Miage
Mont Joly
N
E
S
W
360
Mont Lachat 2115
Col du Mont Lachat 2077
Col des Rognes 2685
Les Rognes 2853
Refuge du Nid d'Aigle
Refuge Tête Rous
Mont Buet
Mont Vorassay
Glacier de Bionnassay
Pointe Baye 4258
Dôme du Go 4304
te Inférieure
Pointe Centrale 3061
Pointe Supérieure 3221
Aiguille de Tricot 3665
Aiguille de Bionnassay 4052
Piton des Italiens 4002
101
100
102
8
7
4
2
1
6
5
3
9

Les Hoches
Le Cret Derriere
La Chapelle
Plan du Moulin
Stage 1b
La Faviere
Le Truc
Auberge du Truc (1750m)
Tête d'Arm
les Contamines (1167m)
La Frasse
Stage v1b
L'Adret
Lac d'Armance
Le Cugnon
Le Lay
le Pontet (1180m)
Combe d
Les Foyères
Parc de loisirs du Pontet
Stage 2a
Stage v2a
Pointe de
Le Pontet
La Gorge
Parc du Chien Polaire
La Sololieu 1490
Notre-Dame-de-la-Gorge
Le Mauvais Pas
Les Rieux
Tête Noire 1973
Refuge de Tré-la-Tête (1969m)
Refuge de Nant-Borrant (1460m)
Stage v2b
La Laya
La Forclaz
La Giettaz
Les Rosières des Prés
La Rollaz
Stage 2b
Pain de sucre du Mont Tondu 3169
Mont Tondu

Stage 1b: Refuge du Fioux to les Contamines

5 See map on p78. From **Refuge du Fioux**, continue descending on the path. Keep SH past the car park at **le Crozat**.

6 0:20: Arrive at the hamlet of **Bionnassay (1326m)**. At **Auberge de Bionnassay**, leave the road, keeping SH on a track. Just afterwards, TL at a junction, passing a little chapel. Descend, cross a footbridge over a torrent and then climb steeply on the other side. TR onto a track.

7 1:15: Descend through **le Champel**. Shortly after a pretty chapel, TL on a road. A few minutes later, at a right-hand hairpin, keep SH on a track.

8 1:40: In the hamlet of **la Villette (1050m)**, follow the road around to the left. Shortly afterwards, TL at a fountain. At the hamlet of **le Gerdil**, TL and climb on a track. 5min later, TL up a road which soon descends again.

9 2:05: TR across a bridge. Shortly afterwards, TR onto a path. After 5min, TL down a road. Soon, follow the road around to the left and descend through **Tresse-d'en-Haut**. Cross a main road and continue SH on a road on the other side. TR at a fork, cross a bridge and follow the road uphill to the right. Keep on the road when it bends left. Soon it becomes a track and then a path.

10 2:30: At **les Hoches**, keep SH and descend on a road. TL at a junction. See map on p80. Shortly afterwards, TL onto a larger road. A few minutes later, cross a bridge. Immediately afterwards, TR on a path, following the river.

11 3:00: TL at a fork to reach **les Contamines (1167m)**.

Stage 1b: les Contamines to Refuge du Fioux

11 See map on p80. From the square/car park next to the **tourist office** in **les Contamines**, pick up a path which descends through trees towards the river. Keep SH at a junction and follow the river N. 20min from the start, TL and cross a bridge over the river: head N along a road. Soon, TR at a junction, heading N on a smaller road. Shortly afterwards, TR at another junction.

10 0:30: See map on p78. At **les Hoches**, TR onto a track. When you meet a road, TL and follow it down to the river. Keep SH across a bridge. Cross a main road and continue SH up **Chemin de Tresse**. At the end of the road, climb E on a path.

9 1:00: TL across a bridge. Then head NW along a road. At **la Gruvaz**, TR onto a track. At the hamlet of **le Gerdil**, TR along a road.

8 1:25: At the hamlet of **la Villette (1050m)**, TR at a junction. Shortly afterwards, TR and climb on a track. Later, keep SH and climb on a road.

7 2:00: Shortly afterwards, TR at a junction in **le Champel**. Pass a pretty chapel. Then climb out of the village on a track. TL at a junction and descend steeply. Cross a footbridge over a torrent and then climb.

6 3:00: Climb NE through the hamlet of **Bionnassay (1326m)**. Head N past the car park at **le Crozat** and continue climbing.

5 3:30: Arrive at **Refuge du Fioux (1505m)**.

v1a/b Les Houches/les Contamines (via Col de Tricot)

This variant is more spectacular than the main Section 1 route. In fact, it offers some of the best views on the whole trek. However, it is much harder than Section 1, with more challenging terrain and a lot of climbing. For some ACW trekkers, this will be an overly demanding day, coming at the start of the TMB before legs have adapted to alpine walking. CW trekkers, on the other hand, should by now be well used to the daily rigours of long-distance hiking and this variant provides a more dramatic and worthy finale to the trek.

Stage v1a (LH/Refuge de Miage): for ACW trekkers, the first part of the route is the same as Stage 1a, involving a straightforward climb on good paths to Col de Voza. However, from there, the routes diverge with Stage v1a aiming upwards instead of following Stage 1a down into the valley. Between Col de Voza and Hotel Bellevue, the views of the Chamonix valley are incredible: you can see all the way to Col de Balme (Section 9). After crossing the ever-popular Bionnassay suspension bridge (which spans a powerful torrent created by the melt-waters of the Glacier de Bionnassay), the path starts its long climb to the spectacular Col de Tricot: on the way up, there are wonderful views of Aiguille de Bionnassay and its glacier. At Col de Tricot, you can spot Refuge du Goûter, the highest manned hut in France, which is the final staging point for climbers aiming for MB's summit. From the col, a long, steep descent leads to Refuge de Miage, one of our favourite places on the TMB: the views of the Dômes de Miage are incredible. Col de Tricot is more difficult for CW trekkers because the climb is steeper in that direction: however, from there, the long descent provides plenty of time to savour the sublime scenery for the last time before you finish the trek at LH.

Stage v1b (Refuge de Miage/LC): ACW trekkers start with a short climb to the beautifully situated Auberge du Truc, enjoying more excellent views of the Dômes de Miage; then descend through trees to the town of les Contamines which is a lovely place to end

	Start	Finish	Time	Distance	Ascent (ACW)	Descent (ACW)	Max Alt
v1a	Les Houches	Refuge de Miage	5:30 4:15	14.3km 8.9miles	1260m 4134ft	711m 2333ft	2120m 6955ft
v1b	Refuge de Miage	Les Contamines	2:15 2:45	7.0km 4.3miles	241m 791ft	633m 2077ft	1750m 5741ft

The permanent snow-pack on Aiguille de Bionnassay

this fantastic TMB variant. CW trekkers have a long, steep slog to reach Auberge du Truc: initially, you climb out of the town on shadeless roads and, on a hot day, it is a relief to enter the forest; you will not leave the trees again until Auberge du Truc. From the auberge, the scenery is divine all the way to Refuge de Miage.

Terrain	**Stage v1a:** between LH and Col de Voza, good paths/tracks which are simple to follow; some short sections along minor roads. Between Col de Voza and Refuge de Miage, the route is more challenging: narrow paths with regular undulations; long, steep climb/descent. The path between Col de Tricot and Refuge de Miage is particularly steep. Sometimes snow lies near Col de Tricot until early July: in such conditions, the climb to, and descent from, the col can be challenging and a fall could be serious. In any difficult conditions, it is preferable to use Section 1. **Stage v1b:** good paths/tracks which are simple to follow; minor roads are used near LC; some steep gradients.
Route-finding	Generally straightforward: there are usually signs at junctions. However, between LH and Col de Voza, follow signs carefully through villages (where there are plenty of different paths/tracks/roads). Take care around Col de Tricot in bad weather, snow or low visibility when navigation can be more tricky at these high altitudes.
Camping	Camping Bellevue at LH. Bivouac areas beside Refuge de Miage and Refuge du Truc. Otherwise, no campsites or places to bivouac legally.
Trail notes	At the time of writing, the snack bar at Col de Voza was closed and it is unclear if it will reopen.
Transport	You can use the Bellevue cable car to shorten Stage v1a: the upper station is 5min from 7. The LC shuttle bus calls at the parking area at la Frasse (between 11 and 13): CW trekkers can use it to avoid part of Stage v1b's climb out of LC. **LH:** see p75. **Col de Voza:** see p75. **Les Contamines:** LC shuttle bus; buses to SGLF.

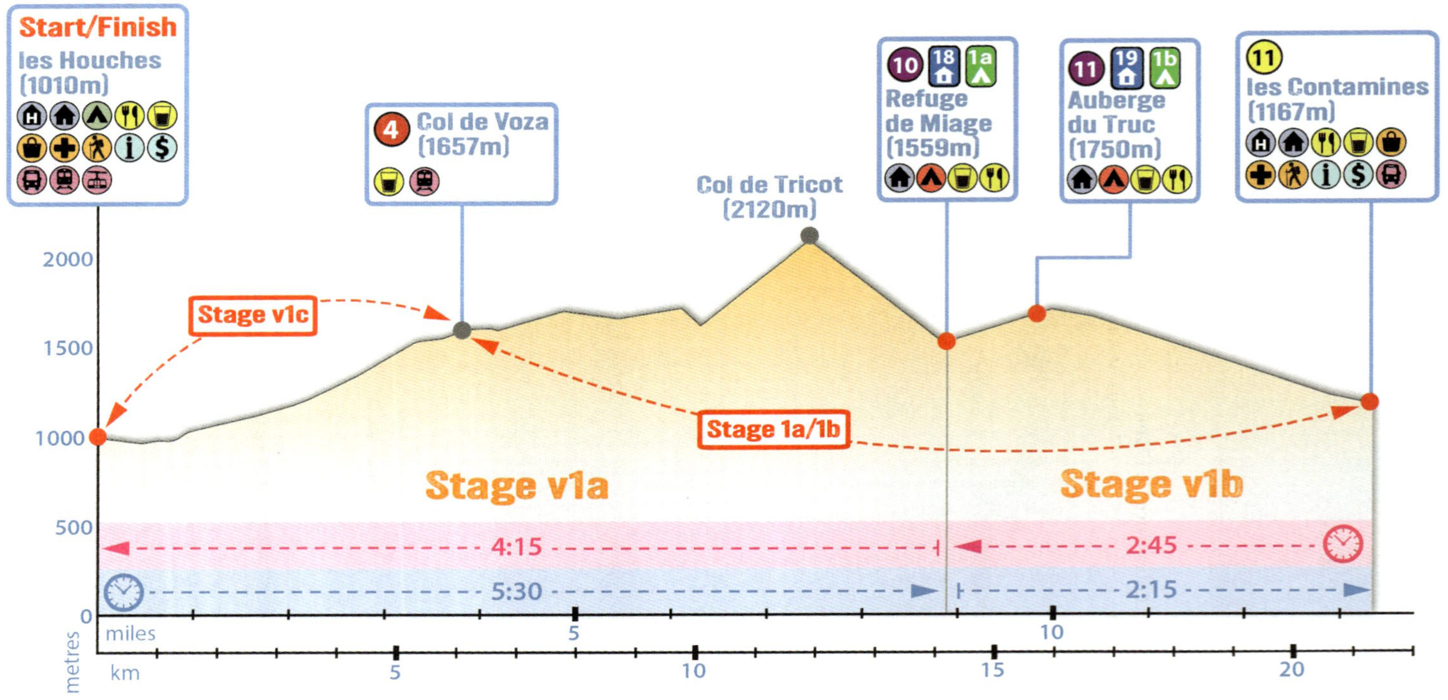

Start/Finish
les Houches
(1010m)
4
Col de Voza
(1657m)
Col de Tricot
(2120m)
10 18 1a
Refuge
de Miage
(1559m)
11 19 1b
Auberge
du Truc
(1750m)
11
les Contamines
(1167m)
Stage v1c
Stage 1a/1b
Stage v1a
Stage v1b
4:15
5:30
2:45
2:15
2000
1500
1000
500
0
metres
miles
5
10
km
5
10
15
20

Stage v1a: les Houches to Refuge de Miage

See map on p79. Follow Stage 1a directions to **Col de Voza** (1653m; 4).

4 2:30: Cross the tracks of the **Tramway du Mont Blanc**. Just afterwards, TL at a junction ('Miage'); alternatively, keep SH for Stage 1a. 20min later, pass **Hotel Bellevue** (which was refurbished but never opened). Shortly afterwards, TR on a path (leaving the track). Just afterwards, keep SH at a junction.

7 2:55: Keep SH at a junction. The path to the left heads to the **Bellevue cable car station**. Soon, fixed cables provide assistance over sections of sloping rocks.

8 3:20: TR at a junction. Descend and cross **Bionnassay suspension bridge**. Shortly afterwards, TL at a junction and climb steeply.

9 4:35: Cross **Col de Tricot (2120m)** and descend steeply to the SW.

10 5:30: TL at a junction to reach **Refuge de Miage (1559m)**.

Stage v1b: Refuge de Miage to les Contamines

10 See map on p78. From **Refuge de Miage**, cross a stream and follow a path SW: pass **Miage bivouac area**. Shortly afterwards, cross a bridge and TL onto a path ('le Truc'): climb steeply and soon enter trees. Above the tree-line, keep SH at a junction: the path on the right leads to the summit of **Mont Truc** (superb views; 15min return).

11 0:30: See map on p80. Pass **Auberge du Truc (1750m)**. Now descend on a track.

12 0:50: TL on a path ('les Contamines').

13 TL when you meet a track: continue descending following waymarks.

11 2:15: Arrive at the church in **les Contamines (1167m)**.

Stage v1b: les Contamines to Refuge de Miage

11 See map on p80. From the church in the centre of LC, climb E on **Chemin du P'Tou**: at junctions, stay on this road. 15min from the start, reach a parking area at **la Frasse**: bus stop, toilet and fountain. Continue climbing E and shortly afterwards, keep SH up a track (into the forest). Shortly afterwards, keep SH at a junction.

13 1:15: TR onto a path (easy to miss).

12 1:40: TR up a track.

11 2:10: Just above the tree-line, reach **Auberge du Truc (1750m)**. See map on p78. Continue SE on a broad path, heading directly towards **Dômes de Miage**. 5min later, keep SH at a junction: the path on the left leads to the summit of **Mont Truc** (superb views; 15min return). Descend steeply through trees. At the bottom of the slope, TR onto a track. Shortly afterwards, pass a **bivouac area**.

10 2:45: Just afterwards, reach **Refuge de Miage (1559m)**.

Stage v1a: Refuge de Miage to les Houches

10 See map on p78. From **Refuge de Miage**, a path heads initially N towards Col de Tricot (which you can see above). Soon the path zigzags steeply upwards.

9 1:20: Cross **Col de Tricot (2120m)** and continue N on a path which contours across the slopes of a ridge (which descends from Mont Vorassay). When you reach the crest of the ridge, there are spectacular views of **Aiguille de Bionnassay** and its glacier. Follow the path down into the valley to the E. TR at a junction ('Bellevue'). Descend steeply on a rocky path. A few minutes later, cross **Bionnassay suspension bridge**.

8 2:00: TL at a junction ('Bellevue'). 5min later, TR at a fork ('Bellevue'). 5min later, fixed cables provide assistance over sections of sloping rocks.

7 2:25: Keep SH at a junction: the path on the right heads to the **Bellevue cable car**. 5min later, TL on a track and follow it to the left of **Hotel Bellevue** (which was refurbished but never opened).

4 2:40: Reach **Col de Voza (1653m)**. Now follow Stage 1a directions (see p77).

4:15: Reach the **TMB arch** in **LH (1010m)**. Congratulations on finishing the trek!

v1c Les Houches/Col de Voza (via le Prarion)

This variant offers a longer, but more spectacular, alternative to Stage 1a. Its main drawcard is the summit of le Prarion which is perhaps the finest place of all from which to view the entire MB massif: by the standards of the Chamonix valley, this outlying peak is relatively small but the views from it are anything but. Because it is set back slightly from the principal peaks, it is a superlative vantage point from which to obtain an overall perspective of the massif: MB and its neighbours are on full display. On a clear day, you will want to spend some time on the summit to identify all the peaks of the range. As a bonus, the route also passes the exceptionally photogenic hamlet of Charousse which has the MB massif as its spectacular backdrop. This hike is not easily forgotten: see the image on p72.

Terrain	Mostly good paths/tracks which are simple to follow. Some short sections along minor roads. The path immediately N of the summit is steep and exposed in places: take care crossing short sections of rocks.
Route-finding	Generally straightforward. However, follow signs carefully through villages (where there are plenty of different paths/tracks/roads). The route near Charousse is a little tricky to follow.
Camping	Camping Bellevue at LH. Otherwise, no campsites or legal bivouac sites.
Trail notes	At the time of writing, the snack bar at Col de Voza was closed and it is unclear if it will reopen.
Transport	Instead of hiking up, ACW hikers can use the Prarion cable car: from the upper station, it is only a short climb to the summit of le Prarion (1km). After visiting the summit, return to the upper station: from there, follow Stage v1c directions to Col de Voza (where you join Stage 1a/v1a). **LH:** see p75. **Col de Voza:** see p75.

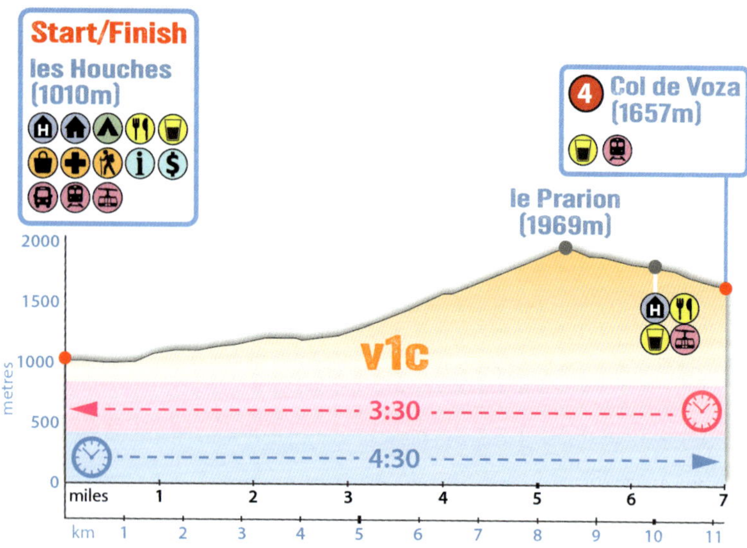

	Start	Finish	Time	Distance	Ascent (ACW)	Descent (ACW)	Max Alt
v1c	Les Houches	Col de Voza	4:30 3:30	11.3m 7.0miles	1003km 3291ft	356m 1168ft	1969m 6460ft

Stage v1c: les Houches to Col de Voza (via le Prarion)

See map on p79. Walk W through **LH**. Pass the **Bellevue lift**. Go through a tunnel.

1 0:20: TL at a building called '**le Grand Balcon**' and climb grassy steps; alternatively, keep SH along the road for the **Prarion lift station**. Then follow a path uphill. Keep SH at a track, still climbing. TL at a junction.

2a 5min later, TR onto a road. Soon, TL onto **Route de la Côte des Chavants**.

1 1:00: TL at a junction. Pass a parking area and keep SH on a track.

2 1:20: Follow a broad path through **Charousse (1210m)**. A few minutes after the hamlet, TL at a junction. Shortly afterwards, TL onto a track.

3 1:45: TR onto a path. When you meet a track, TR.

4 2:30: Shortly afterwards, TL at a junction at **Col de la Forclaz (1533m)**. Just afterwards, TL on a path: soon, climb steeply S.

5 3:50: Reach the summit of **le Prarion (1969m)**. Continue S along the summit ridge. Descend a steep, rocky section.

6 4:15: From the upper station of the **Prarion cable car (1853m)**, descend S on a track.

4 4:30: Arrive at **Col de Voza (1657m)**.

Stage v1c: Col de Voza to les Houches (via le Prarion)

4 See map on p78. From **Col de Voza**, head NW on a track. Shortly afterwards, TL at a junction and climb on a track. At any junctions, continue N.

6 0:40: From the upper station of the **Prarion cable car (1853m)**, climb N on a path ('le Prarion'). Shortly afterwards, TR and head across a section of gravel: on the other side, pick up the path again (yellow waymark). Climb a steep, rocky section.

5 1:05: A few minutes later, reach the summit of **le Prarion (1969m)**. Continue N along the summit ridge and soon start to descend steeply.

4 1:40: TR at **Col de la Forclaz (1533m)**. Shortly afterwards, TR at another junction ('les Houches'). Shortly after that, TL at another junction ('Charousse'): initially, the gradient is gentle but it becomes steeper.

3 2:00: TL onto a track and continue descending. 10min later, TR onto a path ('Charousse'). A few minutes later, TR onto another path and climb for 5min.

2 2:20: Arrive in **Charousse (1210m)**: follow a broad path through the hamlet. Afterwards, keep SH on a track ('les Houches').

1 2:35: At a junction, keep SH, descending on a road ('les Houches'). TR at the next junction, still on the road (yellow sign). At other junctions, continue E.

2a 2:50: TL down a path (easy to miss). A few minutes later, TR onto a track. A few minutes after that, keep SH down a path.

1 3:10: At a building called '**le Grand Balcon**', TR along the road. Pass the **Bellevue lift station**. Go through a tunnel.

3:30: Arrive at the famous arch in **les Houches (1010m)**. Congratulations on completeing the TMB!

Stage 2a (LC/Refuge de Nant-Borrant: ACW trekkers start with a gentle climb alongside the Bon Nant river to the beautiful chapel of Notre Dame de la Gorge; take a break to admire it because the gradient ramps up here. As you ascend steeply through trees on an old Roman road, a torrent gushes through narrow gaps in the rocks: you will pass a thrilling natural stone arch and a Roman bridge. At Refuge de Nant-Borrant, relax on one of the deckchairs in its lovely garden. For CW trekkers, Stage 2a is an easy descent to LC.

Stage 2b (Refuge de Nant-Borrant/Refuge de la Balme): a short but beautiful section of the TMB. For ACW trekkers, it is uphill all the way to Refuge de la Balme, below the dramatic Aiguilles de la Pennaz. Up ahead, to the N, you should see Col du Bonhomme, which you will visit on Stage 2c. CW trekkers have an easy descent.

Stage 2c (Refuge de la Balme/Refuge de la CB): for ACW trekkers, this is where the TMB ramps up a level. The paths get steeper and narrower and the terrain is more exposed. For the first time, you enter properly wild terrain and it is magnificent! This stage also sees the first of the TMB's high passes: Col du Bonhomme is rapidly followed by the beautiful Col de la Croix du Bonhomme. From this second col, a brief descent leads to the wonderfully remote Refuge de la Croix du Bonhomme. Between the cols, there are plenty of ibex, especially in the early morning and evening when most trekkers are safely tucked-up in the huts. For CW trekkers, the descent is stunning although long and tiring.

Stage 2d (Refuge de la CB/les Chapieux): ACW trekkers have a long descent to the pretty hamlet of les Chapieux. It is hard on the knees but the landscape is sublime

	Start	Finish	Time	Distance	Ascent (ACW)	Descent (ACW)	Max Alt
2a	Les Contamines	Refuge de Nant-Borrant	1:55 1:25	5.6km 3.5miles	310m 1017ft	18m 59ft	1459m 4787ft
2b	Refuge de Nant-Borrant	Refuge de la Balme	1:00 0:35	2.5km 1.6miles	247m 810ft	0m 0ft	1706m 5597ft
2c	Refuge de la Balme	Refuge de la CB	2:30 1:30	5.6km 3.5miles	790m 2592ft	53m 174ft	2479m 8133ft
2d	Refuge de la CB	Les Chapieux	1:45 2:50	5.0km 3.1miles	0m 0ft	894m 2933ft	2443m 8015ft

Refuge de la Croix du Bonhomme (Stage 2c/2d)

After the high mountain terrain of the previous stage, the scene is now a bucolic one with remote farms, pastures and herds of cows: the soothing sound of cowbells fills the valley. And the wild-flowers here in spring are staggering. Les Chapieux is a peaceful place to stay. For CW trekkers, Stage 2d is a tough climb: start early because it can be hot here.

Itinerary options: Section v2 (via Refuge de Tré-la-Tête) is a beautiful high level alternative to Stage 2a. See p96.

Stage v3a (via Col des Fours) is a spectacular high level alternative to Stages 2d/3a, travelling directly between Col de la Croix du Bonhomme and Refuge des Mottets (avoiding les Chapieux): see p104.

Terrain	**Stage 2a/2b:** good paths/tracks which are simple to follow; some short sections along minor roads; occasional steep gradients. **Stage 2c/2d:** high altitude routes. Paths/tracks are largely good and simple to follow although the route is more challenging: narrow paths; rocky sections; regular undulations; long, sustained climb/descent with steep gradients. Sometimes snow remains near Stage 2c's cols until early July making the route challenging; in particular, the sloping traverse between the cols can be treacherous in snowy conditions and a fall could be serious.
Route-finding	On Stages 2a/2b, navigation is generally straightforward (with plenty of signs). In good conditions, route-finding on Stages 2c/2d is straightforward too, however, it is more tricky in bad weather, low visibility or snowy conditions.
Camping	Campsite at le Pontet (Stage 2a). Authorised bivouac areas at la Rollaz (Stage 2b), Refuge de la Balme, Refuge de la CB and les Chapieux.
Trail notes	It can be very cold at Refuge de la CB in the evening/early morning. There is little cell network between Refuge de Nant-Borrant and Col de la Seigne (Stage 3b).
Transport	**Les Contamines:** LC shuttle bus; buses to SGLF. **Le Pontet:** LC shuttle bus. **Notre-Dame-de-la-Gorge:** LC shuttle bus. **Les Chapieux:** buses to/from BSM, Ville des Glaciers (Section 3; 27) and Parking des Mottets (Section 3; near Refuge des Mottets 28).

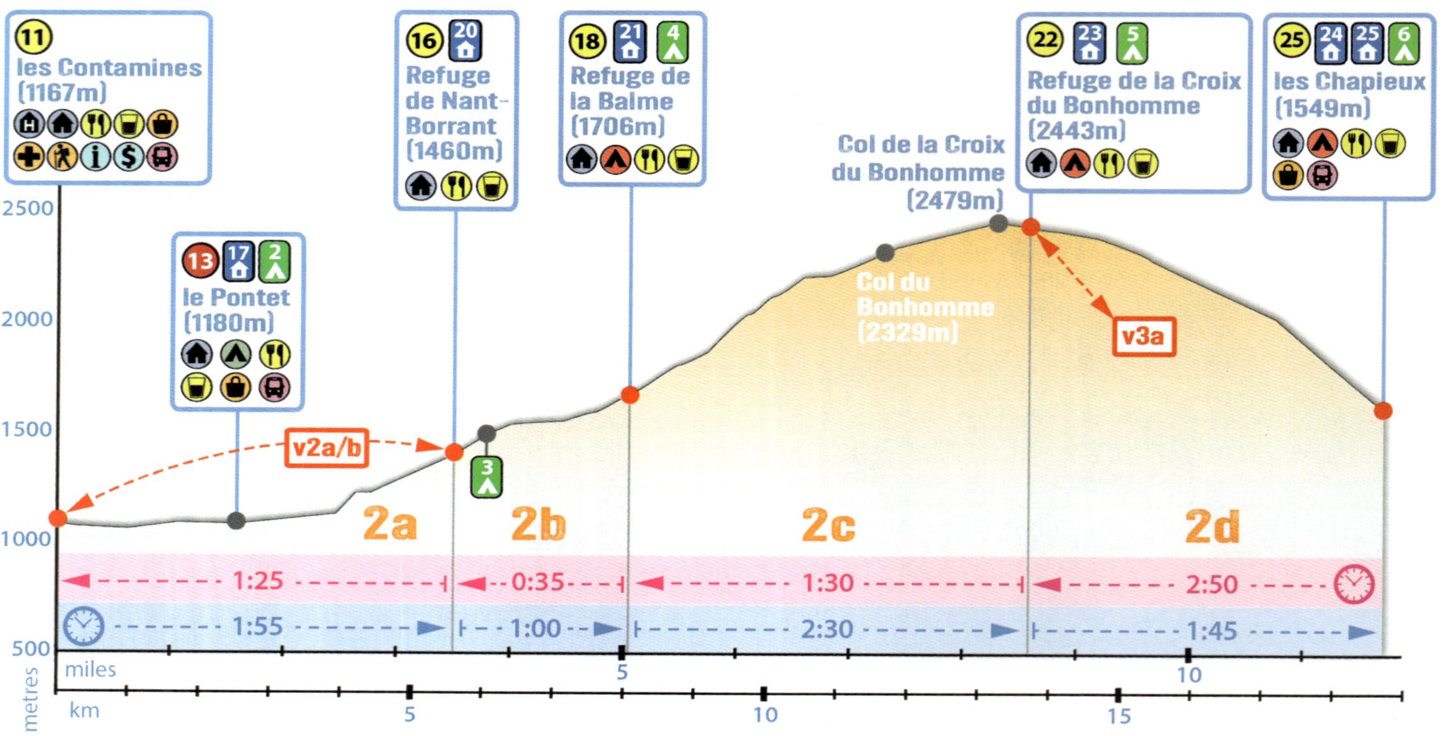

11
les Contamines (1167m)
13 17 2
le Pontet (1180m)
16 20
Refuge de Nant-Borrant (1460m)
18 21 4
Refuge de la Balme (1706m)
3
Col du Bonhomme (2329m)
Col de la Croix du Bonhomme (2479m)
22 23 5
Refuge de la Croix du Bonhomme (2443m)
25 24 25 6
les Chapieux (1549m)
v2a/b
v3a
2a
2b
2c
2d
1:25
0:35
1:30
2:50
1:55
1:00
2:30
1:45
2500
2000
1500
1000
500
metres
miles
km
5
10
15

Stage 2a: les Contamines to Refuge de Nant-Borrant

(11) See map on p80. Head S out of **LC** on the road. Near a road bridge, bear right on a path. Then TR to cross a footbridge. Immediately afterwards, TL and walk upstream.

(12) 0:25: TL across **Pont du Lay**. Immediately afterwards, TR on a path, still walking upstream. Soon, TR and walk alongside a road. Keep SH on a lane when the road bends right. Keep SH when the lane becomes a track.

(13) 0:40: Pass the lake at **le Pontet**. Shortly afterwards, keep SH: alternatively, TR for **Gîte/Camping du Pontet**. Shortly afterwards, TR at a fork. TL at another fork (no waymark). Soon keep SH at a junction.

(14) 1:05: Keep SH at the chapel of **Notre Dame de la Gorge (1210m)** and climb steeply on a stone track (originally laid by the Romans). Pass an interesting **inscription** on the right (see box below) and, after a while, a natural stone arch.

(15) 1:40: Cross a **Roman bridge** across a gorge: the volume of water passing through is incredible.

(16) 1:55: Arrive at **Refuge de Nant-Borrant (1460m)**.

Stage 2b: Refuge de Nant-Borrant to Refuge de la Balme

(16) See map on p80. From **Refuge de Nant-Borrant**, continue S up the track.

(17) 0:10: Pass a sign for the **bivouac area** at **la Rollaz (1535m)**.

(18) 1:00: See map on p92. Arrive at **Refuge de la Balme (1706m)**: bivouac area and public toilets nearby.

Stage 2b: Refuge de la Balme to Refuge de Nant-Borrant

(18) See map on p92. From **Refuge de la Balme**, head N down the track.

(17) 0:30: See map on p80. Pass a sign for the **bivouac area** at **la Rollaz (1535m)**.

(16) 0:35: Arrive at **Refuge de Nant-Borrant (1460m)**.

Stage 2a: Refuge de Nant-Borrant to les Contamines

(16) See map on p80. From **Refuge de Nant-Borrant**, descend N on a stone track (originally laid by the Romans).

(15) 0:05: Cross a **Roman bridge** across a gorge: the volume of water passing through is incredible. Continue descending N on the track. Pass a natural **stone arch** and, after a while, an interesting inscription on the left (see box below).

(14) 0:25: Keep SH at the chapel of **Notre Dame de la Gorge (1210m)**.

(13) 0:40: Keep SH at the lake at **le Pontet**, heading N on a track; alternatively, TL for **Gîte/Camping du Pontet**. Pass a parking area and keep SH on a road. A few minutes later, TL on a path.

(12) 1:00: TL across **Pont du Lay**. Immediately afterwards, TR and walk alongside the river. 10min later, TR and cross a footbridge. Then TL on a path. Soon head N along the road.

(11) 1:25: Arrive at the church in **les Contamines (1167m)**.

The Rock: la Pierre du Pater

Just S of the chapel of Notre Dame de la Gorge, there is an interesting inscription on a rock which is known as 'la Pierre du Pater' (the stone of the Father). The inscription (which has some spelling mistakes!) says *"Passant Honnore an ce lieu la Raine des Cieux 1795"* which broadly means *"Passers-by honour God in this place"*. Some say the engraving commemorates a woodcutter who thanked God for saving him when he fell nearby. Others think that it was intended to instil a fear of the mountains in travellers. The writing was in danger of fading and being lost so it was restored by locals in 2015.

Refuge de la Balme (1706m)
Stage 2c
Aiguilles de la Pennaz 2688
Plan des Dames
Les Thovassets
Col du Bonhomme 2329
Stage 2c
Les Cavets
Tête Nord des Fours 2756
Col des Fours 2665
Tête Sud des Fours 2716
Stage v3a
Col des Tufs
Lac de Mya
Col de la Croix du Bonhomme 2479
Refuge de la Croix du Bonhomme (2443m)
Stage 2d
Chalets de Raja
Route du Cormet
Mont Tondu 3192
Glacier Enclave
N
W
E
S
Mont Buet
Dômes de Miage
Dôme du Goûter
Mont Tondu
Aiguille des Glaciers
Le Grand Mont
Aiguille du Grand Fond
360

Refuge Robert-Blanc
Colle delle Piramidi Calcaree
2622
Pyramides Calcaires-Punta Sud
2691
Tza de la Blanc
a Grande Ecaille
Pointe de la Tépiaz
2694
Col de la Seigne
2516
La Casermetta al Col de la Seigne
Refuge des Mottets (1864m)
Stage 3b
Les Mottets
Pointe Léchaud / Punta Lechaud
3127
Stage 3a
a Ville des Glaciers
Col de l'Oullion
2612
Pic de l'Oullion
2695
Stage 3a
N
Têtes Nord des Fours
Mont Tondu
Mont Blanc
Aiguille des Glaciers
Grand Combin de Grafeneire
W
E
360
Pointe Léchaud
Mont de la Fourclaz
Le Grand Mont
Pointe de la Combe Neuve
Pointe de la Terrasse
S
N
Têtes des Fours
W
Mont Charvin
E
360
Mont Pourri
Aiguille du Grand Fond
Le Grand Mont
Pointe de la Combe Neuve
Pointe de la Terrasse
S
N
Aiguille des Glaciers
Aiguille de Tré-la-Tête
Mont Blanc
Aiguille Blanche/Noire de Peuterey
Grandes Jorasses
Grand Combin de Grafeneire
Mont Vélan
W
Têtes Nord/Sud des Fours
Mont Tondu
E
360
Mont Berrio Blanc
Pointe Léchaud
Mont de la Fourclaz
S
Miravidi
3066
Ruisseau de Chézon

Stage 2c: Refuge de la Balme to Refuge de la CB

18 See map on p92. Take the path climbing SW behind **Refuge de la Balme**. Shortly afterwards, TL at a fork. At a junction, keep SH on a track.

19 0:30: Keep SH at a junction beside a bridge. After 10min, keep SH at a plateau and continue climbing: Col du Bonhomme is visible ahead. After crossing a bridge over the river, a path runs up the E side of the valley.

20 1:45: Cross **Col du Bonhomme (2329m)** and bear left to follow a path traversing upwards across the slope. Later, climb across sloping slabs (slippery): then cross a stream on rocks and climb on a path.

21 2:25: Shortly afterwards, reach the cairn at **Col de la Croix du Bonhomme (2479m)**. Descend S to continue Stage 2c; alternatively, TL and head NE for Stage v3a (to Col des Fours).

22 2:30: Arrive at **Refuge de la Croix du Bonhomme (2443m)**.

Stage 2d: Refuge de la CB to les Chapieux

22 See map on p92. From **Refuge de la CB**, head E on a path and then descend steeply.

23 1:05: Pass **Chalet de Plan Varraro (2013m)**.

24 1:20: Just after **Chalets de Raja (1796m)**, cross a stone bridge. Then TL to descend on a track. After 5min, bear left and descend on a grassy path. After another 5-10min, TL onto a narrow path which descends SE (easy to miss). Afterwards, the path splinters but all branches lead to les Chapieux.

25 1:45: Arrive at the hamlet of **les Chapieux (1549m)**.

Stage 2d: les Chapieux to Refuge de la CB

25 See map on p92. From **les Chapieux**, take a clear path heading up through trees. Soon, TR on a track which zigzags up the slope: paths cut across the track's bends but they are very steep. Soon bear right on a path, leaving the track: the path splinters but all the branches converge later; this section is not well-marked. When you reach a track, TR up it.

24 0:45: Shortly afterwards, TR and cross the bridge at **Chalets de Raja (1796m)**. Immediately afterwards, TL at a fork and climb N.

23 1:25: Climb past **Chalet de Plan Varraro (2013m)**.

22 2:50: Arrive at **Refuge de la Croix du Bonhomme (2443m)**.

Stage 2c: Refuge de la CB to Refuge de la Balme

22 See map on p92. From **Refuge de la CB**, climb N on a path ('Col de la Croix du Bonhomme').

21 0:05: Reach the cairn at **Col de la Croix du Bonhomme (2479m)**. Descend N to continue Stage 2c; alternatively, TR and head NE for Stage v3a to Col des Fours. Shortly afterwards, descend steeply into a gully and cross a stream on rocks. Afterwards, climb across sloping slabs (slippery). Shortly afterwards, pick up the path again. The route undulates for a while as it contours around the slopes, gradually losing height.

20 0:30: At **Col du Bonhomme (2329m)**, TR and descend N. After a while, a path runs down the E side of the valley. Cross a bridge over the river. Then TR and follow a track downstream on the other side.

19 1:10: Keep SH at a junction beside a bridge. A few minutes later, TR at a junction and descend on a path.

18 1:30: Arrive at **Refuge de la Balme (1706m)**: camping area and public toilets nearby.

Wild-flowers in spring (Stage 2d)

v2a/b Les Contamines/Refuge de Nant-Borrant (via Refuge de Tré-la-Tête)

Aiguilles de la Pennaz from Refuge de Tré-la-Tête

This variant offers a more spectacular (but harder) alternative to Stage 2a. Instead of leading you up the floor of the valley, it climbs above the tree-line on the valley's E flank, delivering exquisite views S towards Aiguilles de la Pennaz and Col du Bonhomme (which you will cross on Stage 2c). Refuge de Tré-la-Tête is magnificently situated close to the top of a minor summit (Tête Noir). This variant is useful for those who cannot secure accommodation at Refuge de Nant-Borrant or Refuge de la Balme.

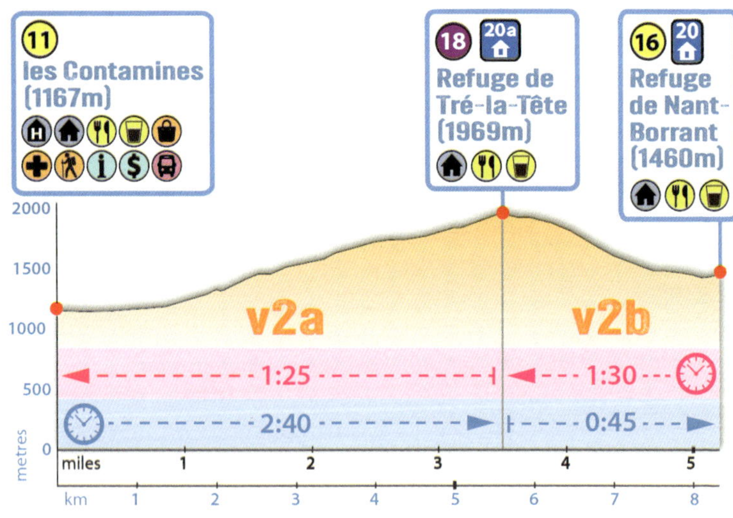

Terrain	Good paths/tracks which are simple to follow: however, they can be muddy after rain. It is a steep climb/descent in either direction. The path immediately N of la Laya is particularly steep and rocky: slippery when wet.
Route-finding	Generally straightforward (with plenty of signs).
Camping	The closest campsite is at le Pontet (Stage 2a). Otherwise, no campsites or places to bivouac legally.
Transport	**Les Contamines:** LC shuttle bus; buses to SGLF

	Start	Finish	Time	Distance	Ascent (ACW)	Descent (ACW)	Max Alt
v2a	Les Contamines	Refuge de Tré-la-Tête	2:40 1:25	5.6km 3.5miles	817m 2680ft	9m 30ft	1969m 6460ft
v2b	Refuge de Tré-la-Tête	Refuge de Nant-Borrant	0:45 1:30	2.7km 1.7miles	29m 95ft	538m 1765ft	1969m 6460ft

Stage v2a: les Contamines to Refuge de Tré-la-Tête

11 See map on p80. Head S out of **les Contamines** on the road. Keep SH past a road bridge. A few minutes later, TL onto **Chemin du Cugnon**. Follow signs up through the hamlet of **le Cugnon**: at junctions, remain on **Chemin du Cugnon**.

14 0:20: At the edge of the hamlet, head S on a path. Soon, keep SH at a junction.

15 0:55: TL at a junction.

16 1:30: TR at a junction.

17 1:50: Keep SH at a junction.

18 2:40: Arrive at **Refuge de Tré-la-Tête (1969m)**.

Stage v2b: Refuge de Tré-la-Tête to Refuge de Nant-Borrant

18 See map on p80. From **Refuge de Tré-la-Tête**, descend SW on a path.

19 0:05: keep SH past a wonderful **viewpoint** and continue descending. Later, TL at a junction (at a beautiful waterfall).

20 A few minutes later, TR at a junction at **la Laya**: the path on the left goes directly to the bivouac area at **la Rollaz** (avoiding Refuge de Nant-Borrant).

16 0:45: Arrive at **Refuge de Nant-Borrant (1460m)**.

Stage v2b: Refuge de Nant-Borrant to Refuge de Tré-la-Tête

16 See map on p80. From a junction immediately E of **Refuge de Nant-Borrant**, descend E on a path through trees ('Combe Noire'). 5min later, TR and cross a bridge over the river. Afterwards, the path starts to climb.

20 0:10: TL at a junction at **la Laya**: the path on the right comes from the bivouac area at **la Rollaz**. A few minutes later, just after a beautiful waterfall, TR at a junction and climb ('Tré-la-Tête').

19 1:20: Pass a wonderful **viewpoint** where the path levels out.

18 1:30: Arrive at **Refuge de Tré-la-Tête (1969m)**.

Stage v2a: Refuge de Tré-la-Tête to les Contamines

18 See map on p80. From **Refuge de Tré-la-Tête**, head NE on a path. Shortly afterwards, TL at a junction ('le Pontet').

17 0:20: Keep SH at a junction.

16 0:30: TL at a junction ('le Pontet').

15 0:50: Reach another junction: TR for LC; alternatively, keep SH if you are staying at le Pontet. 15min later, keep SH at a junction.

14 1:10: Reach a road at **le Cugnon**: head W downhill; alternatively, head S for le Pontet. Follow signs through the hamlet down towards the base of the valley ('les Contamines'). TR and head N along the main road.

11 1:25: Arrive at the church in **les Contamines (1167m)**.

3 Les Chapieux/ Rifugio Elisabetta Soldini

Stage 3a (les Chapieux/Refuge des Mottets): an easy stage through a lovely valley (dominated by the magnificent Aiguille des Glaciers). The views are spectacular all the way. Refuge des Mottets is a working farm with quirky displays of old inventions: this is one of the TMB's best overnight stops and it books up fast. Because of the road section, Stage 3a has developed a reputation as a stage to be skipped: however, we think that is undeserved because the scenery is wonderful and the short stretch of road is more like a quiet lane.

Stage 3b (Refuge des Mottets/Rifugio Elisabetta): you will return to high altitude, climbing relentlessly (in either direction) all the way to Col de la Seigne (on the French/Italian frontier). For ACW trekkers, this is the TMB's first border crossing and the views of MB to the NE are the best so far. Pray for clear weather as this is a trek highlight. On the col, there are two large cairns and an orientation table (identifying the nearby peaks). ACW trekkers descend towards Val Veny: pass beneath the Pyramides Calcaires, limestones peaks which are noticeably different to the higher granite peaks behind; finally, a short, punchy climb leads to Rifugio Elisabetta Soldini. CW trekkers will descend from the col into Vallée des Glaciers to reach Refuge des Mottets (see above).

Itinerary options: many trekkers take the shuttle bus between les Chapieux and Ville des Glaciers/Parking des Mottets. Other trekkers hike Stage v3a (via Col des Fours) in place of Stages 2d/3a: v3a travels directly between Col de la Croix du Bonhomme and Refuge des Mottet, avoiding les Chapieux (see p104). However, although Stage v3a is undeniably spectacular, we do not think that the scenery is vastly superior to the main TMB route and those hiking v3a will forgo a night in delightful les Chapieux.

	Start	Finish	Time	Distance	Ascent (ACW)	Descent (ACW)	Max Alt
3a	Les Chapieux	Refuge des Mottets	2:00 1:25	6.5km 4.0miles	351m 1152ft	30m 98ft	1870m 6135ft
3b	Refuge des Mottets	Rifugio Elisabetta	3:00 2:35	8.1km 5.0miles	686m 2251ft	361m 1184ft	2516m 8255ft

Rifugio Elisabetta

Terrain	**Stage 3a:** good paths/tracks which are simple to follow; there is a section along a quiet road. Gradients are rarely steep. **Stage 3b:** a more challenging route across a high pass with a long climb and a long descent. The route is more difficult for ACW trekkers because there is more altitude gain in that direction. The clear paths are simple to negotiate in good conditions: however, in wet conditions they can be muddy and slippery. The gradient is sometimes steep. Often snow remains near the col until early July: in such conditions, the climb to, and descent from, the col can be challenging.
Route-finding	In good conditions, route-finding is generally straightforward (plenty of signs). However, navigation on the high parts of Stage 3b can be tricky in bad weather, low visibility or snowy conditions. In particular, take care around Col de la Seigne in low visibility: it is possible to drift onto the challenging path to Col des Chavannes instead of the correct path to Rifugio Elisabetta.
Camping	**Stage 3a:** authorised bivouac area at les Chapieux. Unauthorised bivouac area near Refuge des Mottets (not legal). **Stage 3b:** because Col de la Seigne is above 2500m, it is currently legal to bivouac on its Italian side. However, it is an exposed place which is prone to high winds. Some trekkers bivouac amongst the buildings of Lex Blanche (just below Rifugio Elisabetta), however, this is not legal.
Trail notes	At Ville des Glaciers you can buy cheese produced by the local farm. La Casermetta (Stage 3b) is an old military outpost which has been beautifully restored and converted into an education centre. Inside there are exhibits on the nature, geography and history of the region. Open during the summer season: free WiFi and smartphone charging.
Transport	**Les Chapieux:** shuttle bus between BSM, les Chapieux, Ville des Glaciers and Parking des Mottets. **Ville des Glaciers** 27: shuttle bus (see above). **Parking des Mottets** (near Refuge des Mottets 28): shuttle bus (see above).

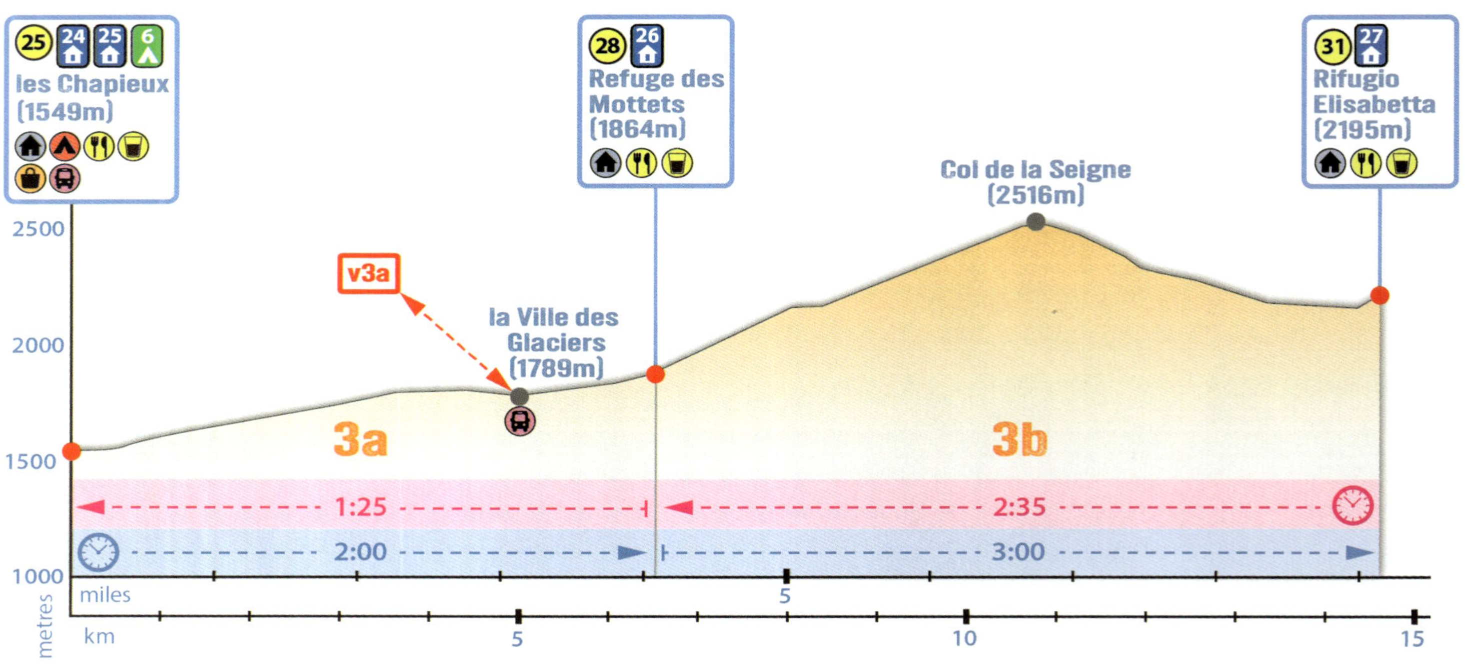
25 24 25 6
les Chapieux
(1549m)
28 26
Refuge des
Mottets
(1864m)
Col de la Seigne
(2516m)
31 27
Rifugio
Elisabetta
(2195m)
v3a
la Ville des
Glaciers
(1789m)
3a
3b
1:25
2:35
2:00
3:00
2500
2000
1500
1000
metres
miles
km
5
10
15

Stage 3a: les Chapieux to Refuge des Mottets

25 See map on p92. From **les Chapieux**, head E and cross a bridge. Then continue NE on a tarmac lane, climbing gently through a narrow valley.

26 0:30: TR onto a path ('Col de la Seigne'). Descend to a footbridge, cross the river and continue upstream on the other side.

27 1:35: Keep SH at a junction below **la Ville des Glaciers**. Continue NE on a path (alongside the river).

28 2:00: Reach a junction beside **Refuge des Mottets (1864m)**: keep SH to head to the refuge or TR to start Stage 3b ('Col de la Seigne').

Stage 3b: Refuge des Mottets to Rifugio Elisabetta

28 See map on p93. From **Refuge des Mottets**, head initially S to pick up the TMB again. Then zigzag up the slope to the E.

29 0:30: TL at a junction. Afterwards, there are some stream crossings: take care in early season when there is plenty of water.

30 1:40: Cross **Col de la Seigne (2516m)** and enter **Italy**. Descend NE. Pass **la Casermetta** (p99). After a while, the path heads down the N flank of the valley.

31 3:00: See map on p102. TL at the ruins at **Lex Blanche** and climb. A few minutes later, reach **Rifugio Elisabetta Soldini (2195m)**.

Stage 3b: Rifugio Elisabetta to Refuge des Mottets

31 See map on p102. From the ruins at **Lex Blanche** (below Rifugio Elisabetta), head SW on a path, climbing the N flank of the valley. See map on p93. Pass **la Casermetta** (p99).

30 1:35: Cross **Col de la Seigne (2516m)** and enter **France**. Descend SW: there are some stream crossings; take care in early season when there is plenty of water.

29 2:15: TR at a junction. Soon zigzag W down the steep slope.

28 2:35: Reach a junction beside **Refuge des Mottets (1864m)**: TR for the refuge or TL for Stage 3a.

Stage 3a: Refuge des Mottets to les Chapieux

28 See map on p93. From **Refuge des Mottets**, head SW on a path alongside the river.

27 0:20: Keep SH at a junction below **la Ville des Glaciers**. Continue SW on a path (beside the river). 35min later, cross the river on a footbridge. Then TL and climb on a path.

26 1:05: TL along a tarmac lane.

25 1:25: Arrive at the hamlet of **les Chapieux (1549m)**.

Les Chapieux

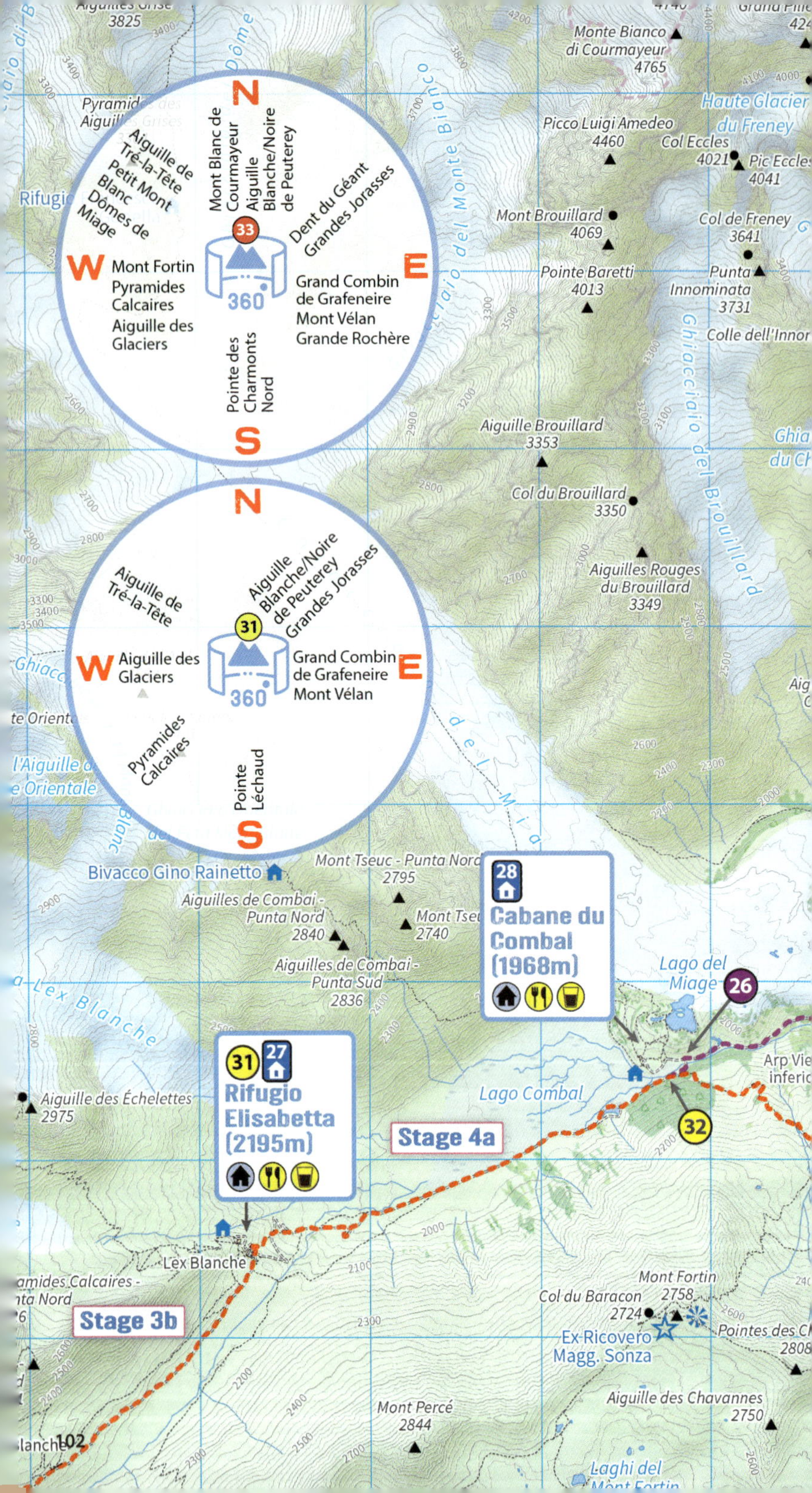

Mont Blanc de Courmayeur
Aiguille Blanche/Noire de Peuterey
Dent du Géant
Grandes Jorasses
Aiguille de Tré-la-Tête
Petit Mont Blanc
Dômes de Miage
Mont Fortin
Pyramides Calcaires
Aiguille des Glaciers
Grand Combin de Grafeneire
Mont Vélan
Grande Rochère
Pointe des Charmonts Nord
Aiguille de Tré-la-Tête
Aiguille Blanche/Noire de Peuterey
Grandes Jorasses
Aiguille des Glaciers
Grand Combin de Grafeneire
Mont Vélan
Pyramides Calcaires
Pointe Léchaud
Monte Bianco di Courmayeur 4765
Picco Luigi Amedeo 4460
Haute Glacier du Freney
Col Eccles 4021
Pic Eccles 4041
Mont Brouillard 4069
Col de Freney 3641
Pointe Baretti 4013
Punta Innominata 3731
Colle dell'Innor
Aiguille Brouillard 3353
Col du Brouillard 3350
Aiguilles Rouges du Brouillard 3349
Ghiacciaio del Brouillard
Bivacco Gino Rainetto
Mont Tseuc - Punta Nord 2795
Aiguilles de Combai - Punta Nord 2840
Mont Tseuc 2740
Aiguilles de Combai - Punta Sud 2836
28
Cabane du Combal (1968m)
Lago del Miage
26
Arp Vieille inferiore
Lago Combal
32
Stage 4a
31
27
Rifugio Elisabetta (2195m)
Aiguille des Échelettes 2975
Lex Blanche
Stage 3b
Mont Fortin 2758
Col du Baracon 2724
Ex-Ricovero Magg. Sonza
Pointes des Ch 2808
Aiguille des Chavannes 2750
Mont Percé 2844
Laghi del Mont Fortin

Entrèves
la Palud
Traforo del Mo
Punta Gugliermina
3893
Aiguille Noire
de Peuterey
3772
Punta Ottoz
3742
Aiguille Noire
de Peuterey
2928
Glacier de
Combalet
Picco Gamba
3067
Col des
Chasseurs
2741
Mont Rouge
de Peuterey
2941
Stage v4b
v4c
Peuterey
Peindein
Tête Neyron
2044
Cuignon
Plan Vény
Freney
Dora di Veny
Stage v4b
Col
Chécrouit
1952
Stage 4
Rifugio Maison
Vieille (1956m)
Lago
Chécrouit
la Visaille
(1659m)
Stage 4b
Lac des Vesses
2442
Stage 4b
Col de la You
2661
Fourches de la
2808
Mont Nix
2918
Pointe des
Charmonts Nord
2951
Col du Berrio Blanc
2818
Ex Rico
Magg. Reggia
Glacier de
la Plate
Laghi de la Plate
N
S
W
E
Mont Blanc de
Courmayeur
Aiguille
Blanche/Noire
de Peuterey
la Tour Ronde
Pointe
Helbronner
Dent du Géant
Grandes Jorasses
Pyramides
Calcaires
Aiguille des
Glaciers
Aiguille de
Tré-la-Tête
Testa di Liconi
Grivola
Tête d'Arp
360

Refuge de la Croix du Bonhomme/ Refuge des Mottets (via Col des Fours)

This high variant provides a more direct route between Col de la Croix du Bonhomme and Refuge des Mottets. However, it is more difficult than the main route (Stages 2d/3a). The terrain is wonderfully varied with the barren, rocky landscape around Col des Fours contrasting starkly with the flower-filled pastures further E. At 2665m, Col des Fours is the same height as Fenêtre d'Arpette (Stage v8b) and they are the joint highest points on the TMB. The high altitude means that the views are wonderfully far-reaching and the landscape between 22 and 24 is sublime.

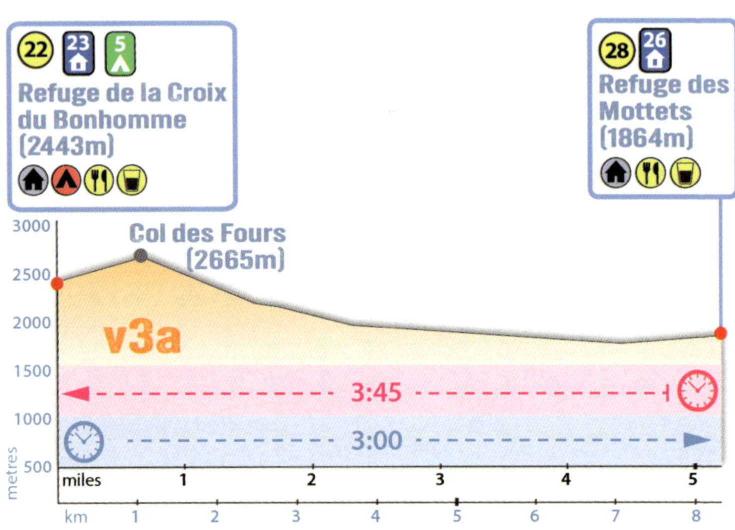

Terrain	This stage is not for the faint-hearted, involving some of the TMB's most difficult terrain. Immediately E of Col des Fours, the route crosses a steep and unstable slope: take care. Near the col, snow tends to lie later than almost anywhere else on the TMB: do not attempt Stage v3a in snowy conditions when the steep terrain can be treacherous and a fall could be serious. Between 22 and 23, there are stream crossings which are not difficult in good conditions: however, in June/early July, snow bridges form over the streams which are prone to collapse; in recent years, at least one TMB trekker has died crossing these snow bridges.
Route-finding	The route between 21 and 23 is sometimes hard to follow: rockfall and landslides can obscure parts of the path. Otherwise, route-finding is largely straightforward in good conditions. However, avoid this route in bad weather/low visibility/snowy conditions when navigation is tricky.
Camping	No campsites or official bivouac sites. Some trekkers bivouac on the grassy slopes E of Col des Fours but this may not be legal. Unauthorised bivouac area near Refuge des Mottets (not legal).
Trail notes	At Ville des Glaciers you can buy cheese produced by the local farm.
Transport	**Ville des Glaciers** 27: shuttle bus to les Chapieux and BSM. **Parking des Mottets** (near Refuge des Mottets 28): shuttle bus to les Chapieux and BSM.

	Start	Finish	Time	Distance	Ascent (ACW)	Descent (ACW)	Max Alt
v3a	Refuge de la CB	Refuge des Mottets	3:00 3:45	8.3km 5.2miles	310m 1017ft	889m 2917ft	2665m 8743ft

Stage v3a: Refuge de la CB to Refuge des Mottets (via Col des Fours)

22 See map on p92. From **Refuge de la CB**, climb N on the path back up to Col de la Croix du Bonhomme.

21 0:05: TR at the cairn at **Col de la Croix du Bonhomme (2479m)** and climb the crest of a ridge.

21 0:45: Keep SH across the barren **Col des Fours (2665m)**. Descend SE across shale on a path: watch your footing and follow the path carefully.

22 1:10: Keep SH at a junction and head NE over rough terrain: the path to the right heads to **Lac de Mya**. Soon keep SH past another junction. Descend further and enter flower-filled pastures.

23 1:35: TR at a junction and descend alongside a stream (a branch of **Ruisseau des Tufs**). Soon, cross the stream.

24 2:05: TR on a track. Shortly afterwards, just after the buildings at **les Tufs (1993m)**, TR down a path. 10min later, TR down a track.

25 2:35: At **la Ville des Glaciers (1789m)**, keep SH past the chapel. Then descend to the river and cross a bridge.

27 Immediately afterwards, TL at a junction and head NE on Stage 3a.

28 3:00: Reach a junction beside **Refuge des Mottets (1864m)**: keep SH to head to the refuge or TR to start Stage 3b.

Stage v3a: Refuge des Mottets to Refuge de la CB (via Col des Fours)

28 See map on p93. From **Refuge des Mottets**, head SW on a path beside the river.

27 0:20: TR at a junction, cross a bridge and climb.

25 Shortly afterwards, keep SH past the chapel at **Ville des Glaciers (1789m)**. Climb W on a track. Soon TL on a path: you can also remain on the track all the way to les Tufs but it takes longer.

24 1:00: At the buildings at **les Tufs (1993m)**, TL on a track. Shortly afterwards, TL on a path. Soon, there are streams to cross.

23 1:50: TL and climb S.

22 2:35: Keep SH at a junction and climb W over rough terrain: the path to the left heads to **Lac de Mya**.

21 3:20: From the barren **Col des Fours (2665m)**, descend SW on a rocky path. Soon the path splinters but the branches converge later.

21 3:40: Reach the cairn at **Col de la Croix du Bonhomme (2479m)**. TL to head to Refuge de la CB; alternatively, TR for Stage 2c to Refuge de la Balme.

22 3:45: Arrive at **Refuge de la Croix du Bonhomme (2433m)**.

4 Rifugio Elisabetta Soldini/ Courmayeur

Mont Blanc de Courmayeur (Stage 4b)

Stage 4a (Rifugio Elisabetta/Combal): although short, this stage is a delight. A level track along Val Veny runs most of the way between Rifugio Elisabetta and Cabane du Combal, enabling you to fully enjoy the wonderful views of the distinctive spear-headed Aiguille Noire de Peuterey (to the NE); to the W, Aiguille des Glaciers looks fabulous. Cabane du Combal is set at the foot of Glacier du Miage and is a lovely place to stay: it can be more peaceful than some of the TMB's other refuges.

Stage 4b (Combal/Maison Vieille): this is a highlight of the TMB offering sublime vistas. In ether direction, the climb to 33 is quite tough although it is steeper for ACW trekkers. However, the magnificent scenery should take your mind off the exertions. Mont Blanc de Courmayeur (a peak on the SE ridge of MB's summit) looks amazing from this angle: although you cannot quite see the main summit, you would never have known if we had not told you! You get plenty of time to study the massif as you proceed along a fabulous balcony directly opposite it. In fine conditions, this path is world class but incredibly, it is only one of three such balconies on the TMB! The other two are on Sections 5 and 11.

	Start	Finish	Time	Distance	Ascent (ACW)	Descent (ACW)	Max Alt
4a	Rifugio Elisabetta	Combal	0:50 1:10	3.3km 2.1miles	15m 49ft	235m 771ft	2195m 7201ft
4b	Combal	Rifugio Maison Vieille	3:00 3:00	7.5km 4.7miles	460m 1509ft	479m 1572ft	2430m 7972ft
4c	Rifugio Maison Vieille	Courmayeur	1:30 2:45	5.4km 3.4miles	20m 66ft	766m 2513ft	1956m 6417ft

Col Chécrouit, at the E end of Stage 4b, is a beautiful location with mountains on all sides: to the SE, you can see Gran Paradiso National Park. Although there is ski infrastructure near the col, you will hardly notice it. There are two places to stay (which book up fast): Rifugio Maison Vieille and Gîte le Randonneur.

Stage 4c (Maison Vieille/Courmayeur): although the scenery is beautiful, this is far from the most popular part of the TMB. ACW trekkers have a knee-jerking descent across ski slopes to the town of Courmayeur; CW trekkers endure a brutal climb. Courmayeur is a lovely town with a magnificent setting. There are plenty of bars/restaurants and you can enjoy some of the best food on the TMB: food is worshipped in Italy. There are luxurious hotels/spas too and many trekkers take a day off in Courmayeur to rejuvenate tired legs.

Itinerary options: many trekkers use the ski-lifts to travel between Col Chécrouit and Dolonne (close to Courmayeur), skipping most of Stage 4c; see below.

ACW trekkers can leave the main TMB at (32), continuing NE on Stage v4b's easy track down Val Veny (p114). The main reason for doing this would be to avail of one of Val Veny's campsites (there are none along the main route between les Chapieux and Courmayeur). Stage v4b also offers a safer route in bad weather conditions. However, if you hike Stage v4b all the way to Courmayeur, you miss out on Stage 4b's incredible balcony path. Alternatively, if you do not want to miss Stage 4b, you can access Val Veny's campsites using Stage v4c from Col Chécrouit (p116). We describe further solutions on p114.

Hutters who cannot find accommodation at Col Chécrouit, can also use Stage v4c to descend to Rifugio Monte Bianco.

Terrain	**Stage 4a:** at the W end of the stage (between Lex Blanche and the valley floor), the steep, rocky path cuts across the hairpins of a track. If you prefer, you can avoid the path by taking the longer, easier route down the track. The track along the valley floor is level and easy. **Stage 4b:** high altitude route which is quite challenging: narrow and/or rocky sections; regular undulations; long, sustained climb/descent with some steep gradients. The route is exposed in places: a fall would be serious. Snow can remain into July making the sloping traverses of the balcony slippery and dangerous: in such conditions, use Stage v4b instead. **Stage 4c:** good paths/tracks/lanes; some sections along minor roads; gradients are occasionally steep.
Route-finding	On Stage 4c, there is a labyrinth of paths, tracks and pistes through Courmayeur's ski-slopes: follow signposts carefully. Otherwise, route-finding is largely straightforward in good conditions. However, avoid Stage 4b in bad weather, low visibility or snowy conditions: use Stage v4b instead.
Camping	There are no campsites or places to bivouac legally. Trekkers sometimes bivouac beside Rifugio Maison Vieille, with permission from the hut manager: they may allow it if you buy dinner; they will inform you that it is not technically legal.
Trail notes	Between (36) and Plan Chécrouit, there are two possible routes. The old TMB route descended E from (36) on a steep path through trees (purple on the map on p110). However, at the time of writing, this path was closed and the TMB had been re-routed towards the open ski-slopes to the S (red on the map). It is unclear whether the re-routing is permanent.
Transport	**La Visaille** (27) (2.8km hike from Cabane du Combal): shuttle bus to Courmayeur and Val Veny's campsites. **Rifugio Maison Vieille/Col Chécrouit:** Maison Vieille chair-lift between Col Chécrouit (35) and Plan Chécrouit (37); and Dolonne gondola between Plan Chécrouit (37) and Dolonne. **Courmayeur:** buses and cable cars (see p46 and p49).

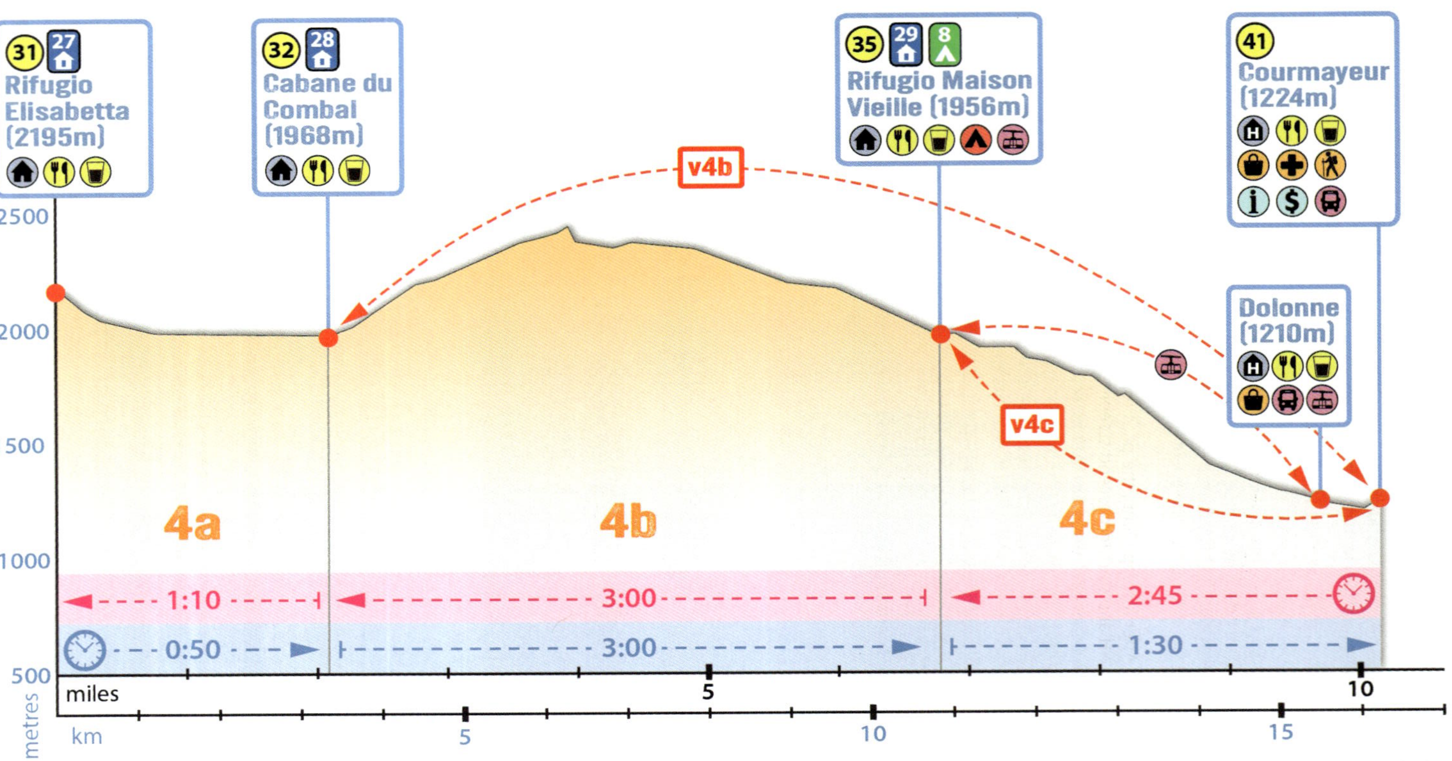
31
27
Rifugio Elisabetta (2195m)
32
28
Cabane du Combal (1968m)
35
29
8
Rifugio Maison Vieille (1956m)
41
Courmayeur (1224m)
Dolonne (1210m)
v4b
v4c
4a
4b
4c
1:10
3:00
2:45
0:50
3:00
1:30
2500
2000
1500
1000
500
metres
miles
5
10
km
5
10
15

Stage 4a: Rifugio Elisabetta to Combal

31 See map on p102. From **Rifugio Elisabetta**, descend back to the ruins at **Lex Blanche**. Then TL and follow a path heading NE, down into the valley: it cuts across the hairpins of a track. At the valley floor, keep SH, heading NE on the track.

32 0:50: Reach a **junction**: TR for Stage 4b. Alternatively, for Cabane du Combal (5min) and Stage v4b, keep SH: shortly afterwards, cross a bridge and then TL to reach **Cabane du Combal (1968m)** or TR for v4b.

Stage 4b: Combal to Rifugio Maison Vieille

32 See map on p102. From the **junction**, climb steeply E on a path.

33 1:45: After a steep climb, the path tops out at a little ledge (with incredible views). Keep SH and start to descend steeply: watch your footing. Soon the gradient eases and you continue downhill, traversing across the slopes.

34 2:40: Keep SH at a junction (yellow arrows). Soon afterwards, continue descending, gently at first and then more steeply.

35 3:00: Arrive at **Rifugio Maison Vieille** at **Col Chécrouit (1956m)**.

Stage 4b: Rifugio Maison Vieille to Combal

35 See map on p103. From **Rifugio Maison Vieille**, climb SW on a path.

34 0:30: Keep SH at a junction (yellow arrows) and continue climbing.

33 1:55: After a steep climb, the path tops out at a little ledge (with incredible views). Keep SH and start to descend.

32 3:00: Reach a **junction**: TL for Stage 4a. Alternatively, TR for Cabane du Combal (5min): shortly afterwards, cross a bridge and then TL to reach **Cabane du Combal (1968m)**.

Stage 4a: Combal to Rifugio Elisabetta

32 See map on p102. From the **junction**, head SW on a track which is level at first and then gains height slowly. Later, the gradient increases as the track heads W up a slope: paths cut steeply across the track's hairpins.

31 1:10: TR at the ruins at **Lex Blanche** and climb. A few minutes later, reach **Rifugio Elisabetta Soldini (2195m)**.

Gîte le Randonneur (Stage 4c)

Entrèves (1306m)/ la Palud (1370m)
Stage v5a
La Palud
Chapy
Rifugio Pavillon
Rifugio Bertone (1991m)
Stage v4b
Stage v4b
v4c
v4c
Peindein
Mont Chétif 2343
Dolonne (1210m)
Les Forges
Stage 4c
Tête Neyron 2044
Col Chécrouit 1952
Plan Chécrouit
Rifugio Maison Vieille (1956m)
Courmayeur (1224m)
Champtoret
Praleux Desot
Villair Desot
Torrente Sapin
Rochefort
Plampincieux
Meyen
Entrèves
Dora di Veny
Dora Baltea
Traforo del Mo
Mostra dei Cristalli
Rifugio Torino Nuovo
Rifugio Torino Vecchio
Tour de Jétoula 3339
Dent de Jétoula 3304
Flambeau 3569
5b

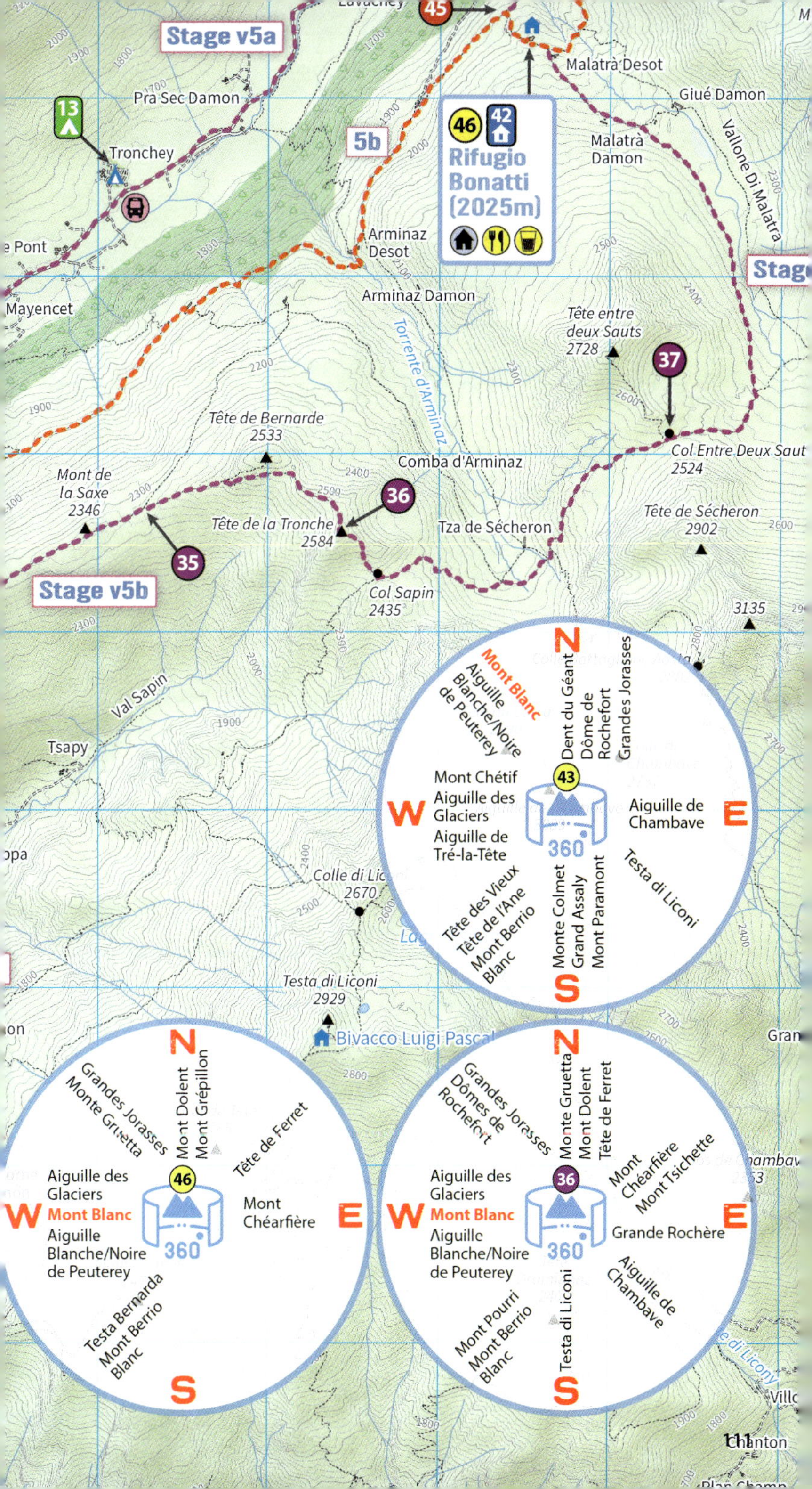

Stage v5a
Pra Sec Damon
Tronchey
e Pont
Mayencet
5b
46
42
Rifugio Bonatti (2025m)
Malatrà Desot
Giué Damon
Malatrà Damon
Vallone Di Malatra
Arminaz Desot
Arminaz Damon
Torrente d'Arminaz
Tête entre deux Sauts 2728
37
Col Entre Deux Saut 2524
Tête de Bernarde 2533
Comba d'Arminaz
Mont de la Saxe 2346
36
Tête de la Tronche 2584
Tza de Sécheron
Tête de Sécheron 2902
35
Stage v5b
Col Sapin 2435
3135
Val Sapin
Tsapy
Colle di Liconi 2670
Testa di Liconi 2929
Bivacco Luigi Pascal
N
Mont Blanc
Aiguille Blanche/Noire de Peuterey
Dent du Géant
Dôme de Rochefort
Grandes Jorasses
W
Mont Chétif
Aiguille des Glaciers
Aiguille de Tré-la-Tête
43
360
E
Aiguille de Chambave
Testa di Liconi
Tête des Vieux
Tête de l'Ane
Mont Berrio Blanc
Monte Colmet
Grand Assaly
Mont Paramont
S
N
Grandes Jorasses
Monte Gruetta
Mont Dolent
Mont Grépillon
Tête de Ferret
W
Aiguille des Glaciers
Mont Blanc
Aiguille Blanche/Noire de Peuterey
46
360
E
Mont Chéarfière
Testa Bernarda
Mont Berrio Blanc
S
N
Grandes Jorasses
Dômes de Rochefort
Monte Gruetta
Mont Dolent
Tête de Ferret
W
Aiguille des Glaciers
Mont Blanc
Aiguille Blanche/Noire de Peuterey
36
360
E
Mont Chéarfière
Mont Tsichette
Grande Rochère
Aiguille de Chambave
Testa di Liconi
Mont Pourri
Mont Berrio Blanc
S
Chanton

Les Grandes Jorasses seen on the Stage 4b traverse

Stage 4c: Rifugio Maison Vieille to Courmayeur

35 See map on p110. From **Rifugio Maison Vieille**, head E on a broad path. Shortly afterwards, keep SH at a junction and head downhill on a steep track alongside a ski-lift. Keep SH past **Gîte le Randonneur** and **Ristorante Ollier**. Soon, TR at a junction in front of a café. Shortly afterwards, TR just before a small ski-lift and descend on a steep, narrow path.

36 0:15: TR at a junction and descend on a path. Shortly afterwards, TL down a winding ski piste.

37 0:30: At **Plan Chécrouit** ski station, TL onto another track. Shortly afterwards, at the upper station of the **Dolonne ski-lift**, pick up a path on the left: descend E (steeply through trees).

38 0:50: TL onto a track. Immediately afterwards, TL down a path. 10min later, TR at a junction. Shortly afterwards, leave the forest and enjoy fabulous views of Courmayeur. Just afterwards, TL onto a lane and continue descending.

39 1:05: Enter the village of **Dolonne (1210m)**. At a road junction, keep SH and continue descending. Keep SH on a narrow street between buildings: the yellow waymarks are hard to spot. Just before the church, TR onto another street and descend.

40 1:15: At a T-junction, TL to descend on a road. After 5min, keep SH at a junction to cross the river on a road bridge. Just afterwards, follow the road around to the right and climb. Soon, pass under a bridge.

41 1:30: Just afterwards, enter **Courmayeur (1224m)**: the tourist office/bus station is just across the square.

Stage 4c: Courmayeur to Rifugio Maison Vieille

41 **See map on p110.** From the **tourist office**, head W. Pass under a bridge and descend NW on a road. TL and cross a bridge over the river. Then follow the road upwards.

40 0:15: TR at a junction. Immediately afterwards, bear left and climb between buildings into the village of **Dolonne (1210m)**. At the top of the street, TL on a narrow street between buildings: the yellow waymarks are hard to spot. The street bends right.

39 0:25: Keep SH at a junction and climb W out of the village on a lane. 5min later, TR onto a path. Soon, TL at a junction.

38 1:00: TR onto a track. Immediately afterwards, TR up a path and climb through trees. At the upper station of the **Dolonne ski-lift**, head W on a track.

37 1:50: Shortly afterwards, bear right and follow a ski-piste W. 20min later, TR on a path.

36 2:15: Shortly afterwards, TL up a steep path. At a café, pick up a track. Keep SH past **Gîte le Randonneur** and **Ristorante Ollier**. Then climb SW.

35 2:45: Arrive at **Rifugio Maison Vieille** at **Col Chécrouit (1956m)**.

v4b Cabane du Combal/Courmayeur (via Val Veny)

The 30.8km stretch between les Chapieux and Courmayeur is probably the hardest part of the TMB to plan and book: there is not enough accommodation and the distance is too great for most trekkers to hike it all in one day. Furthermore, there are no campsites along the main route and there are few places to bivouac legally. However, the three campsites on Stage v4b (in Val Veny) offer a solution both for those with their own tents and those without: as well as tent pitches, they all have fixed tents for rent and Camping Monte Bianco la Sorgente has a dormitory. Stage v4b also offers a bad weather alternative to the exposed Stage 4b.

Although this is a valley route, the scenery is spectacular: between 26 and 31, you are directly below MB and only a stone's throw from the distinctive Aiguille Noire de Peuterey. However, it cannot compete with the superlative balcony path on Stage 4b (which you will miss out on if you hike v4b all the way between 26 and Courmayeur).

Itinerary options: to avoid missing out on Stage 4b, you could, hike Stage 4b to Rifugio Maison Vieille and then descend to the Val Veny campsites using Stage v4c (p116). Alternatively, you could spend two nights at the Val Veny campsites: for example, ACW trekkers can hike in one day from les Chapieux/Refuge des Mottets to Val Veny; after the first night in a Val Veny campsite, leave your tent pitched (so that you can travel light) and hike back up to 26; from there, hike the Stage 4b balcony to Rifugio Maison Vieille; then use Stage v4c to descend back to your tent in Val Veny; spend a second night in Val Veny and the following morning hike (or take the bus) to Courmayeur.

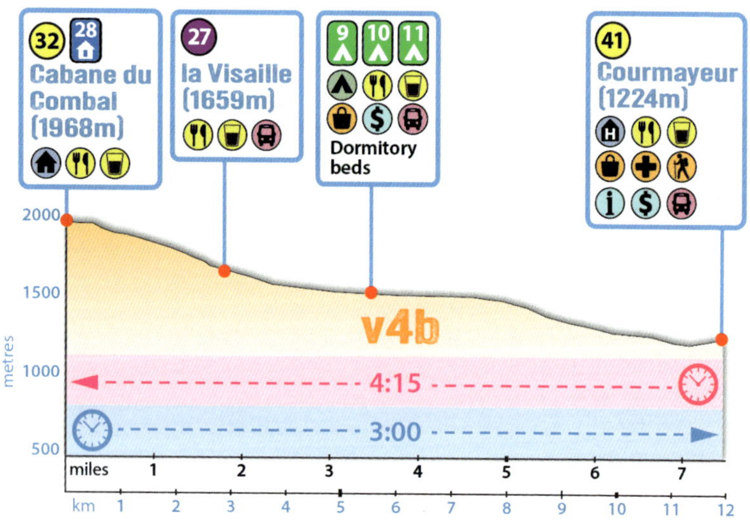

	Start	Finish	Time	Distance	Ascent (ACW)	Descent (ACW)	Max Alt
v4b	Combal	Courmayeur	3:00 4:15	11.9km 7.4miles	92m 302ft	836m 2743ft	1968m 6457ft

Terrain	At the time of writing, parts of the path between 27 and 28 had been washed away. It was possible to hop across rocks at the edge of the river but this might be difficult in early season when there is more water: it can be safer to follow the road between 27 and 28. Otherwise, the paths/tracks/roads are simple to negotiate: there is a lot of road walking.
Route-finding	Straightforward.
Camping	Three campsites but no legal bivouac sites.
Trail notes	The Val Veny campsites can be busy with holidaymakers (quite noisy).
Transport	Val Veny shuttle bus runs hourly between la Visaille 27 and Courmayeur (stopping at the campsites).

Stage v4b: Combal to Courmayeur (via Val Veny)

26 See map on p102. From a **junction**, head E down a road. 30min later (at around 1750m), TR down a path to cut across a hairpin. Then continue NE along the road.

27 0:45: Shortly after the restaurant at **la Visaille** (Chalet del Miage), TL on a path which descends (sometimes steeply) alongside the river.

28 0:55: TR onto a track alongside the river. Soon, TL to reach a car park: pick up a path heading downstream. At **Hobo Camping**, TL along the road. Soon, pass **Camping Aiguille Noire**.

29 1:40: 10min later, keep SH at a junction; alternatively, TL for **Camping Monte Bianco la Sorgente** (0.5km OR).

30 1:50: Keep SH at a junction. See map on p110.

31 2:00: Pass a souvenir shop and the **Sanctuary of Notre-Dame de la Guérison**.

32 2:35: Keep SH on a track. Soon keep SH on a quiet road. Cross a bridge over the river and climb on a road. TR on a main road. Shortly afterwards, TL on **Strada della Villette**: at the end of it, TL. Just afterwards, TR at a roundabout and climb S up **Via Roma/Viale Monte Bianco**.

41 3:00: Reach **Piazza Abbé Henry** in **Courmayeur (1224m)**.

Stage v4b: Courmayeur to Combal (via Val Veny)

41 See map on p110. From **Piazza Abbé Henry** in **Courmayeur**, head N down **Via Roma/Viale Monte Bianco**. TL at a roundabout. Just afterwards, TR and head NW on **Strada della Villette**. 5min later, TR on a main road. Shortly afterwards, TL and descend on a small road. Cross the river and then TR, climbing on a quiet road. 10min later, keep SH on a sealed track. There are lovely views of the MB massif.

32 0:30: 5min later, keep SH up a road.

31 1:20: Pass a souvenir shop and the **Sanctuary of Notre-Dame de la Guérison**.

30 1:30: See map on p103. TR at a fork; alternatively, TL for v4c to Rifugio Monte Bianco.

29 1:45: Keep SH at a junction; alternatively, TR for **Camping Monte Bianco la Sorgente** (0.5km OR). 10min later, pass **Camping Aiguille Noire**. A few minutes later, TR at **Hobo Camping** into a parking area: follow a path upstream. Soon walk through another car park and pick up a track heading gently uphill alongside the river.

28 2:45: TL at a junction, following a path which climbs alongside the river ('Val Veny').

27 3:00: At **la Visaille**, TR along the road. Pass a restaurant (Chalet del Miage). 5-10min later, when the road bends right at a hairpin, keep SH and climb steeply on a path. After a few minutes, TL up the road again.

26 4:15: Reach a **junction**: TR for Cabane du Combal (5min); alternatively, TL for Stage 4a to Rifugio Elisabetta.

v4c Rifugio Maison Vieille/Courmayeur (via Rifugio Monte Bianco)

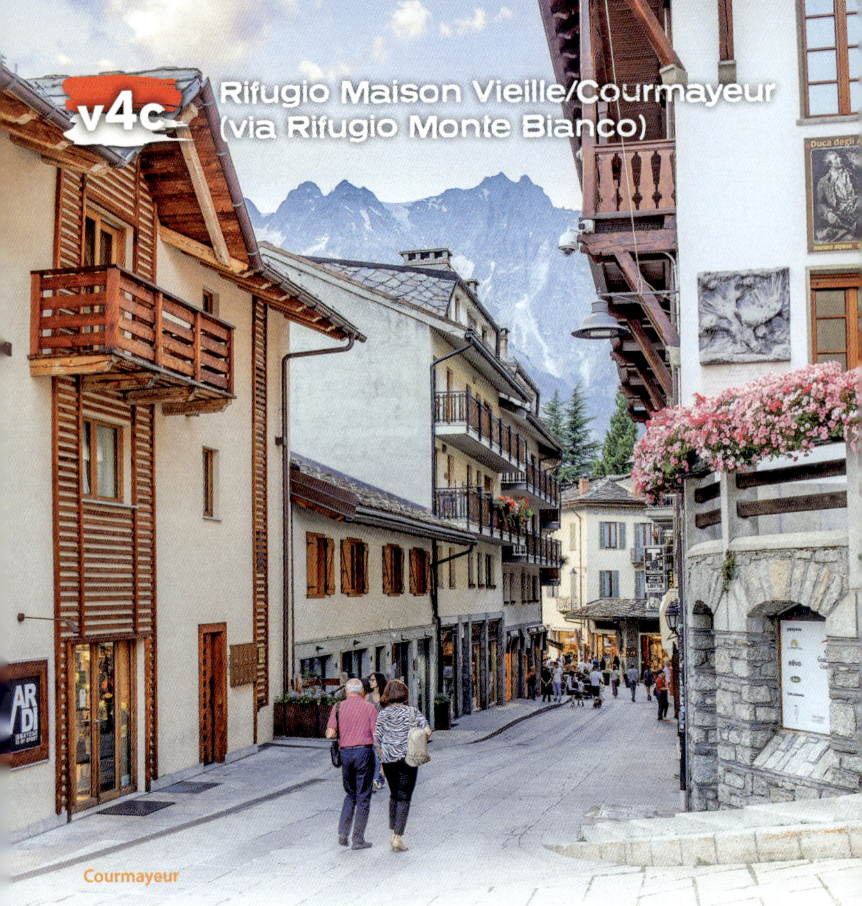

Courmayeur

This variant provides an alternative to Stage 4c of the main route. It is useful for those who cannot find accommodation at Col Chécrouit because it passes Rifugio Monte Bianco: with superb views of Glacier de la Brenva and Aiguille Noire, it is a wonderful place to spend the night and is quieter than the accommodation along the TMB's main route. The stage is also useful for campers who want to stay at one of Val Veny's campsites (there are none along the main route between les Chapieux and Courmayeur): using v4c, you can access the campsites without having to miss out on Stage 4b's magnificent balcony.

Stage v4c avoids the steeper, knee-jerking descent on Stage 4c but the distance to Courmayeur is longer. At 30 (a short distance N of Rifugio Monte Bianco), Stage v4c meets v4b (which you then follow between 30 and Courmayeur).

Terrain	Good paths/tracks which are simple to follow. Between 30 and Courmayeur there is a lot of road walking.
Route-finding	Straightforward.
Camping	Three campsites in Val Veny but no legal bivouac sites.
Trail notes	The Val Veny campsites can be busy with holidaymakers (quite noisy).
Transport	Val Veny shuttle bus runs hourly between la Visaille 27 and Courmayeur (stopping at the campsites and 30).

	Start	Finish	Time	Distance	Ascent (ACW)	Descent (ACW)	Max Alt
v4c	Rifugio Maison Vieille	Courmayeur	1:55 3:15	7.6km 4.7miles	41m 135ft	773m 2536ft	1956m 6417ft

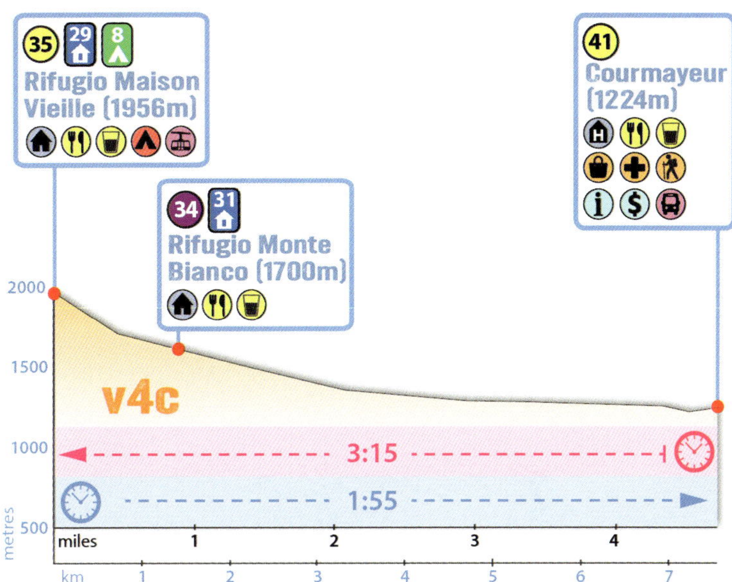

Stage v4c: Rifugio Maison Vieille to Courmayeur

35 See map on p103. From **Rifugio Maison Vieille**, head W. Soon, descend on a path through trees.

33 0:10: TR near a **ski-station** to descend NE across the slope.

34 0:25: Arrive at **Rifugio Monte Bianco (1700m)**. Descend N on a road. Shortly afterwards, there is a path on the left which drops down to the road in Val Veny: use this if you wish to head to the valley's campsites; ignore the path if you are heading for Courmayeur.

30 0:55: TR at a road junction and follow Stage v4b's directions (see p115).

41 1:55: Arrive in **Courmayeur (1224m)**.

Stage v4c: Courmayeur to Rifugio Maison Vieille

41 See map on p110. From **Courmayeur**, follow Stage v4b's directions to 30 (see p115).

30 1:50: TL at a road junction and climb.

34 2:30: Arrive at **Rifugio Monte Bianco (1700m)**. Climb S.

33 2:55: See map on p103. TL after a **ski-station** and climb E on a path through trees.

35 3:15: Arrive at **Rifugio Maison Vieille** at **Col Chécrouit (1956m)**.

5 Courmayeur/ Rifugio Walter Bonatti

Stage 5a (Courmayeur/Rifugio Bertone): ACW trekkers have a steep and relentless climb to Rifugio Bertone which has one of the finest settings on the TMB: it looks straight across Val Veny towards MB. In good weather, a night here will not be easily forgotten. CW trekkers, on the other hand, have a tiring, knee-jerking descent into Courmayeur.

Stage 5b (Rifugio Bertone/Rifugio Bonatti): pray for a fine day because this is a highlight of the trek. The views of the MB massif (on the second of the TMB's great balcony paths) are exquisite and you feel closer to it than almost anywhere else along the route: Glacier de la Brenva, which begins near MB's summit, is so close that you can almost touch it! The setting of Rifugio Bonatti is magnificent (facing directly onto the Grandes Jorasses) but it is extremely busy. There are more peaceful accommodation options along the route of Section 6 but they are too far away for some hikers to reach from Courmayeur in one day.

Itinerary options: although Stage 5b is spectacular, the v5b high variant is even better (p126).

	Start	Finish	Time	Distance	Ascent (ACW)	Descent (ACW)	Max Alt
5a	Courmayeur	Rifugio Bertone	2:30 1:30	5.3km 3.3miles	781m 2562ft	0m 0ft	1991m 6532ft
5b	Rifugio Bertone	Rifugio Bonatti	2:30 2:25	7.9km 4.9miles	300m 984ft	266m 873ft	2025m 6644ft

Mont Blanc viewed from near Rifugio Bertone (Stage 5a)

In bad weather, you can avoid Section 5 by taking the bus from Courmayeur to 39 in Italian Val Ferret (see p122). From there, it is a short climb to Rifugio Bonatti using the Bonatti Link Route (p121).

Terrain	**Stage 5a:** good paths/tracks/roads which are simple to follow. Between 42 and 43, the gradient is often steep: it is a long, hard climb for ACW trekkers; for CW trekkers, the long descent is tough on the knees. **Stage 5b:** paths are largely clear and simple to follow although the route is quite challenging: it undulates relentlessly and is more tiring than it looks on the map; narrow and/or rocky sections. Snow can remain into July making some sloping traverses of the balcony slippery. In June, take care on snow bridges which form over the torrents: they melt from underneath and can be fragile. If in doubt, do not cross and try to find a safer way across either above or below the snow bridge. In such conditions, consider using Stage v5a instead (see p122).
Route-finding	The route heads generally NE all the way between 44 and 45: take care not to stray onto one of the paths descending W into Val Ferret. Otherwise, navigation is generally straightforward (with plenty of signs).
Camping	Along the main route, there are no campsites or places to bivouac legally. Some trekkers bivouac SE of Rifugio Bonatti (along the route of Stage v5b) but this is not legal (because it is under 2500m). The highest parts of Stage v5b are above 2500m though so it may be possible to bivouac legally there.
Transport	**Courmayeur:** buses and cable cars (see p46 and p49).

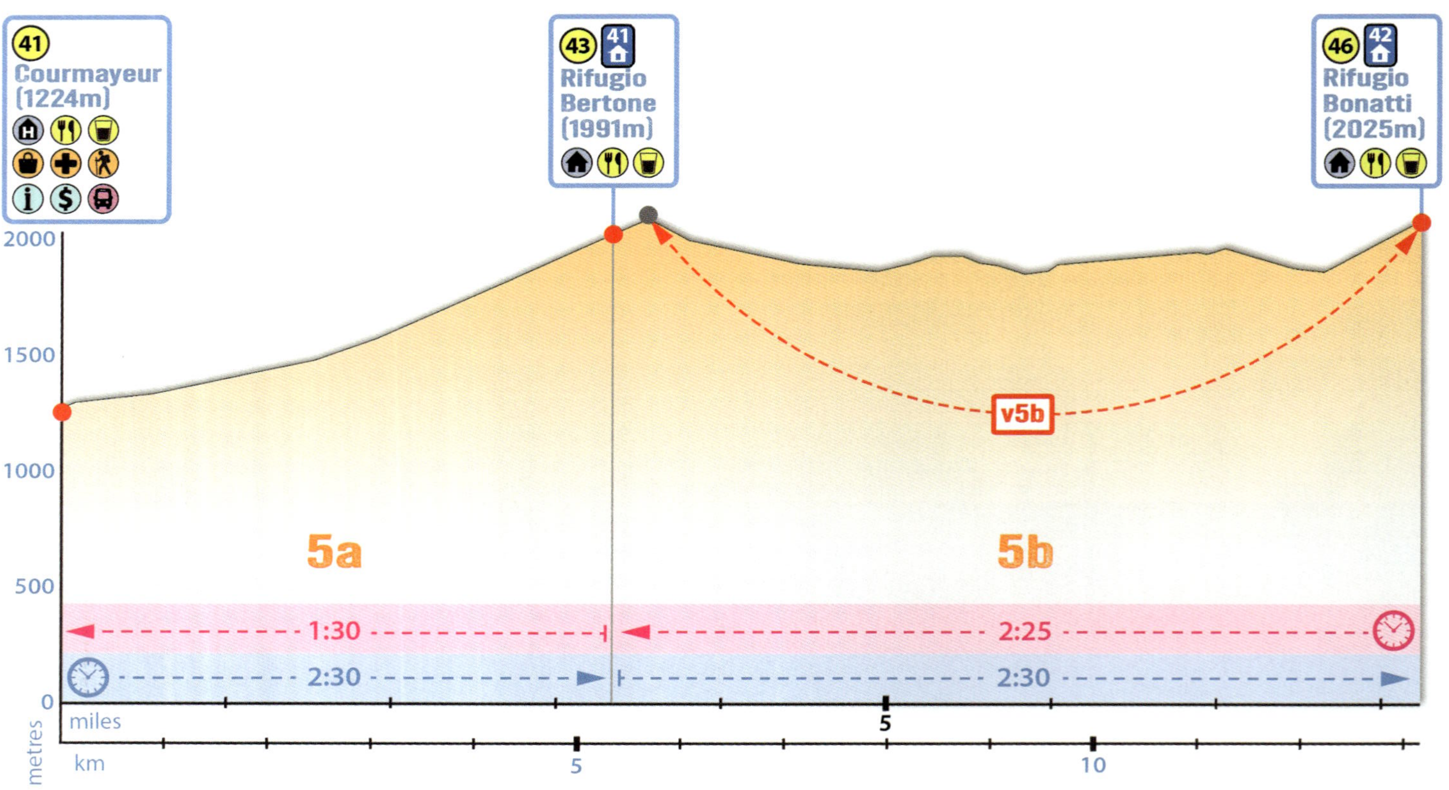
41
Courmayeur
(1224m)
43
41
Rifugio
Bertone
(1991m)
46
42
Rifugio
Bonatti
(2025m)
2000
1500
1000
500
0
metres
v5b
5a
5b
1:30
2:25
2:30
2:30
miles
5
km
5
10

Stage 5a: Courmayeur to Rifugio Bertone

(41) See map on p110. From **Courmayeur's tourist office**, head E up **Via Croux** towards the church. Shortly afterwards, keep SH at a junction onto **Via Vicolo della Chiesa**. Keep SH at the next junction onto a cobbled path. Soon climb some steps. TL along **Via Roma** to reach **Piazza Abbé Henry**. Just after the church, TR on **Strada del Villair**. 5min later, keep SH at a junction, still on **Strada del Villair**.

(42) 0:55: Soon after the road becomes a track, TL, cross a bridge and continue uphill. Soon, TR onto a path and climb through trees. When you meet a track, cross it and continue climbing on a path.

(43) 2:30: Arrive at **Rifugio Bertone (1991m)**.

Stage 5b: Rifugio Bertone to Rifugio Walter Bonatti

(43) See map on p110. From **Rifugio Bertone**, climb on a path. TR at a fork.

(44) 0:10: Arrive at a junction: keep SH (N) for Stage 5b; alternatively, TR and climb NE for Stage v5b (p126). Afterwards, the path undulates and contours around the hillside.

(45) 2:20: TR at a junction and head straight up the hillside.

(46) 2:30: Arrive at **Rifugio Walter Bonatti (2025m)**.

Stage 5b: Rifugio Walter Bonatti to Rifugio Bertone

(46) See map on p111. From **Rifugio Bonatti**, descend NW on a path.

(45) 0:05: TL at a junction. Afterwards, the path undulates and contours around the hillside.

(44) 2:20: Keep SH at a junction: the path joining from the left is Stage v5b.

(43) 2:25: Arrive at **Rifugio Bertone (1991m)**.

Stage 5a: Rifugio Bertone to Courmayeur

(43) See map on p110. From **Rifugio Bertone**, descend S on a path. Later, when you meet a track, cross it and continue descending on a path. Soon, TL down the track.

(42) 0:50: Shortly afterwards, cross a bridge. Immediately afterwards, TR down a track. Keep SH onto **Strada del Villair** and follow it all the way into Courmayeur.

(41) 1:30: Reach **Piazza Abbé Henry** in **Courmayeur (1224m)**. Buses leave from the tourist office in Piazza Monte Bianco (at the bottom of the town).

Bonatti Link Route

See map on p125.

ACW: 50min; 1.5km; +330m.

From (39), climb S on a path through trees. After 40min, TL at (45), still climbing. 5-10min later, reach **Rifugio Bonatti (2025m)**.

CW: 25min; 1.5km; -330m.

From **Rifugio Walter Bonatti**, descend N on a path. 5min later, TR at (45): soon, descend NW through trees. 20min later, reach (39).

Courmayeur/Chalet Val Ferret-Arnuova (via Italian Val Ferret)

The 34km stretch between Courmayeur and la Fouly (Sections 5 and 6) is another hard part of the TMB to plan and book: there is insufficient accommodation and the distance is too great for most trekkers to hike it all in one day. Furthermore, there are no campsites along the main route between Courmayeur and la Fouly, or in Courmayeur itself; and there are few places to bivouac legally. However, the two campsites on Stage v5a (along Italian Val Ferret) offer a solution for those with their own tents. There are also a few accommodation options in Italian Val Ferret for those who cannot find a bed along the main route. Furthermore, Stage v5a offers a safer route in bad weather than the higher Stage 5b.

However, although the scenery is beautiful, Stage v5a cannot compete with the exquisite balcony path on Stage 5b or the superlative Stage v5b high variant: you will miss out on those delights if you hike v5a. Furthermore, the route largely uses the road along Italian Val Ferret so it is hardly a wilderness experience.

Itinerary options: you can access Stage v5a directly from Stage v4b, without having to hike all the way into Courmayeur: the two routes meet at (32); in total, this avoids 3.5km of walking, making it easier to hike between the campsites of Val Veny and the campsites of Italian Val Ferret in one day.

To avoid missing out on Stage 5b/v5b, ACW campers could hike Stage 5b/v5b to Rifugio Bonatti and then descend to (39) (using the Bonatti Link Route; p121): from (39), head SW along v5a to the Italian Val Ferret campsites (on foot or by bus); the following morning, hike (or take the bus) back to (39) to resume the trek.

Alternatively, ACW trekkers could spend two nights at the Italian Val Ferret campsites: hike (or take the bus) to a Val Ferret campsite from either Courmayeur or (32). After the first night, leave your tent pitched (so that you can travel light) and hike along v5a to (39); from there, use the Bonatti Link Route to climb to Rifugio Bonatti (46); then hike Section 5 CW to Courmayeur. From there, take the bus back to your tent in Italian Val Ferret and spend a second night there. The following morning resume your ACW trek. CW trekkers can also use the campsites in a similar way.

Terrain	Easy road walking.
Route-finding	Straightforward.
Camping	Two campsites but no legal bivouac sites.
Trail notes	There are various bars/restaurants scattered along Italian Val Ferret.
Transport	The Val Ferret shuttle bus runs hourly between Courmayeur's Tourist Office in Piazzale Monte Bianco and Chalet Val Ferret-Arnuova (49). It stops at various places in Italian Val Ferret including (32) (the bus stop is on Strada Larzey-Entrèves), Entrèves, Val Ferret's campsites and (39) (for access to Rifugio Bonatti).

	Start	Finish	Time	Distance	Ascent (ACW)	Descent (ACW)	Max Alt
v5a	Courmayeur	Chalet Val Ferret (Arnouva)	4:25 3:20	13.8km 8.6miles	591m 1939ft	44m 144ft	1771m 5810ft

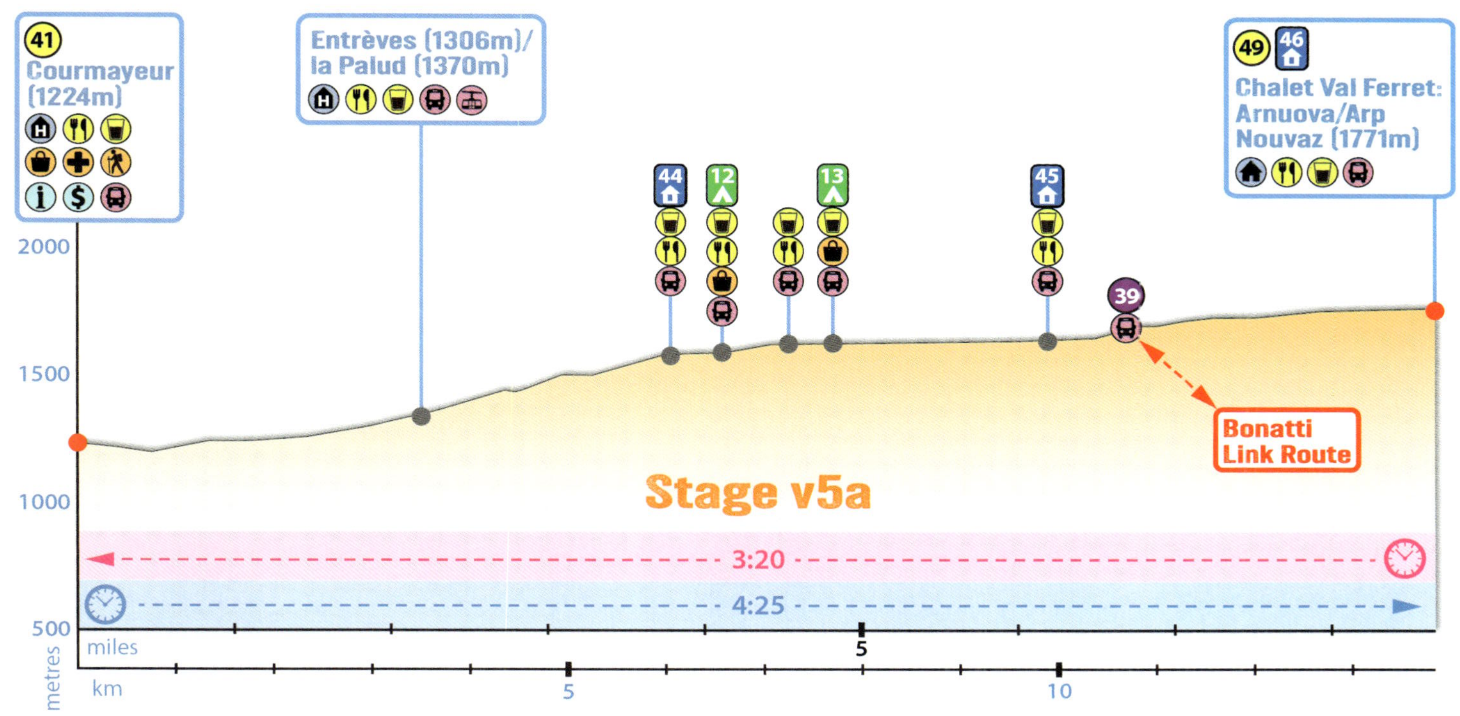
41
Courmayeur (1224m)
Entrèves (1306m)/
la Palud (1370m)
44
12
13
45
39
49
46
Chalet Val Ferret:
Arnuova/Arp
Nouvaz (1771m)
Bonatti
Link Route
Stage v5a
3:20
4:25
2000
1500
1000
500
metres
miles
km
5
5
10

Stage v5a: Courmayeur to Chalet Val Ferret-Arnuova

41 See map on p110. From **Piazza Abbé Henry** in **Courmayeur**, head N down **Via Roma/Viale Monte Bianco**. TL at a roundabout. Just afterwards, TR and head NW on **Strada della Villette**. 5min later, TR on a main road. Shortly afterwards, TL and descend on a small road. Cross the river and then TR, climbing on a quiet road. 10min later, keep SH on a sealed track. There are lovely views of the MB massif.

32 0:30: 5min later, TR on a road and cross a bridge. Shortly afterwards, TL at a junction onto **Strada Larzey-Entrèves**: supermarket near the junction. From **la Palud**, follow a road NE up **Val Ferret**.

38 2:00: TR onto a path which heads NE across grassy slopes. 10min later, TR and head up the road again.

12 2:25: Continue up the road past **Camping Grandes Jorasses**.

13 2:45: Continue up the road past **Camping Tronchey**.

45 3:20: See map on p125. Continue up the road past **Hotel Lavachey**.

39 3:30: Keep SH at a junction: the path to the right is the **Bonatti Link Route** (p121).

49 4:25: Arrive at **Chalet Val Ferret** at **Arnuova/Arp Nouvaz (1771m)**.

Stage v5a: Chalet Val Ferret-Arnuova to Courmayeur

49 See map on p125. From **Arnuova/Arp Nouvaz**, head SW along the road.

39 0:45: Keep SH at a junction: the path to the left is the **Bonatti Link Route** (p121).

45 0:55: Continue SW on the road past **Hotel Lavachey**.

13 1:30: See map on p111. Continue SW on the road past **Camping Tronchey**.

12 1:45: Continue SW on the road past **Camping Grandes Jorasses**. TL onto a path which heads SW across grassy slopes.

38 2:05: 10min later, TL and head SW down the road again. From **la Palud**, follow **Strada la Palud**, and then **Strada Larzey-Entrèves**. Later, TR at a junction onto **Via Valveny** ('Val Veny'): supermarket near the junction.

32 2:55: Just after crossing a bridge, TL onto a track. Soon keep SH on a quiet road. Cross a bridge over the river and climb on a small road. TR on a main road. Shortly afterwards, TL on **Strada della Villette**: at the end of it, TL. Just afterwards, TR at a roundabout and climb S up **Via Roma/Viale Monte Bianco**.

41 3:20: Reach **Piazza Abbé Henry** in **Courmayeur (1224m)**.

Stage v5a runs along Italian Val Ferret

Rifugio Elena (2061m)
Chalet Val Ferret: Arnuova/Arp Nouvaz (1771m)
Rifugio Bonatti (2025m)
Stage 6b
Stage v5a
Stage 6a
Stage v5b
Aiguille Rouge de Triolet
Mont Dolent
Mont Grépillon
Tête de Ferret
Monte Gruetta
Testa Bernarda
Mont Berrio Blanc
Bella Comba
Mont Chéarfière
Aiguille Rouge de Triolet
Aiguille de Triolet
Mont Dolent
Mont de la Fouly
La Tsavre
Grandes Jorasses
Monte Gruetta
Grand Combin de Grafeneire
Mont Vélan
Mont Berrio Blanc
Mont Tapie
Aiguille de Bonalex
Grande Rochère
Grand Golliat
Cima Centrale 3332
Aiguille Rouge de Triolet 3289
Bivacco Fiorio
Petit Col Ferret 2486
Le Chantonnet 2576
Col Chantonnet 2540
Pré de Bar Desot
Pré de Bar Damon
Arnuova Desot
Arnuova Damon
Tza de Jean Desot
Ex Bivacco Fréboudze
Belle Combe
Vallon de la Belle Co
Bella Comba 2701
Giué Desot
Malatra Desot
Giué Damon
Malatra Damon
Vallone Di Malatra
Arminaz Desot
Arminaz Damon
Tête entre
Aiguille d'Artan 3069
Dora di Ferret

v5b Rifugio Bertone/Rifugio Bonatti (via Mont de la Saxe)

Mont de la Saxe

Choosing an absolute highlight of the consistently superlative TMB is a difficult task. However, if pressed, you might choose this variant stage. On a clear sunny day, the scenery is exquisite: the MB massif is only a stone's throw away and you have plenty of time to enjoy the vistas as you travel along the high ridge of Mont de la Saxe and across the summit of Tête de la Tronche. Vallon d'Arminaz (between Col Sapin and Col Entre-Deux-Sauts) is magnificent too. However, the sublime scenery is not given away cheaply because this variant is much harder than the main route (Stage 5b).

Terrain	High altitude route with challenging paths: remote terrain with fewer hikers; narrow and/or rocky sections; regular undulations; long, sustained climbs/descents with steep gradients. Sometimes snow remains until early July and this part of the TMB gets tracked less quickly than the main route: in such conditions, steep gradients make the route challenging and a fall could be serious.
Route-finding	In Vallon d'Arminaz (between 36 and 37), there are a number of different paths: follow the map/directions carefully. The path E of Col Entre-Deux-Sauts can be faint. Otherwise, route-finding is straightforward in good conditions. However, navigation can be tricky in bad weather, low visibility or snowy conditions: in particular, it is easy to become disorientated in the remote Vallon d'Arminaz. Accordingly, it is not wise to attempt Stage v5b in bad conditions.
Camping	No official campsites. The terrain around Tête de Bernarde, Tête de la Tronche and Col Entre-Deux-Sauts is above 2500m so bivouac is possible: however, these places are pretty exposed.
Transport	None

	Start	Finish	Time	Distance	Ascent	Descent	Max Alt
v5b	Rifugio Bertone	Rifugio Bonatti	4:00 4:00	10.3km 6.4miles	903m 2963ft	869m 2851ft	2584m 8478ft

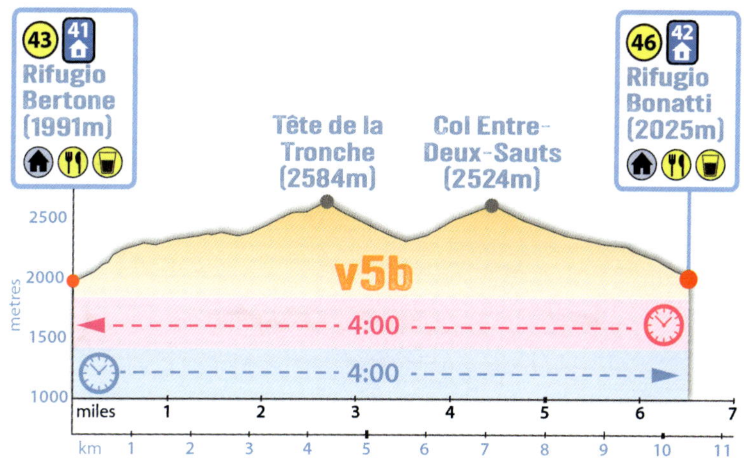

Stage v5b: Rifugio Bertone to Rifugio Bonatti

(43) See map on p110. From **Rifugio Bertone**, climb N on a path. TR at a fork.

(44) 0:10: TR at a junction and climb steeply to the NE. Continue NE along the crest of the ridge, on a path which levels and then undulates. There are numerous paths on the ridge: stay close to the top for the best views. Continue NE across the summit of **Mont de la Saxe (2346m)**.

(35) 1:25: Climb steeply again, still on the crest of the ridge. Take care climbing over a small section of rocks. Follow the path just to the right of **Tête de Bernarde (2533m)**. Shortly afterwards, TR at a junction on a saddle and continue climbing.

(36) 2:05: Cross the summit of **Tête de la Tronche (2584m)**. Descend steeply SE to **Col Sapin (2435m)**. Then head E into the lovely **Vallon d'Arminaz**. Contour around the slopes, ignoring paths descending to the left.

(37) 3:10: Cross **Col Entre-Deux-Sauts (2524m)**. Then descend E. Soon bear left to head N down another valley: the path is faint. Keep to the left of the stream running down the valley. At **Malatrà Damon**, TL at a junction. Keep SH at the junction at **Malatrà Dèsot**.

(46) 4:00: Shortly afterwards, arrive at **Rifugio Walter Bonatti (2025m)**.

Stage v5b: Rifugio Bonatti to Rifugio Bertone

(46) See map on p111. From **Rifugio Bonatti**, head E on a path. Shortly afterwards, TR at a junction at **Malatrà Dèsot** and climb SE up the valley. At **Malatrà Damon**, TR at a junction: climb S along the W side of the stream. Later the path drifts right, climbing W (directly up the slope).

(37) 1:45: Cross **Col Entre-Deux-Sauts (2524m)**. Contour around the slopes of **Vallon d'Arminaz**, ignoring paths heading down to the right. At **Col Sapin (2435m)**, TR and climb steeply NW.

(36) 2:50: Cross the summit of **Tête de la Tronche (2584m)** and descend NW. Soon the path bends left and passes to the left of **Tête de Bernarde (2533m)**.

(35) Keep SH, descending SW along a ridge. Cross the summit of **Mont de la Saxe (2346m)**. Continue SW along the ridge.

(44) 3:55: TL at a junction.

(43) 4:00: Arrive at **Rifugio Bertone (1991m)**.

6 Rifugio Walter Bonatti/la Fouly

Stage 6a (Rifugio Bonatti/Chalet Val Ferret): a superb traverse across open slopes with amazing views of the Grandes Jorasses and MB. ACW trekkers finish by descending to Italian Val Ferret's wonderful Chalet Val Ferret (which books up lightning fast); for CW trekkers, this is a punchy climb.

Stage 6b (Chalet Val Ferret/Rifugio Elena): a magnificent stage linking Chalet Val Ferret with Rifugio Elena. The views are stunning, both S down Italian Val Ferret and NW towards Glaciers Triolet and Pré de Bar. However, Rifugio Elena steals the show with its long terrace facing Glacier de Pré de Bar. ACW trekkers tackle the stage in an uphill direction whereas CW trekkers descend all the way.

Stage 6c (Rifugio Elena/Alpage de la Peule): the crossing of Grand Col Ferret, between Italy and Switzerland, is another highlight of the TMB. It is particularly dramatic for CW trekkers because the MB massif is suddenly revealed as you approach the top. There are awesome views throughout the stage but the col itself is a particularly special place with a 360° panorama: to the W, the Grandes Jorasses, Monte Gruetta, Aiguille de Triolet and Mont Dolent look fabulous; to the E, you get a good look at the Combins massif. For ACW trekkers, the descent towards Swiss Val Ferret is sublime and we highly recommend a stay at Gîte Alpage de la Peule: its remote location ensures that it is one of the TMB's most peaceful overnight stops.

Stage 6d (Alpage de la Peule/Ferret): the sound of cow bells will sooth ACW trekkers as they descend on easy paths/tracks into beautiful Swiss Val Ferret. Upon reaching the valley floor, follow the road to the neat little hamlet of Ferret with its hotel and scenic

	Start	Finish	Time	Distance	Ascent (ACW)	Descent (ACW)	Max Alt
6a	Rifugio Bonatti	Chalet Val Ferret	1:20 1:45	5.1km 3.2miles	60m 197ft	323m 1060ft	2025m 6644ft
6b	Chalet Val Ferret	Rifugio Elena	0:55 0:35	2.2km 1.4miles	293m 961ft	0m 0ft	2062m 6765ft
6c	Rifugio Elena	Alpage de la Peule	2:30 2:30	6.5km 4.0miles	475m 1558ft	464m 1522ft	2536m 8320ft
6d	Alpage de la Peule	Ferret	1:15 1:50	4.6km 2.9miles	30m 98ft	401m 1316ft	2071m 6795ft
6e	Ferret	La Fouly	0:40 0:50	2.8km 1.7miles	0m 0ft	100m 328ft	1700m 5577ft

The E side of Grand Col Ferret

chapel. For CW trekkers, an overnight stay at Gîte Alpage de la Peule is recommended to break up the long climb to Grand Col Ferret.

Stage 6e (Ferret/la Fouly): an easy hike between Ferret and the superbly situated village of la Fouly where you can stock up on supplies. There are a few shops and restaurants and plenty of places to stay.

Terrain	**Stage 6a:** the traverse undulates continuously and is quite tiring. Snow can remain into July making paths slippery. In a few places, the route crosses streams in gullies: in good conditions, crossing is not difficult; however, take care in June/early July when snow bridges can form. This stage is harder for CW trekkers who have a steep climb between Chalet Val Ferret and 48. **Stage 6b:** Some steep slopes. In snowy conditions, the route can be slippery and a fall could be serious: it can be safer to use the vehicle track (up the valley floor) between 50 and Rifugio Elena. **Stage 6c:** a challenging route across a high pass with a long climb and a long descent. The gradient is sometimes steep. In wet conditions, paths can be slippery. Sometimes snow remains near the col until early July: in such conditions, the climb to, and descent from, the col are tougher; in particular, the steep zigzags just above Rifugio Elena can be treacherous. **Stages 6d/6e:** good paths/tracks/roads which are simple to follow. These stages are harder for CW trekkers who have a lot of climbing.
Route-finding	Stage 6c is a high altitude route: although navigation is straightforward in good conditions, it is more difficult in bad weather, low visibility or snow: do not attempt Stage 6c in such conditions. Otherwise, navigation is generally straightforward throughout Section 6 (plenty of signs).
Camping	Campsite at la Fouly. Bivouac is sometimes permitted at Gîte Alpage de la Peule. Because the Italian side of Grand Col Ferret is above 2500m, bivouac used to be permitted: however, signs at the col now state that bivouac is prohibited to protect the sensitive environment. Some trekkers bivouac at the parking area at 54: this may not be legal but it seems to be tolerated.
Transport	From Rifugio Bonatti, you can descend to 39 using the Bonatti Link Route (p121): the Italian Val Ferret shuttle bus between Courmayeur and Chalet Val Ferret stops there (see p122). **Chalet Val Ferret (Arnouva/Arp Nouvaz):** Italian Val Ferret shuttle bus. **Ferret:** bus 272 to/from la Fouly, Praz-de-Fort (Stage 7), Issert (Stage 7) and Orsières. **La Fouly:** bus 272 to/from Ferret, Praz-de-Fort (Stage 7), Issert (Stage 7) and Orsières.

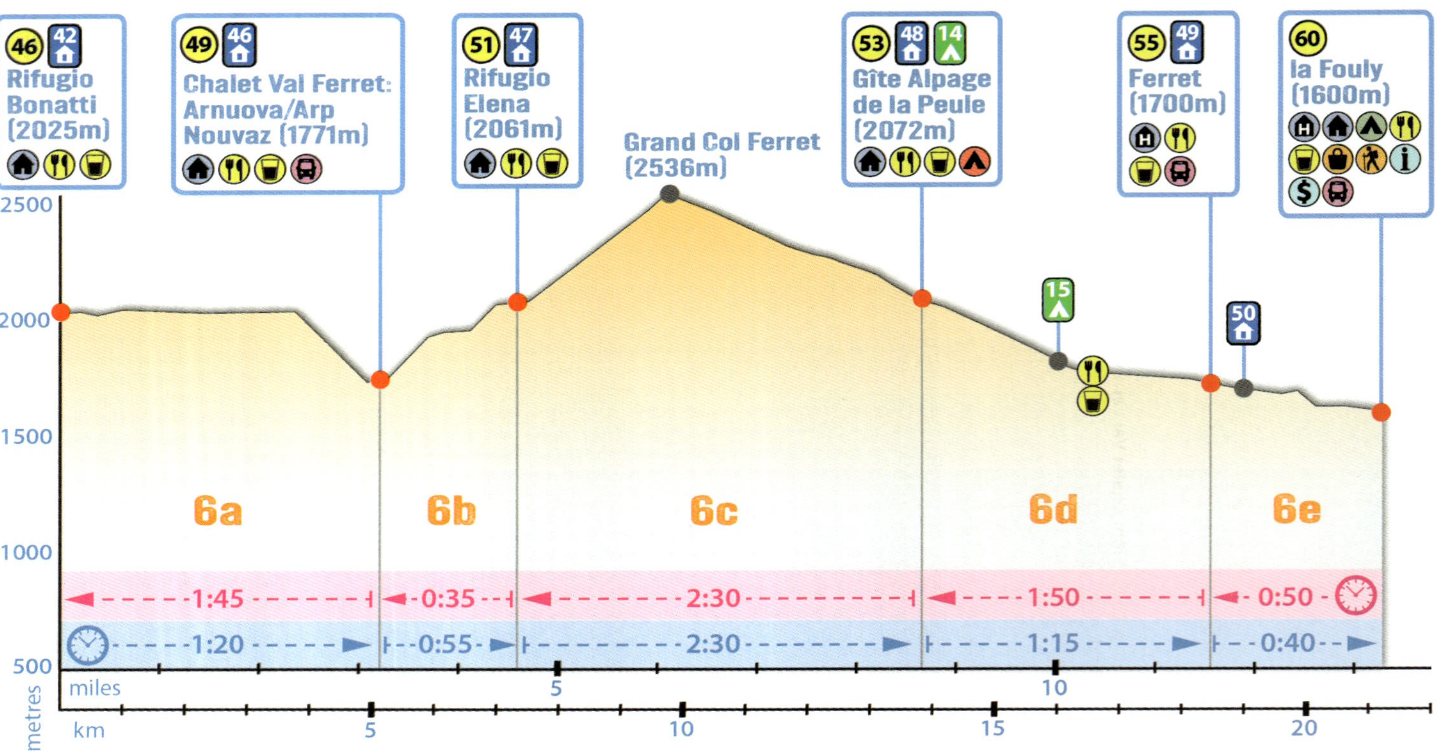
46 42 Rifugio Bonatti (2025m)
49 46 Chalet Val Ferret: Arnuova/Arp Nouvaz (1771m)
51 47 Rifugio Elena (2061m)
Grand Col Ferret (2536m)
53 48 14 Gîte Alpage de la Peule (2072m)
15
55 49 Ferret (1700m)
50
60 la Fouly (1600m)
2500
2000
1500
1000
500
metres
6a
6b
6c
6d
6e
1:45
0:35
2:30
1:50
0:50
1:20
0:55
2:30
1:15
0:40
miles
5
10
km
5
10
15
20

Stage 6a: Rifugio Bonatti to Chalet Val Ferret

46 See map on p125. Climb briefly SE above **Rifugio Bonatti**. At the buildings of **Malatrà Dèsot**, TL on a path which contours NE around the slopes. After crossing two streams, TL at a junction.

47 0:10: At **Giué Dèsot**, keep SH (NE).

48 1:00: TL at a junction near a building and descend. TR at the next fork.

49 1:20: Arrive at **Chalet Val Ferret (1771m)**.

Stage 6b: Chalet Val Ferret to Rifugio Elena

49 See map on p125. From **Chalet Val Ferret**, head briefly W on a tarmac lane. TR to cross a bridge and then continue on a track.

50 0:05: TR on a path and climb steeply. After a while, the path levels out and contours NE across the slopes.

51 0:55: Arrive at **Rifugio Elena (2061m)**: the views from the terrace are incredible.

Stage 6c: Rifugio Elena to Alpage de la Peule

51 See map on p125. From **Rifugio Elena**, head N. Shortly afterwards, TR at a junction onto a path zigzagging upwards (to the E). At around **2300m**, the path turns left to climb N.

52 1:30: Cross **Grand Col Ferret (2536m)** and enter **Switzerland**. Bear left on a path and head N. See map on p132. Soon the path bends to the E as it makes its way down the left flank of the valley.

53 2:30: Arrive at **Gîte Alpage de la Peule (2072m)**.

Stage 6c: Alpage de la Peule to Rifugio Elena

53 See map on p132. From **Gîte Alpage de la Peule**, head N. Just afterwards, TL at a junction and climb initially N: soon, the path turns left to climb SW.

52 1:35: See map on p125. Cross **Grand Col Ferret (2536m)** and enter **Italy**. Descend S on a path. At around **2300m**, the path turns right to descend W: soon, it zigzags down the slope.

51 2:30: Arrive at **Rifugio Elena (2061m)**.

Stage 6b: Rifugio Elena to Chalet Val Ferret

51 See map on p125. From **Rifugio Elena**, head S on a path which contours across the slopes.

50 0:30: TL on a track. Just after crossing a bridge, TL and head E on a tarmac lane.

49 0:35: Shortly afterwards, reach **Chalet Val Ferret (1771m)**.

Stage 6a: Chalet Val Ferret to Rifugio Bonatti

49 See map on p125. From **Chalet Val Ferret**, zigzag up to the E on a path.

48 0:45: TR at a junction near a building and contour SW across the slopes.

47 1:35: At **Giué Dèsot,** keep SH. Shortly, head S at a junction: cross two streams. At the buildings of **Malatrà Dèsot**, TR and head W.

46 1:45: Shortly afterwards, arrive at **Rifugio Walter Bonatti (2025m)**.

Prayon
Torrent Idroz
Combe B
Cabane de l'A Neuve CAS
N
W
E
S
Aiguille de l'Amône
Aiguille Rouge de Dolent
Tour Noir
60
360
Mont de la Fouly
Petit Grépillon
La Maye
Dranse de Ferret
Stage 7
61
Forêt des Places
Torrent d
Crêtet
Ravines
60
la Fouly (1600m)
55
16
54
51
52
53
La Maye 2642
Bivouac du Dolent
Ravines
50
Gîte de la Léchère (1700m)
59
Le Clou
Stage 6e
58
55
49
Ferret (1700m)
Reuses du Dolent
57
Crêtet de la Gouille 2083
La Tsavre
56
Planproz
Crêtet de la Perche 2289
Savolayres
Mont Allobrogia 3171
Les Ars
Stage 6d
Peule-Ferret Alt
Les Creuses
54
15
La Dotse 2491
Col Ferret 2486
Le Chantonnet 2576
Chantonnet 2575
Tête de Ferret 2714
Arête des Planfins
La Peule
53
48
14
Gîte Alpage de la Peule (2072m)
Stage 6c
52
Grand Col Ferret 2536
Torrent de la Peule
2631
Pré de Bar
Damon
132
Grand Creux
Six Blanc 2795
Arête des Econdu

Stage 6d: Alpage de la Peule to Ferret

53 See map on p132. Head S along the front of **Gîte Alpage de la Peule**. Shortly afterwards, follow a track around to the left: follow waymarks to descend to the river, using both the track and paths which cut across the track's hairpin bends.

54 0:40: Cross a bridge over the **Dranse de Ferret**. Immediately afterwards, TL onto a track and walk alongside the river. Soon, keep SH at a junction and descend on a road.

55 1:15: Arrive at the hamlet of **Ferret (1700m)**.

Stage 6e: Ferret to la Fouly

55 See map on p132. From the S side of **Ferret**, descend W on a path ('la Fouly').

56 Shortly afterwards, cross a footbridge over the river and continue downstream. Soon the path shifts away from the river and then crosses another stream (on a bridge).

57 0:10: Shortly afterwards, keep SH at a junction: alternatively, TL for **Gîte de la Léchère** (5min). Shortly after that, TL onto a track.

58 0:15: Keep SH at a junction: the track on the left comes from **Gîte de la Léchère** (5min).

59 0:20 At a left-hand bend in the track, take a small path running downhill to the right (NE). Cross the river (on a bridge) and then TL to climb on a track. Shortly afterwards, TL onto a road.

60 0:40: Enter **la Fouly (1600m)**.

Stage 6e: la Fouly to Ferret

60 See map on p132. From **la Fouly**, head S on the road. After 15min, TR down a track. Cross the river (on a bridge) and then TL. Shortly afterwards, TR and climb on a path.

59 0:25: TL along a track.

58 0:30: Keep SH at a junction: alternatively, TR for **Gîte de la Léchère** (5min).

57 0:35: TR on a path. Shortly afterwards, keep SH at a junction: the path to the right comes from **Gîte de la Léchère** (5min). Soon, cross a bridge and head SE on a path.

56 0:45: TL and cross a bridge over the **Dranse de Ferret**.

55 0:50: Arrive at the hamlet of **Ferret (1700m)**.

Stage 6d: Ferret to Alpage de la Peule

55 See map on p132. From **Ferret**, climb SE on the road. TR at a junction at **les Ars**.

54 0:30: Cross a bridge over the **Dranse de Ferret** and climb on a track. Soon, TL on a path. When you reach the track again, TL up it. Shortly afterwards, TR on a path (easy to miss). Shortly after that, keep SH across the track. When you meet the track again, TL up it.

53 1:50: TR at a junction to reach **Gîte Alpage de la Peule (2072m)**.

Peule-Ferret Alternative Route

ACW (1hr; 3.5km; ⬆50m; ⬇426): from **Gîte Alpage de la Peule**, head N. Just afterwards, TR at a junction ('Ferret'): the path contours N around the slopes. Later, head around the spur of a ridge and descend: the views are amazing. After a building at **Planproz**, the path bears right and descends NE. When you reach 56, TR for **Ferret** or TL for **la Fouly**.

CW (1.5hr; 3.5km; ⬆426; ⬇50): From 56, climb W on a path. Soon TL at a junction, climbing SW. Near a building at **Planproz**, the path bears left to head E. Head around the spur of a ridge and contour SE around the slopes. Eventually, reach **Gîte Alpage de la Peule**.

7 La Fouly/Champex

View from la Fouly

This valley walk is far removed from the high mountain stages of the previous few days. This part of the Swiss Val Ferret is gentle and green: forests of larch and pine interspersed with the bucolic, flower filled, 'Sound of Music' pastures that one associates with Switzerland. And dotted around the slopes are the neat and tidy chalets found only in Switzerland. A sparkling river runs through the middle of the valley and the TMB leads you along its unpopulated left bank. It is a lovely walk.

ACW trekkers will stay in Champex, at the N end of the stage: it is a pretty lakeside town with bars, restaurants, hotels, gîtes and a campsite. If you arrive early, you can enjoy a relaxed lunch, rent a rowing boat on the lake, or take a stroll around it. Alternatively, Champex is a good place in which to take a day off. As is often the case with place names in French, the correct pronunciation of 'Champex' is not immediately obvious (even to French speakers) and is the subject of much discussion amongst trekkers: some French speakers pronounce the 'x' but most locals do not. CW trekkers will stay at la Fouly (p129).

Terrain	Good paths/tracks which are simple to negotiate. Some short sections along minor roads. ACW trekkers have a long, easy descent near the valley floor, followed by a stiff climb up its W flank. CW trekkers, on the other hand, have a steep descent followed by a gentle climb.
Route-finding	The directions for this stage are a little fiddly but the route is quite well marked. Follow signs carefully through villages (where there are plenty of different paths/tracks/roads).
Camping	Campsites at la Fouly and Champex. No places to bivouac legally.
Trail notes	If you cannot find accommodation in Champex, consider Gîte Bon Abri (1.5km NW of Champex, along Stage 8a). Alternatively, stay at the wonderful Relais d'Arpette (2km W of Champex, at the W end of Stage v8a): the following morning, ACW trekkers could either hike the superlative Stage v8b across Fenêtre d'Arpette (p146) or retrace their steps slightly to get back onto Stage 8a.
Transport	**La Fouly:** bus 272: N to Praz-de-Fort, Issert and Orsières; S to Ferret. **Praz-de-Fort:** bus 272: N to Issert and Orsières; S to la Fouly and Ferret. **Issert:** bus 272: N to Orsières; S to Praz-de-Fort, la Fouly and Ferret. **Champex:** Bus 271 to Orsières. For further info, see p47.

	Start	Finish	Time	Distance	Ascent (ACW)	Descent (ACW)	Max Alt
7	La Fouly	Champex	4:30 5:00	15.5km 9.6miles	474m 1555ft	607m 1991ft	1600m 5249ft

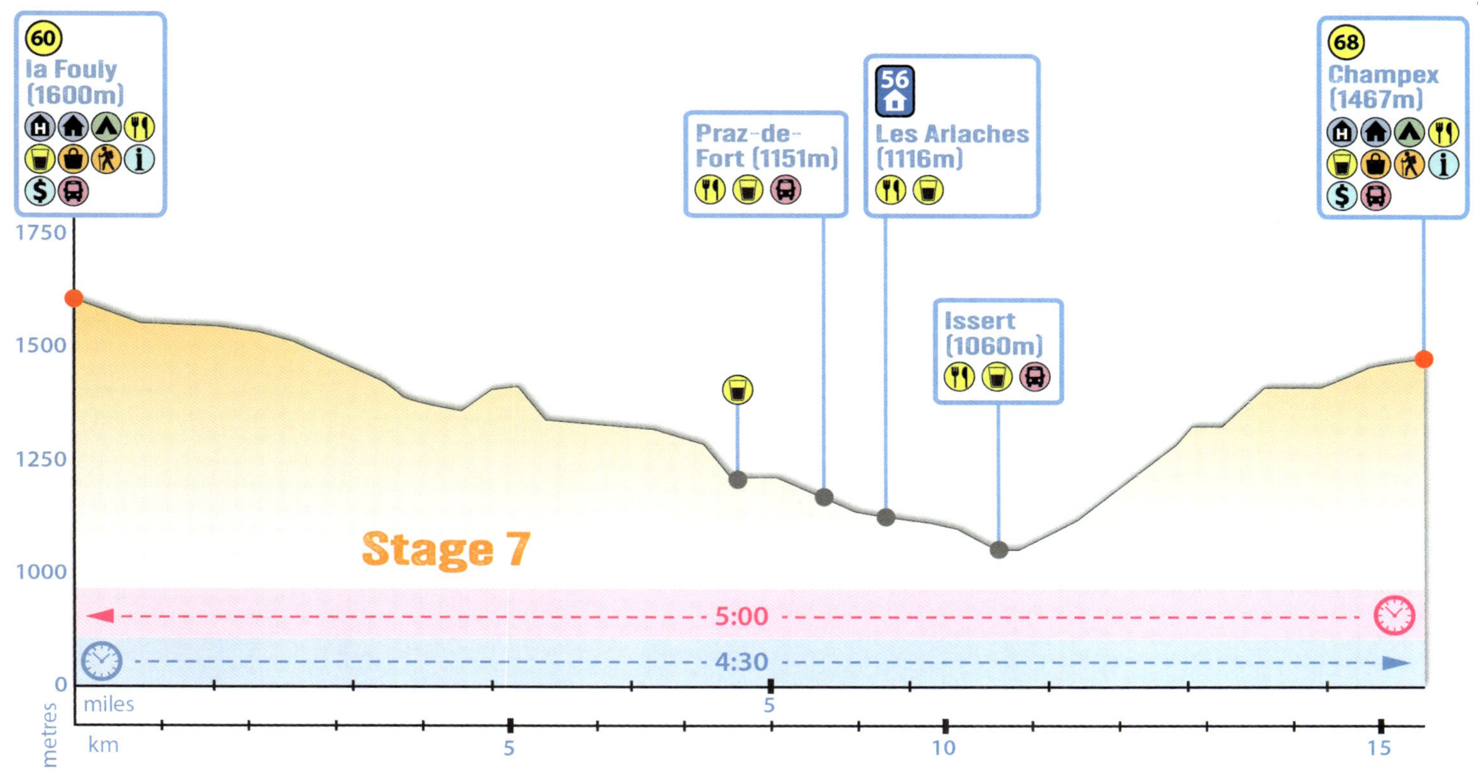

60
la Fouly
(1600m)
Praz-de-
Fort (1151m)
56
Les Arlaches
(1116m)
Issert
(1060m)
68
Champex
(1467m)
Stage 7
1750
1500
1250
1000
0
metres
miles
km
5
10
15
5
5:00
4:30

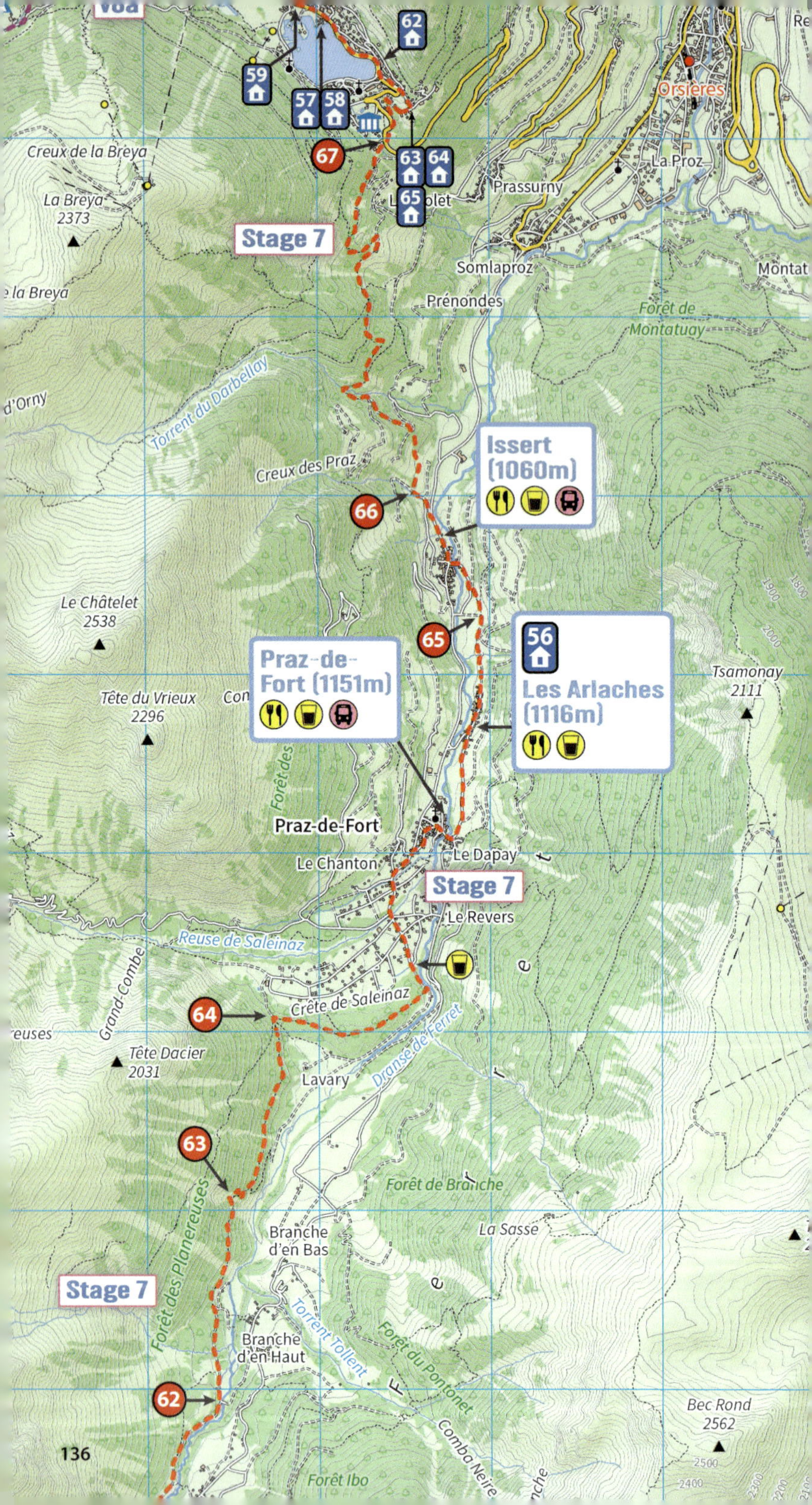

Stage 7
Creux de la Breya
La Breya
2373
Orsières
La Proz
Prassurny
Somlaproz
Prénondes
Montat
Forêt de Montatuay
Torrent du Darbellay
Creux des Praz
Issert (1060m)
Le Châtelet
2538
Praz-de-Fort (1151m)
Les Arlaches (1116m)
Tsamonay
2111
Tête du Vrieux
2296
Praz-de-Fort
Le Chanton
Le Dapay
Le Revers
Reuse de Saleinaz
Crête de Saleinaz
Grand Combe
Tête Dacier
2031
Lavary
Dranse de Ferret
Forêt de Branche
La Sasse
Branche d'en Bas
Forêt des Planereuses
Branche d'en Haut
Torrent Tollent
Forêt du Pontonet
Bec Rond
2562
Comba Neire
Forêt Ibo

Stage 7: la Fouly to Champex

60 See map on p132. Walk N along the main road through **la Fouly**. Just after **Grand Hôtel**, TL onto a path. Soon, keep SH across a junction of tracks to descend to the river. Just after crossing a bridge, TR on a small road. Shortly afterwards, TR on a track.

61 0:15: Keep SH at a junction.

62 1:00: See map on p136. Keep SH at a junction. 15min later, at a right-hand bend in the track, TL on a path.

63 1:20: The path narrows and skirts the edge of a steep gully: fixed chains to assist.

64 1:40: TR at a junction. 10-15min later, TL onto a track. Shortly afterwards, keep SH at a junction on a road through a hamlet. Cross a bridge and keep SH on the road. Keep SH at a crossroads. Soon, TR on **Chemin de la Vallo** and pass through the magnificent old buildings of **Praz-de-Fort (1151m)**. TR on **Coin du Village**. Shortly afterwards, TR onto **Route de Ferret** and cross a bridge over the river. Soon, TL onto a lane. Pass through the beautiful old hamlet of **les Arlaches (1116m)**, following waymarks: afterwards, keep SH, climbing on a lane.

65 2:35: When the track bends left (heading towards the main road), keep SH on a grassy path. Soon, TL onto a track. Immediately afterwards, TR onto another track. Cross a bridge over the river at the village of **Issert**: keep SH up between houses. Soon afterwards, TR onto a road. After 5min, TL onto a small road and start climbing.

66 2:50: Soon, TR onto a path: climb through forest, following waymarks. At a track, TL: immediately afterwards, TR and keep climbing; there are wooden carvings scattered throughout the forest. At a left-hand hairpin, TR. At a junction with a carving of an ibex, TL (no waymark). TL at a fountain and continue climbing.

67 4:15: Cross a road and TL, walking up a path alongside it. Shortly afterwards, the path heads around the right side of a small building and continues climbing. TL onto a minor road. TL after **Hotel Belvédère** and walk down a street to arrive at the SE side of Champex-Lac. Head NW along the lake.

68 4:30: See map on p143. Reach the centre of **Champex-Lac (1467m)**.

Stage 7: Champex to la Fouly

68 See map on p143. From the centre of **Champex**, walk SE alongside the lake: just after it, TL on a road. TR before **Hotel Belvédère**. Shortly afterwards TR on a path.

67 0:15: Cross a road and descend on a path through forest (following waymarks). See map on p136. TR at a fountain and continue descending through the forest. At around 1200m, TL down a track. Just after a hairpin, TR down a path.

66 1:05: TL down a lane. Soon, TR along a road. Shortly, TL in **Issert**: descend between houses. Cross a bridge over the river. Immediately afterwards, TR at a junction, climbing S on a track. At a junction, TL onto another track: immediately afterwards, TR on a path.

65 1:20: Keep SH on a track/lane. Pass through the beautiful old hamlet of **les Arlaches (1116m)**, following waymarks. TR onto **Route de Ferret** and cross a bridge over the river at **Praz-de-Fort (1151m)**. Just afterwards, TL on **Coin du Village**. TL on **Chemin de la Vallo** and pass some magnificent old buildings. Soon, TL at a staggered junction. Keep SH at a crossroads. Cross a bridge and keep SH on the road. When the road bends left, keep SH on a track. Soon, TR and climb on a path through trees.

64 2:55: TL at a junction. The path is level for a while and then climbs steeply.

63 3:25: Cross an exposed ravine (chains for safety). 10-15min later, keep SH on a track.

62 3:45: Keep SH at a junction.

61 See map on p132. Keep SH at a junction, climbing on a track. TL on a road (toilets). Shortly afterwards, TL and cross a bridge: alternatively, keep SH for the campsite. Afterwards, keep SH at a junction, climbing on a path. At the next junction, keep SH.

60 5:00: Shortly afterwards, TR along the road to enter **la Fouly (1600m)**.

8 Champex/Trient (via Bovine)

Although Section 8 is part of the TMB's main route, it tends to be underrated because its alternative (Section v8) is so spectacular. In fact, many people walk Section 8 only if the weather is too bad to undertake v8. However, we think that is a shame because Section 8 is a very beautiful route in its own right, visiting one of the TMB's best lunch stops. Furthermore, Section 8 is much easier than v8 (which has notoriously challenging boulder crossings and a lot more ascent/descent).

Stage 8a (Champex/Col de la Forclaz): in either direction, there is a long climb to the stunning pastures around Bovine where you will find a fabulous restaurant: stop for a drink or some food, enjoying the sublime views of the Rhône valley (stretching out to the NE). Afterwards, descend through aromatic forest with tantalising views of the high peaks between the trees. The slopes are covered with alpenrose which is a vibrant pink colour in June/July. ACW trekkers can stay at the hotel at Col de la Forclaz: it is popular with groups so reserve in advance. CW trekkers will stay at Champex (see p134).

Stage 8b (Col de la Forclaz/Trient): this short hike links Col de la Forclaz with Trient. It is downhill for ACW trekkers and uphill for CW trekkers. Trient is a lovely little village with a distinctive pink church: there are a few places to stay but they fill up quickly.

	Start	Finish	Time	Distance	Ascent	Descent	Max Alt
8a	Champex	Col de la Forclaz	4:50 4:45	14.6km 9.1miles	790m 2592ft	741m 2431ft	2049m 6722ft
8b	Col de la Forclaz	Trient	0:30 0:45	1.5km 0.9miles	13m 43ft	239m 784ft	1526m 5007ft

Views of the Rhône valley from Bovine.

Itinerary options: if the weather is fine and you are in good shape, you can also travel between Champex and Col de la Forclaz using the spectacular Section v8 high variant (p146).

You can hike directly between Col de la Forclaz and le Peuty (avoiding Trient): see p156.

Terrain	Paths and tracks are clear and well maintained but they are sometimes steep and rocky. In particular, the route between Plan de l'Au and Bovine is steep in places (with loose rock). There is a short road section near Champex: take care at blind corners.
Route-finding	Straightforward
Camping	Campsites at Champex, Hotel du Col de la Forclaz and Trient. No places to bivouac legally.
Trail notes	If you are unable to find accommodation at Col de la Forclaz/Trient, consider staying at le Peuty (at the S end of Stage 9a). Alternatively, you could use bus 213 to head to Martigny (40min) where there are more hotels: the following morning, you can take the bus back up to Trient/Col de la Forclaz.
Transport	**Champex:** Bus 271 to Orsières. For further info, see p47. **Col de la Forclaz:** Bus 213: NE to Martigny; W to Trient and le Châtelard (MBE station). **Trient:** Bus 213: NE to Col de la Forclaz/Martigny; W to le Châtelard (MBE station).

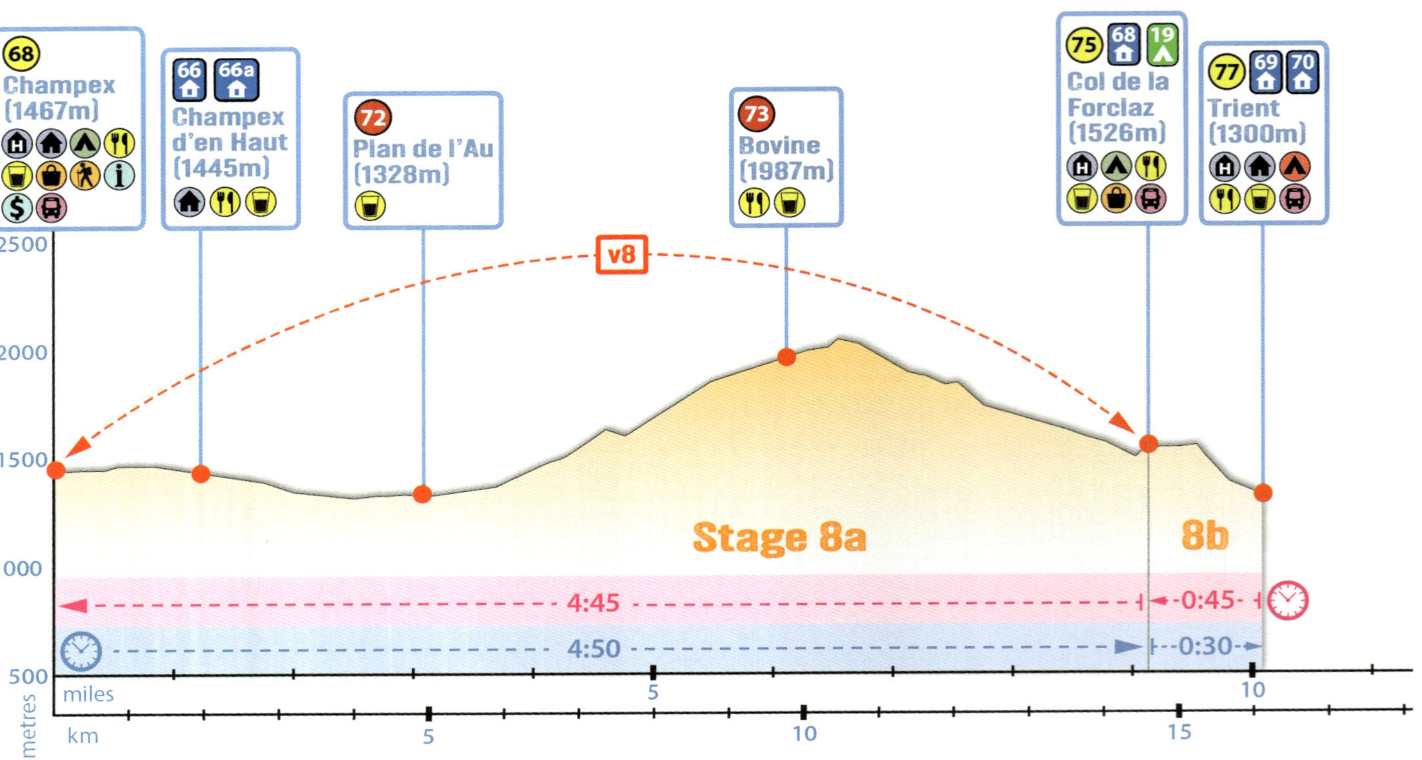

68
Champex
(1467m)
66
66a
Champex d'en Haut
(1445m)
72
Plan de l'Au
(1328m)
73
Bovine
(1987m)
75
68
19
Col de la Forclaz
(1526m)
77
69
70
Trient
(1300m)
v8
Stage 8a
8b
4:45
0:45
4:50
0:30
2500
2000
1500
1000
500
metres
miles
km
5
10
15

Stage 8a: Champex to Col de la Forclaz (via Bovine)

68 See map on p143. Head W on the main road out of **Champex**. Pass the **campsite**.

69 0:20: Ignore a track on the left and continue on the road. Shortly afterwards, TL on a forest track and descend. After 5min, take a small path on the right if you wish to go to **Champex-d'en-Haut (1445m)**: otherwise, keep SH.

70 0:35: TR at a junction and descend. A few minutes later, TL. Pass through **Champex-d'en-Bas**.

71 0:50: TL onto a path, cross a bridge and continue W on a track. Shortly afterwards, TR at a junction. At a fork, TL on a path. TL onto a road.

72 1:10: Shortly afterwards, pass the buvette at **Plan de l'Au (1328m)**. Contour around the hillside. Take care crossing a few streams (particularly in early summer when there is plenty of water). Soon climb steeply, eventually rising above the tree-line.

73 3:30: Pass the idyllic farm at **Bovine** (1987m; lovely restaurant).

74 3:45: Cross a small col and start to descend.

75 4:50: Arrive at the road at **Col de la Forclaz (1526m)**.

Stage 8b: Col de la Forclaz to Trient

75 See map on p145. Head S from the hotel at **Col de la Forclaz**, crossing a road to reach a yellow signpost. Keep SH ('Fenêtre d'Arpette') and continue S on a path.

76 0:10: TR at a junction, descending on a path. Cross a footbridge over a road. Then follow a track S: alternatively, take a more direct path that descends more steeply to the W. At a four-way junction, TR and descend N. 5-10min later, TL at a junction. Shortly afterwards, TR along the road.

77 0:30: Shortly afterwards, reach the village of **Trient (1300m)**.

Stage 8b: Trient to Col de la Forclaz

77 See map on p145. From **Trient**, head S along the road which leads to Col de la Forclaz. Shortly afterwards, TL onto a path which climbs S across the slope. At a four-way junction, TL and climb N. Cross a bridge over a road and climb steeply on a path.

76 0:35: Reach a junction; TL to head to Col de la Forclaz; alternatively, TR to start Stage v8b (avoiding Col de la Forclaz).

75 0:45: Arrive at **Col de la Forclaz (1526m)**.

Stage 8a: Col de la Forclaz to Champex (via Bovine)

75 See map on p142. From the hotel at **Col de la Forclaz**, head E across the road and pick up a path to the left of the shop. Soon, start to climb through forest.

74 1:55: Cross a small col and descend.

73 2:10: Pass the idyllic farm at **Bovine (1987m)** where there is a lovely restaurant. Keep descending as the path contours around the hillside with magnificent views of the **Rhône valley**. After a while, drop below the tree-line and descend more steeply: watch out for loose rocks. Take care crossing a few streams (particularly in early summer when there is plenty of water).

72 3:25: Pass the little buvette at **Plan de l'Au**. Shortly afterwards, TR onto a path. At a junction, keep SH on a track. Keep SH at another junction. Just afterwards, cross a bridge.

71 3:45: Immediately afterwards, TR. Pass through **Champex-d'en-Bas**. Soon TR at a junction and climb: alternatively, keep SH for **Champex-d'en-Haut (1445m)**.

70 4:10: A few minutes later, TL onto a forest track.

69 4:35: After 20min, TR onto a main road. Pass Champex's **campsite** on the left.

68 4:45: Arrive at **Champex-Lac (1467m)**.

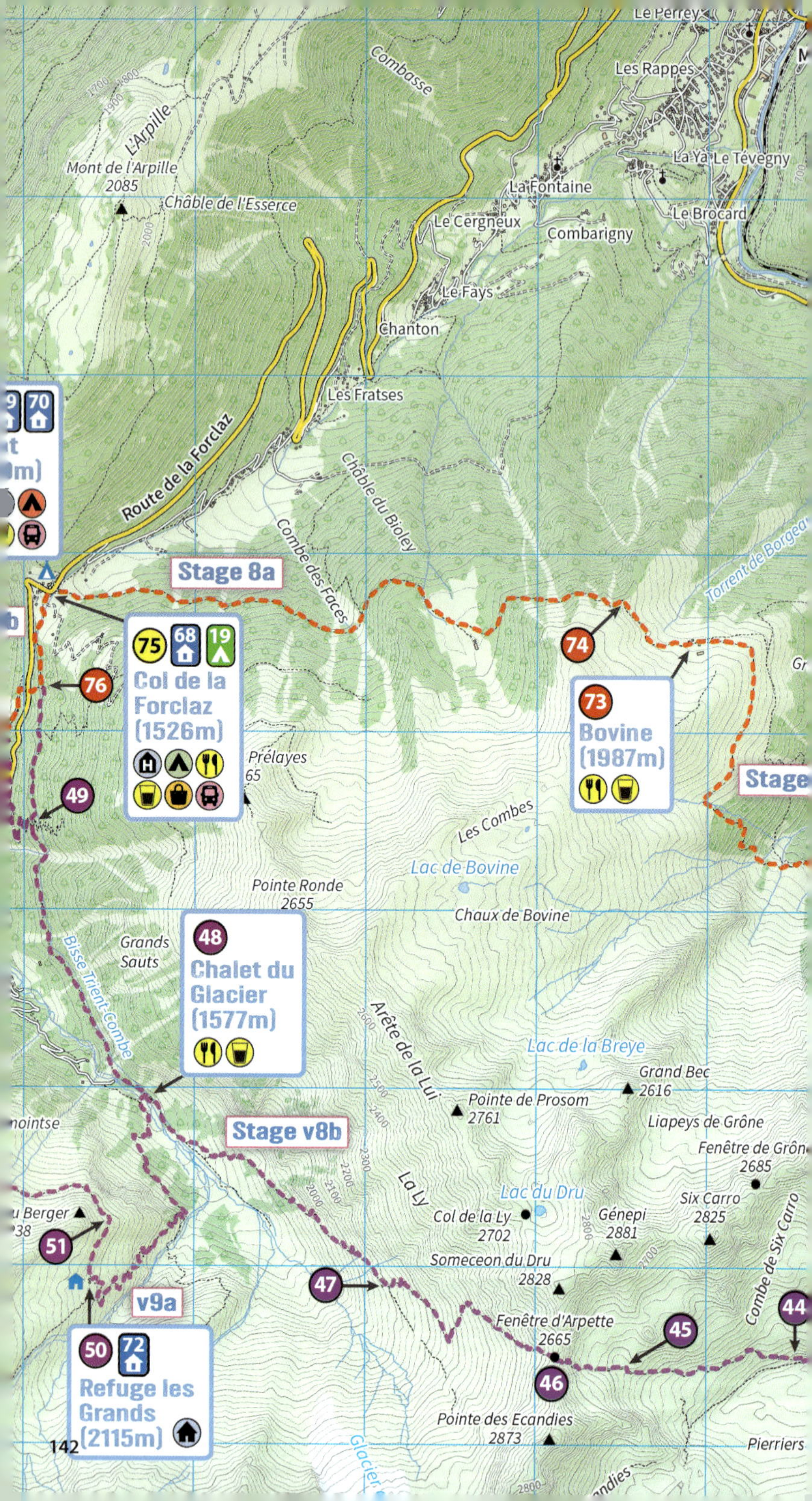

Le Perrey
Les Rappes
Combasse
L'Arpille
Mont de l'Arpille
2085
Châble de l'Esserce
La Ya
Le Tévegny
La Fontaine
Le Brocard
Le Cergneux
Combarigny
Le Fays
Chanton
Les Fratses
Route de la Forclaz
Châble du Bioley
Combe des Faces
Torrent de Borgeat
Stage 8a
75
68
19
Col de la Forclaz (1526m)
76
74
73
Bovine (1987m)
Prélayes
49
Les Combes
Lac de Bovine
Pointe Ronde
2655
Chaux de Bovine
Grands Sauts
48
Chalet du Glacier (1577m)
Bisse Trient-Combe
Arête de la Lui
Lac de la Breye
Grand Bec
2616
Pointe de Prosom
2761
Liapeys de Grône
Stage v8b
Fenêtre de Grône
2685
La Ly
Lac du Dru
Col de la Ly
2702
Génepi
2881
Six Carro
2825
51
Someceon du Dru
2828
Combe de Six Carro
47
v9a
Fenêtre d'Arpette
2665
45
44
46
50
72
Refuge les Grands (2115m)
Pointe des Ecandies
2873
Pierriers

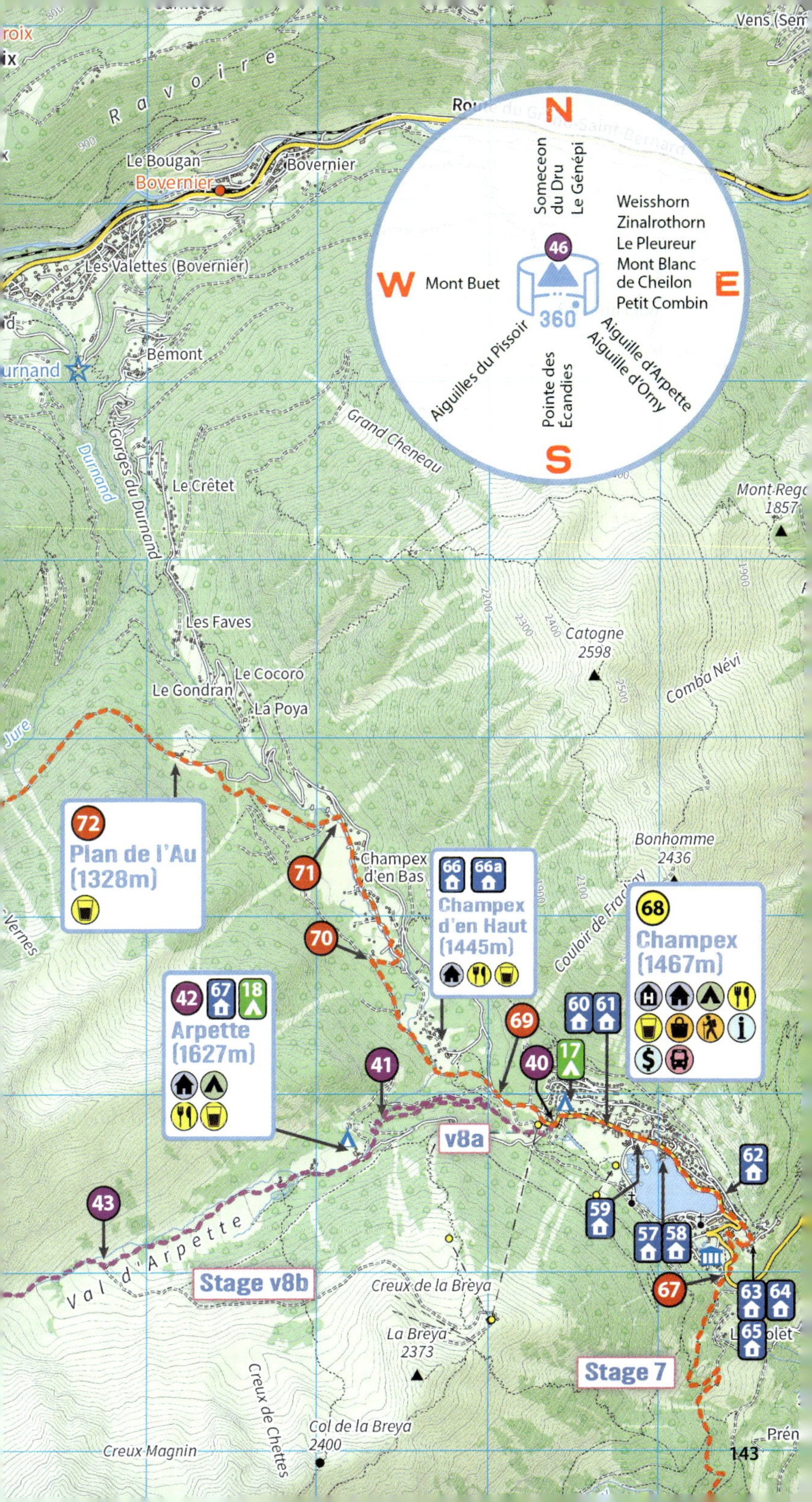
Ravoire
Route du Grand-Saint-Bernard
Le Bougan
Bovernier
Les Valettes (Bovernier)
Bémont
Gorges du Durnand
Durnand
Le Crêtet
Grand Cheneau
Les Faves
Le Cocoro
Le Gondran
La Poya
Catogne
2598
Comba Névi
Mont Regard
1857
Bonhomme
2436
Couloir de Fracley
Champex d'en Bas
72
Plan de l'Au
(1328m)
66
66a
Champex d'en Haut
(1445m)
68
Champex
(1467m)
42
67
18
Arpette
(1627m)
N
S
W
E
46
360
Someceon
du Dru
Le Génépi
Weisshorn
Zinalrothorn
Le Pleureur
Mont Blanc de Cheilon
Petit Combin
Mont Buet
Aiguilles du Pissoir
Pointe des Écandies
Aiguille d'Arpette
Aiguille d'Orny
71
70
69
41
40
17
60
61
62
59
57
58
67
63
64
65
43
v8a
Stage v8b
Val d'Arpette
Creux de la Breya
La Breya
2373
Stage 7
Col de la Breya
2400
Creux Magnin
Creux de Chettes
Vens
Prén

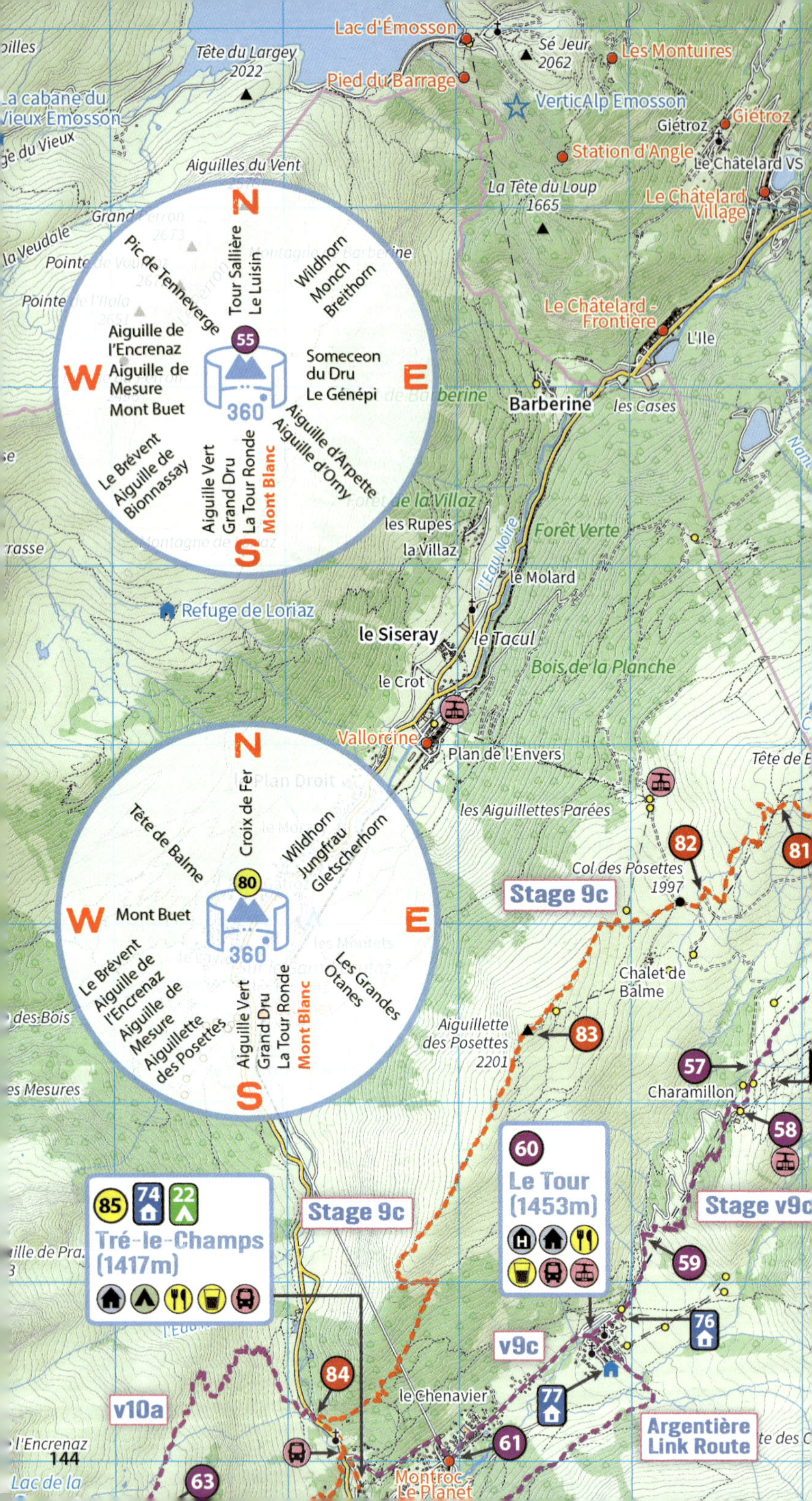
Lac d'Émosson
Tête du Largey
2022
Sé Jeur
2062
Les Montuires
Pied du Barrage
La cabane du
Vieux Emosson
VerticAlp Emosson
Giétroz
Giétroz
Station d'Angle
Le Châtelard VS
Aiguilles du Vent
La Tête du Loup
1665
Le Châtelard
Village
N
Tour Sallière
Le Luisin
Pic de Tenneverge
Wildhorn
Monch
Breithorn
55
Aiguille de
l'Encrenaz
Aiguille de
Mesure
Mont Buet
W
Someceon
du Dru
Le Génépi
E
360
Le Brévent
Aiguille de
Bionnassay
Aiguille Vert
Grand Dru
La Tour Ronde
Mont Blanc
Aiguille d'Arpette
Aiguille d'Orny
S
Le Châtelard -
Frontière
L'Ile
Barberine
les Cases
Forêt de la Villaz
les Rupes
la Villaz
Forêt Verte
l'Eau Noire
le Molard
Refuge de Loriaz
le Siseray
le Tacul
Bois de la Planche
le Crot
Vallorcine
Plan de l'Envers
N
Croix de Fer
Tête de Balme
Wildhorn
Jungfrau
Gletscherhorn
80
W
Mont Buet
E
360
Le Brévent
Aiguille de
l'Encrenaz
Aiguille de
Mesure
Aiguillette
des Posettes
Aiguille Vert
Grand Dru
La Tour Ronde
Mont Blanc
Les Grandes
Otanes
S
les Aiguillettes Parées
82
81
Col des Posettes
1997
Stage 9c
Chalet de
Balme
Aiguillette
des Posettes
2201
83
57
Charamillon
58
60
Le Tour
(1453m)
Stage v9c
85
74
22
Tré-le-Champs
(1417m)
Stage 9c
59
76
v9c
84
le Chenavier
77
v10a
61
Argentière
Link Route
Montroc-
Le Planet
63

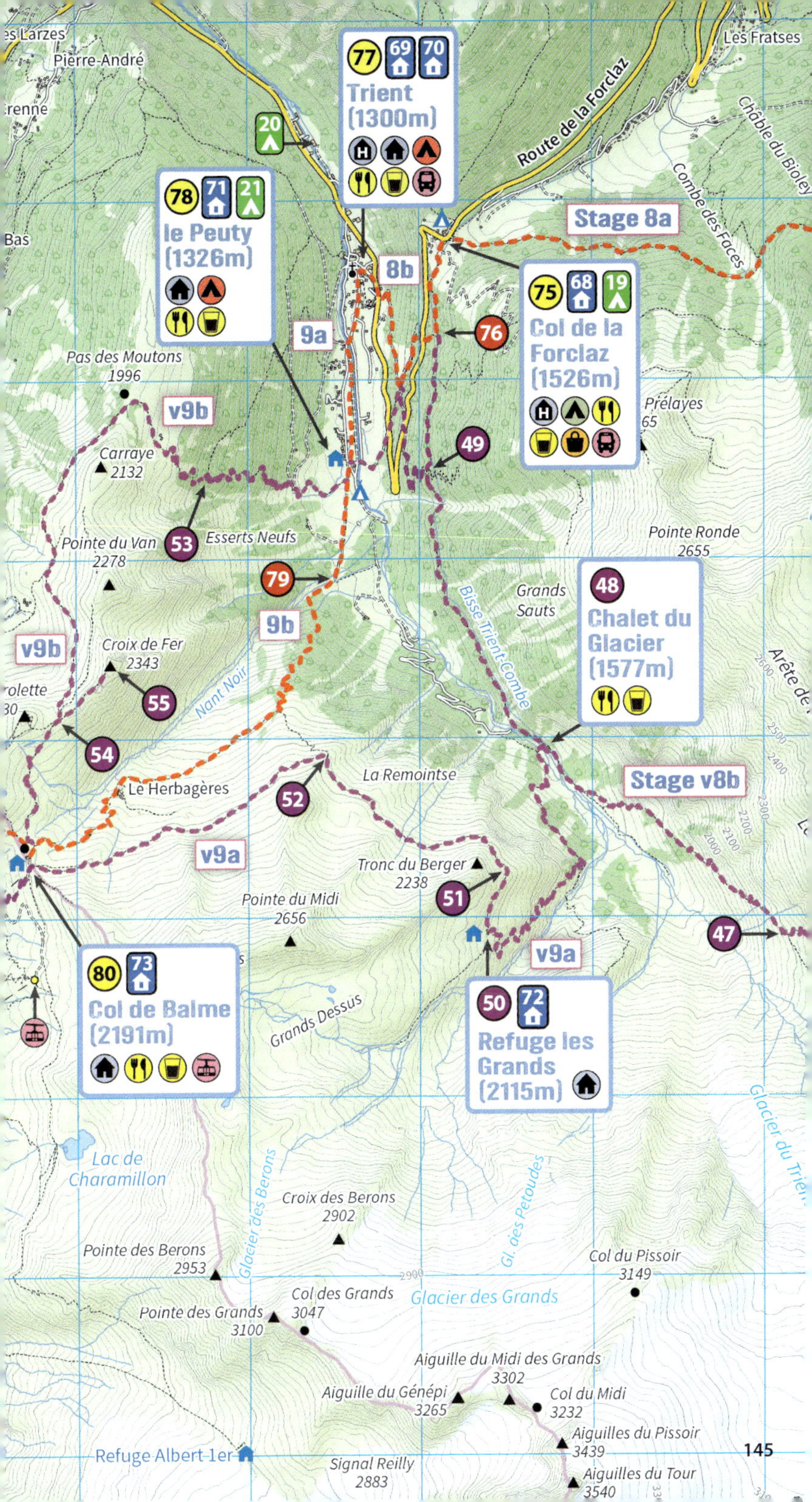

Les Larzes
Pierre-André
Les Fratses
Route de la Forclaz
Châble du Bioley
Combe des Faces
20
77 69 70
Trient (1300m)
78 71 21
le Peuty (1326m)
Stage 8a
8b
75 68 19
Col de la Forclaz (1526m)
76
9a
Pas des Moutons 1996
v9b
Prélayes
49
Carraye 2132
Esserts Neufs
53
Pointe du Van 2278
Pointe Ronde 2655
79
Grands Sauts
48
Chalet du Glacier (1577m)
Bisse Trient-Combe
9b
v9b
Croix de Fer 2343
Nant Noir
55
54
Le Herbagères
La Remointse
52
Stage v8b
v9a
Tronc du Berger 2238
51
Pointe du Midi 2656
47
v9a
80 73
Col de Balme (2191m)
Grands Dessus
50 72
Refuge les Grands (2115m)
Lac de Charamillon
Glacier des Berons
Gl. des Petoudes
Croix des Berons 2902
Pointe des Berons 2953
Col du Pissoir 3149
Col des Grands 3047
Glacier des Grands
Pointe des Grands 3100
Aiguille du Midi des Grands 3302
Aiguille du Génépi 3265
Col du Midi 3232
Aiguilles du Pissoir 3439
Refuge Albert 1er
Signal Reilly 2883
Aiguilles du Tour 3540

v8a/b Champex/Col de la Forclaz (via Fenêtre d'Arpette)

Although it is not part of the TMB's main route, the Section v8 variant is a highlight of the trek, leading you across the spectacular pass known as Fenêtre d'Arpette (*the window of Arpette*): at 2665m, it is the same height as Col des Fours (Stage v3a) and they are the joint highest points on the TMB. However, with such high altitude comes plenty of hard work and the crossing of Fenêtre d'Arpette is one of the most notorious parts of the TMB with heaps of steep climbing/descending and challenging boulder crossings. Section v8 is significantly harder than the main route (Section 8; p138).

Stage v8a (Champex/Relais d'Arpette): this short, straightforward route connects Champex and the superbly situated Relais d'Arpette (an excellent alternative to a night in Champex).

Stage v8b (Relais d'Arpette/Col de la Forclaz): this stage involves crossing the difficult Fenêtre d'Arpette. Pray for a clear day as the views of the Glacier du Trient to the SW are exceptional: it is hard to convey just how close to it you find yourself. One TMB hiker complained to us that, after posting selfies of himself with the glacier on social media, he was bombarded with accusations of photo tampering! However, Stage v8b is not all about Fenêtre d'Arpette because the scenery on both sides of it is amazing too.

Itinerary options: ACW trekkers can leave Stage v8 at Chalet du Glacier 48 and transfer onto Stage v9a. You could then overnight at the basic Refuge les Grands (although you need to bring your own food): this is a stunning option but it makes for a long day. Very fit trekkers could even continue further along v9a that same day and stay at Col de Balme.

Stage v8b ends/starts at Col de la Forclaz. However, in fact, you do not need to go all the way to the col unless you are staying there. Instead, there are paths leading directly from the route of Stage v8b to Trient and le Peuty, saving you time and energy: an easy path connects 49 with le Peuty; and Stage 8b connects 76 to Trient.

	Start	Finish	Time	Distance	Ascent (ACW)	Descent (ACW)	Max Alt
v8a	Champex	Relais d'Arpette	0:55 0:40	2.6km 1.6miles	160m 525ft	0m 0ft	1627m 5338ft
v8b	Relais d'Arpette	Col de la Forclaz	5:50 6:00	12.9km 8.0miles	1048m 3438ft	1149m 3770ft	2665m 8743ft

The view E from Fenêtre d'Arpette

Terrain	**Stage v8a:** paths and tracks are clear and well maintained. Short section along the road near Champex: take care at blind corners. **Stage v8b:** this is probably the TMB's hardest route and should not be underestimated. Paths are often exposed, rocky, uneven and tiring. Furthermore, at times, there are no paths at all. There are some very steep gradients and a lot of climbing/descent. The shale slope immediately E of the pass is steep and unstable. There are tricky boulder crossings on both sides of the pass but the E side is more challenging: slippery in wet conditions; some scrambling required; in many places, a fall would be serious so take it slowly and choose your steps carefully. Sometimes snow lies near the pass until early July: in such conditions, the route is treacherous and it is unwise to attempt it. In any difficult conditions, it is safer to use Section 8 (p138).
Route-finding	The directions for Stage v8a are a little fiddly. Stage v8b is a challenging high mountain route: in good conditions, the red/white waymarks are mostly straightforward to follow; however, there are a few sections without paths and places where cairns/waymarks are sporadic or hard to spot; in particular, follow waymarks carefully amongst the boulders on the E side of the pass. Do not attempt v8b in bad weather/low visibility/snowy conditions when navigation is more tricky and straying from the route can be dangerous.
Camping	Campsites at Champex, Relais d'Arpette, Hotel du Col de la Forclaz and Trient.
Trail notes	Fenêtre d'Arpette is a small place and you are unlikely to have it to yourself: start early to beat the crowds. The hotel at Col de la Forclaz is popular with groups: reserve in advance; for alternatives, see p139.
Transport	**Champex:** Bus 271 to Orsières. For further info, see p47. **Col de la Forclaz:** Bus 213: NE to Martigny; W to Trient and le Châtelard (MBE station). **Trient:** Bus 213: NE to Col de la Forclaz/Martigny and W to le Châtelard (MBE station).

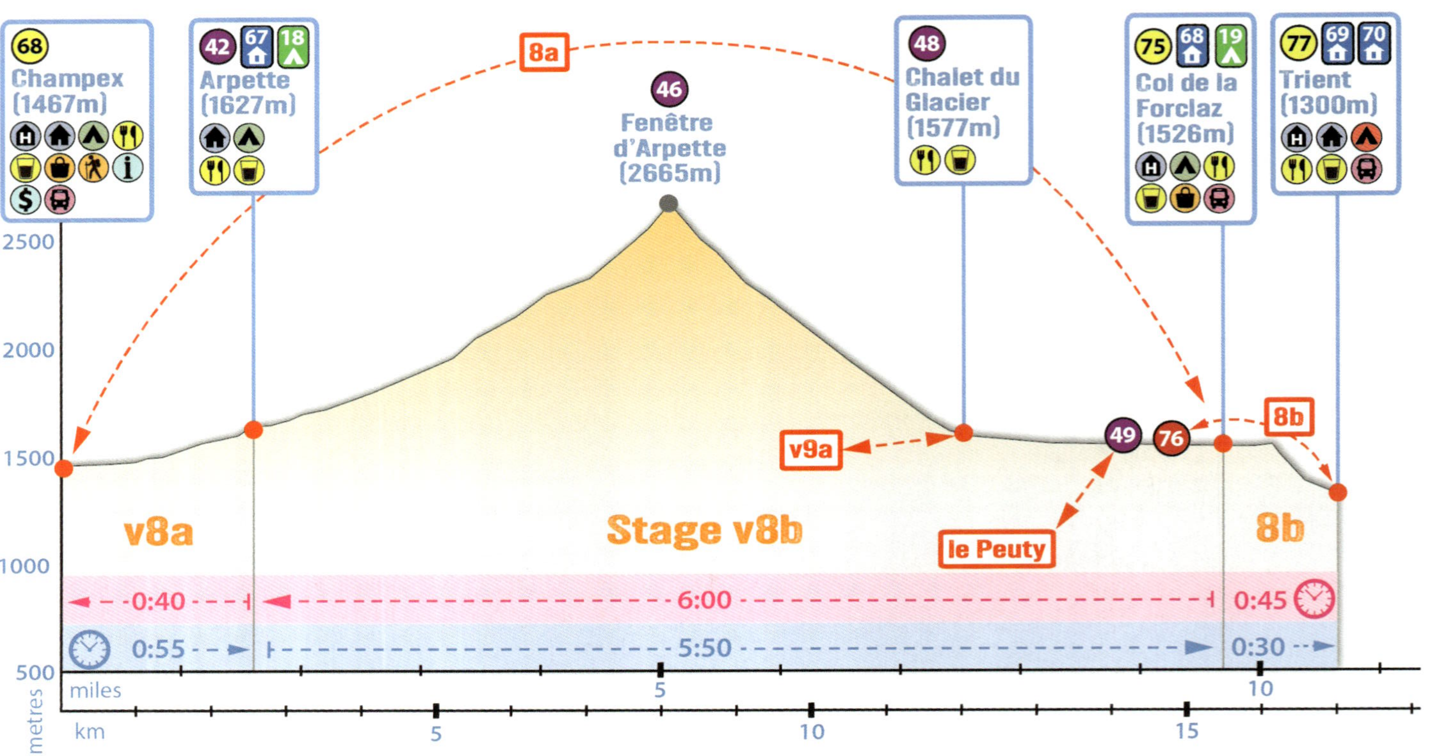

68
Champex
(1467m)
42
67
18
Arpette
(1627m)
8a
46
Fenêtre
d'Arpette
(2665m)
48
Chalet du
Glacier
(1577m)
75
68
19
Col de la
Forclaz
(1526m)
77
69
70
Trient
(1300m)
2500
2000
1500
1000
500
metres
v9a
49
76
8b
le Peuty
v8a
Stage v8b
8b
0:40
6:00
0:45
0:55
5:50
0:30
miles
5
10
km
5
10
15

The trail to Fenêtre d'Arpette

Stage v8a: Champex to Relais d'Arpette

68 See map on p143. Head W on the main road out of **Champex**. Pass the campsite.

40 0:10: At a right-hand bend, TL onto another road. Shortly afterwards, TR on a path and head under a ski-lift. Follow a path NW into forest. Shortly afterwards, TL at a fork. At the following junction, TR and head W on a path beside an irrigation canal: equally, you could TL at this junction because the two paths converge near 41.

41 0:40: Shortly after the two paths converge, cross a stream on a bridge. Then TL and climb alongside the stream. After a few minutes, TL on a track and cross the stream again. Immediately afterwards, TR and climb on a path. Then TR onto a small road.

42 0:55: Reach **Relais d'Arpette (1627m)**.

Stage v8b: Relais d'Arpette to Col de la Forclaz

42 See map on p143. From **Relais d'Arpette**, head SW. Shortly afterwards, at some chalets, keep SH through a gate and climb on a track.

43 0:50: TR at a junction.

44 1:40: TR at a junction, climbing the right flank of the valley.

45 2:45: Arrive at the dreaded section of boulders, some of which must be scrambled over as you climb steeply: follow waymarks/cairns; this section is challenging and the route is hard to follow. After the boulders, climb a steep unstable shale slope. The path soon splinters into a series of interlinking ones.

46 3:45: Cross the narrow **Fenêtre d'Arpette (2665m)**. To descend, bear right and scramble down steep rocks (following waymarks NW). After a while, pick up a clear path again.

47 4:15: Pass to the right of an old cabin. Take care on a precipitous section of path protected by a rope: a fall would be serious. Keep descending NW at any junctions.

48 5:10: Keep SH past **Chalet du Glacier (1577m; restaurant)**. Shortly afterwards, reach a junction: TR to continue on Stage v8b; alternatively, TL for Stage v9a (to les Grands). A beautiful balcony path runs beside an old irrigation canal.

49 5:30: Keep SH at a junction ('Col de la Forclaz'); alternatively, TL to head to le Peuty.

76 5:40: At a junction, keep SH for Col de la Forclaz: alternatively, TL for Trient (Stage 8b).

75 5:50: Arrive at the road at **Col de la Forclaz (1526m)**.

Col de Balme & Croix de Fer viewed from near Col de la Forclaz

Stage v8b: Col de la Forclaz to Relais d'Arpette

75 See map on p142. Head S from the hotel at **Col de la Forclaz**, crossing a road to reach a yellow signpost. Keep SH ('Fenêtre d'Arpette') and continue on a path contouring around the hillside (shared with Stage 8b). Keep SH past 76 and 49. Soon, walk beside an old irrigation canal.

48 0:40: TL at a junction to pass **Chalet du Glacier (1577m; restaurant)**. Just afterwards, bear left ('Arpette'). After 10min, TL at a junction ('Fenêtre d'Arpette'). As the path climbs, you get closer to the glacier. Take care on a precipitous section of path protected by a rope: a fall would be serious.

47 2:00: After a while, pass to the left of an old cabin. Eventually, bear left and climb a rocky gully, following waymarks: watch your footing. Finally, scramble up a very steep section.

46 3:30: Cross the narrow **Fenêtre d'Arpette (2665m)**. On a fine day, you will want to spend some time here. Descend steeply E on a path that soon splinters into a series of interlinking ones: watch your footing as the surface is unstable.

45 3:45: In a rocky gully, follow waymarks and cairns across large boulders. This section is challenging and the route is hard to follow. After another steep descent, enter a huge mountain bowl: the path descends (more gently now) along its left flank.

44 4:45: TL at a junction.

43 5:25: TL at a junction ('Champex') and descend on a track.

42 6:00: Pass through a gate at some chalets and descend on a track. Soon afterwards, arrive at **Relais d'Arpette (1627m)**.

Stage v8a: Relais d'Arpette to Champex

42 See map on p143. From **Relais d'Arpette**, descend on the road. Shortly afterwards, TL on a path ('Champex'). After a few minutes, TL across a bridge. Just afterwards, TR on a path heading downhill alongside a torrent.

41 0:15: Soon, cross the torrent again on a bridge. Shortly afterwards, TL at a junction: equally, you could TR at this junction because the two paths converge later. After a while, TL on another path. Shortly afterwards, TL at a ski-lift. Keep SH under the cables of another ski-lift. Just afterwards, TL onto a road ('Champex').

40 0:30: Shortly afterwards, TR onto a main road. Pass Champex's campsite on the left.

68 0:40: Arrive at **Champex-Lac (1467m)**.

Stage 9a (Trient/le Peuty): a short, easy walk between Trient and le Peuty (set amongst grassy pastures which are littered with wild-flowers in early season). Refuge du Peuty is a peaceful place to stay and there is an authorised bivouac area beside it. CW trekkers can stay at Trient (see p138).

Stage 9b (le Peuty/Col de Balme): ACW trekkers have a long climb to Col de Balme which offers the TMB's first clear views of Vallée de l'Arve (the Chamonix valley). MB's snowy summit looks fabulous from here (and ACW trekkers will not have seen it since Stage 6a). It is a great setting for the refuge which was built in 1877 and was occupied by German troops during WW2. Near the front of the refuge, there is a much-photographed stone marker indicating the Swiss/French frontier: for ACW trekkers, this is the third (and last) of the TMB's border crossings; for CW trekkers, it is the first.

Stage 9c (Col de Balme/Tré-le-Champs): between Col de Balme and Col des Posettes, the route follows clear paths along open grassy slopes with sublime views of the MB massif: between Col de Balme and (81), a magnificent rolling traverse gives you plenty of time to relax and enjoy the scenery. However, the highlight of the stage is the crossing of the summit of l'Aiguillette des Posettes: a wild, exposed place, high above the valley; the slopes here are covered with myrtille and alpenrose and, if you are lucky, you may spot some chamois; there are super views of the Aiguilles Rouges to the SW. Auberge la Boerne is the only place to stay/camp at Tré-le-Champs and it books up fast.

Itinerary options: Stage v9b (p160) is a spectacular alternative to Stage 9b. You could also use v9a (p158) to travel between Col de la Forclaz and Col de Balme (avoiding Trient).

	Start	Finish	Time	Distance	Ascent (ACW)	Descent (ACW)	Max Alt
9a	Trient	Le Peuty	0:20 0:20	1.2km 0.7miles	26m 85ft	0m 0ft	1326m 4350ft
9b	Le Peuty	Col de Balme	2:30 1:40	4.6km 2.9miles	865m 2838ft	0m 0ft	2191m 7188ft
9c	Col de Balme	Tré-le-Champs	2:45 3:45	8.1km 5.0miles	228m 748ft	1002m 3287ft	2191m 7188ft

Refuge du Col de Balme (with MB to the right)

In snowy conditions, bad weather or low visibility, it is safer to avoid Stage 9c and hike Stage v9c instead (see p162). Alternatively, you could use the Charamillon/Autannes ski-lifts to ascend/descend between Autannes (0.7km from Col de Balme) and le Tour: from le Tour, a short low level hike (along v9c) leads to Tré-le-Champs. Furthermore, 0.6km from Col des Posettes, there is another cable car which travels to Vallorcine: from there, the MBE heads to Chamonix/Martigny.

You can hike directly between Col de la Forclaz and le Peuty (avoiding Trient): see p156.

Terrain	**Stage 9a:** easy paths/tracks/roads. **Stage 9b:** paths/tracks are clear and well maintained but sometimes steep and rocky. ACW trekkers have a long climb; CW trekkers descend. **Stage 9c:** between (80) and (82), paths are clear and well maintained. Between (82) and (84), the route is wilder, rougher and steeper with exposed sections: avoid this section in snow/bad weather/low visibility. ACW trekkers have a long descent; for CW trekkers, it is a steep climb.
Route-finding	Navigation is straightforward in good conditions. Because, Stages 9b/9c are high mountain routes, navigation can be more difficult in bad weather/low visibility. Sometimes snow remains on the high parts of the route until early July: in such conditions, the route is more challenging and navigation can be tricky, especially between (82) and (84).
Camping	Campsites at Trient, le Peuty and Argentière (OR; near Tré-le-Champs). Bivouac permitted at Auberge la Boerne in Tré-le-Champs. Bivouac is prohibited around Col/Aiguillette des Posettes and in the parts of the Réserve Naturelle des Aiguilles Rouges crossed by Stage 9c.
Trail notes	There is only one place to stay in Tré-le-Champs. Otherwise, Gîte le Moulin in les Frasserands is not too far away: see Stage v9c.
Transport	**Trient:** Bus 213 heads NE to Col de la Forclaz/Martigny and W to le Châtelard (MBE station). **Col de Balme:** Autannes/Charamillon ski-lifts between Autannes (0.7km from Col de Balme) and le Tour. **Col des Posettes:** Vallorcine ski-lift between Vallorcine and 1950m (0.6km from Col des Posettes). **Tré-le-Champs:** bus between Tré-le-Champs and Argentière.

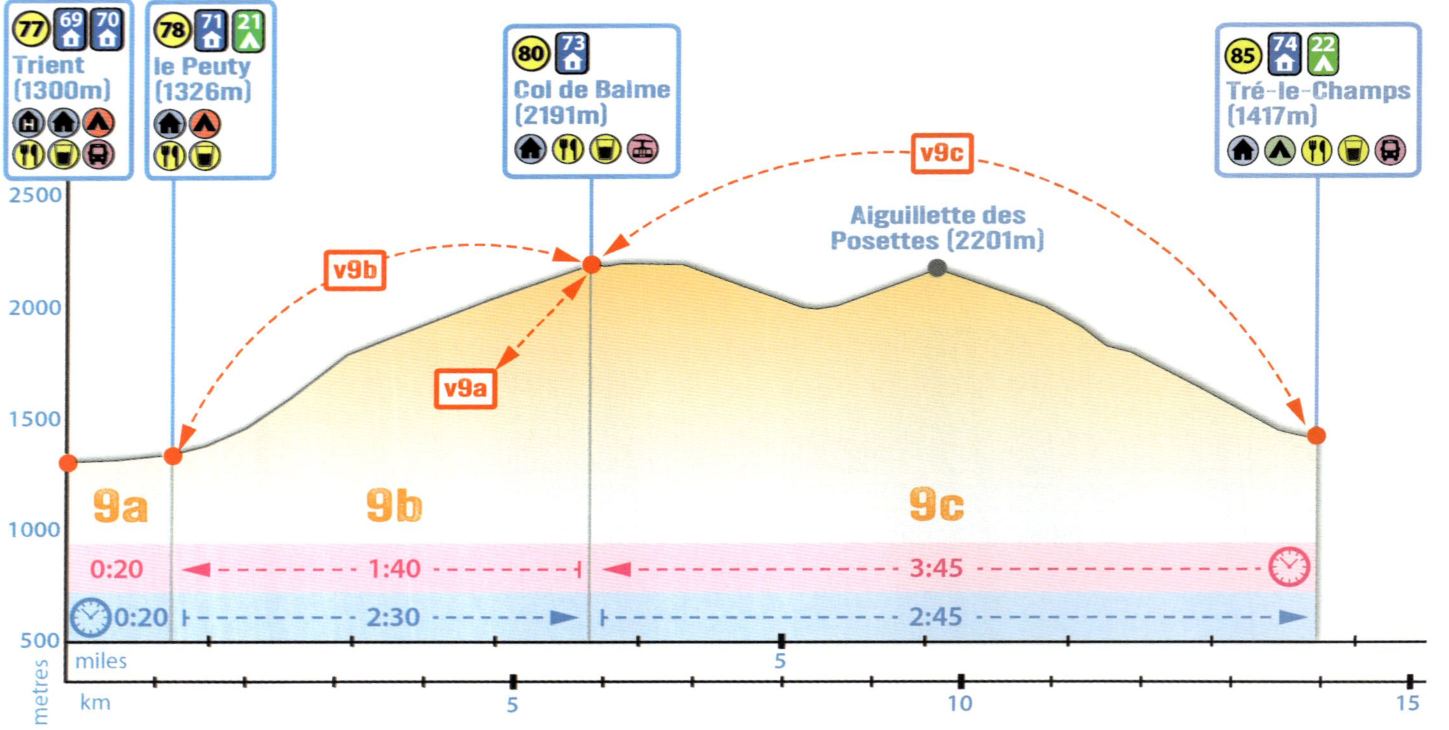

77 69 70
Trient
(1300m)
78 71 21
le Peuty
(1326m)
80 73
Col de Balme
(2191m)
85 74 22
Tré-le-Champs
(1417m)
Aiguillette des
Posettes (2201m)
v9a
v9b
v9c
9a
9b
9c
0:20
1:40
3:45
0:20
2:30
2:45
2500
2000
1500
1000
500
metres
miles
km
5
10
15

The approach to Col de Balme (Stage 9c)

Stage 9a: Trient to le Peuty

(77) See map on p145. From the pink chapel in **Trient**, head S on a road. 10min later, TR at a junction and cross a bridge over the river. Immediately afterwards, head S on a path/track beside the river: alternatively, you can head S along the road. Pass a well preserved old watermill.

(78) 0:20: Reach **Refuge du Peuty (1326m)**.

Stage 9b: le Peuty to Col de Balme

(78) See map on p145. Climb S from **Refuge du Peuty** on a broad path. After 5min, keep SH at a junction.

(79) 0:10: Soon, ford a river on rocks: take care in early season when there is a lot of water. Afterwards, the climb begins in earnest: just keep climbing (generally SW) on the main path.

(80) 2:30: Arrive at **Col de Balme (2191m)**.

Stage 9b: Col de Balme to le Peuty

(80) See map on p145. Head NE from **Refuge du Col de Balme**, descending the right flank of the Nant Noir valley. At any junctions, keep descending generally NE.

(79) 1:30: Ford a river on rocks: take care in early season when there is a lot of water. After a few minutes, keep SH at a junction.

(78) 1:40: Arrive at **Refuge du Peuty (1326m)**. For Trient, head N on Stage 9a. Alternatively, to head directly to Col de la Forclaz (avoiding Trient), see p156.

Stage 9a: le Peuty to Trient

(78) See map on p145. From **Refuge du Peuty**, head N: you can either use the road or follow a path/track beside the river (which passes an old watermill). After 10min, cross a bridge over the river. Then TR at a fork in the road.

(77) 0:20: Reach the pink chapel in the village of **Trient (1300m)**.

Pastures overlooked by MB (Stage 9c)

Direct route: Col de la Forclaz to le Peuty

75 See map on p145. Head S from the hotel at **Col de la Forclaz**, crossing a road to reach a yellow signpost. Keep SH ('Fenêtre d'Arpette') and continue S on a path.

76 0:10: TR at a junction, descending on a path. Cross a footbridge over a road. Then follow a track S. At a four-way junction, take the lower of two paths to the left and head downhill. A few minutes later, cross the road again and descend on a track.

78 0:30: Arrive at **Refuge du Peuty (1326m)**.

Direct route: le Peuty to Col de la Forclaz

78 See map on p145. From **le Peuty** head E on a small road which becomes a track. Cross a road and climb N on a path. 20min from the start, at a junction, there are two paths heading towards the N: climb on the right-hand one. Cross a footbridge over a road and climb steeply on a path.

76 0:35: Soon, at a junction, TL to head to Col de la Forclaz: alternatively, TR to start Stage v8b, (avoiding Col de la Forclaz).

75 0:45: Arrive at **Col de la Forclaz (1526m)**.

Stage 9c: Col de Balme to Tré-le-Champs

80 **See map on p145.** From **Refuge du Col de Balme**, head N ('Croix de Fer'). Shortly afterwards, TL at a junction: the path bends left. Just afterwards, reach a fork: TL and head W on a path that contours around the slopes.

81 0:15: Pass under a ski-lift and zigzag down to the SW: pass back and forth under the cables.

82 0:40: TR onto a track. Shortly afterwards, reach **Col des Posettes (1997m)**. Head SW on a path and soon start to climb towards a ridge. When the path passes over a series of rocks, it is harder to follow. Eventually, the path turns left and heads straight up the ridge's crest: rocky and uneven. Towards the top, the path splinters but all branches head to the summit.

83 1:40: Arrive at the summit of **l'Aiguillette des Posettes (2201m)**. Follow a path SW down the ridge's crest. After a few minutes, keep SH at a junction, staying on the ridge ('Col des Montets'). Soon the gradient becomes very steep. Later, the path bends left and continues descending. Afterwards, TR at any junctions.

84 2:40: Just before a road, TL on a path and walk alongside it. When the path meets the road, walk down it. Shortly afterwards, TL on a track.

85 2:45: Ignore a path on the left and shortly afterwards, enter **Tré-le-Champs (1417m)**.

Stage 9c: Tré-le-Champs to Col de Balme

85 **See map on p144.** From **Tré-le-Champs**, head N on a track. Soon, keep SH up the road. Shortly, TR on a path.

84 0:10: A few minutes later, TR at a junction and climb on a path. Afterwards, TL at any junctions. At around **1800m**, the path bends right and continues climbing N along the crest of a ridge.

83 2:10: Reach the summit of **l'Aiguillette des Posettes (2201m)**. Follow a path NE down the ridge's crest: the rocky, uneven path splits a number of times but the branches should all head to the same place. Later the path bends right and descends off the ridge. At **Col des Posettes (1997m)**, TR along a track.

82 2:40: Soon TL and climb on a path (which zigzags up to the NE): pass back and forth under a ski-lift.

81 3:25: Pass under the ski-lift one more time and then head E on a path that contours around the slopes.

80 3:45: Arrive at **Refuge du Col de Balme (2191m)**.

l'Aiguillette des Posettes

v9a Col de la Forclaz/Col de Balme (via Refuge les Grands)

This alternative trail between Col de la Forclaz and Col de Balme is scenically superior to the main route (Stages 8b/9a/9b). It is also more peaceful because fewer people hike it. In particular, the section between Refuge les Grands and Col de Balme is exquisite, leading you along a magnificent balcony: the views of Glacier du Trient and Glacier des Grands are sublime. The slopes are covered with alpenrose and myrtille.

Although Refuge les Grands is superbly situated, it is pretty basic, hard to book and does not serve meals. Accordingly, most trekkers continue past, without stopping. Refuge les Grands also has a winter room in the bergerie next door (although it is not always open). For information on Col de Balme and Col de la Forclaz, see p152 and p138 respectively.

Itinerary options: after crossing Fenêtre d'Arpette (on Stage v8b), ACW trekkers can transfer onto Stage v9a at Chalet du Glacier (48) and overnight at Refuge les Grands; this is a stunning option although it makes for a very long day. Very fit trekkers could even complete Stages v8b and v9a in full, overnighting at Col de Balme. CW trekkers can avoid Col de la Forclaz by transferring from v9a onto Stage v8b at (48) and proceeding directly to Arpette to spend the night.

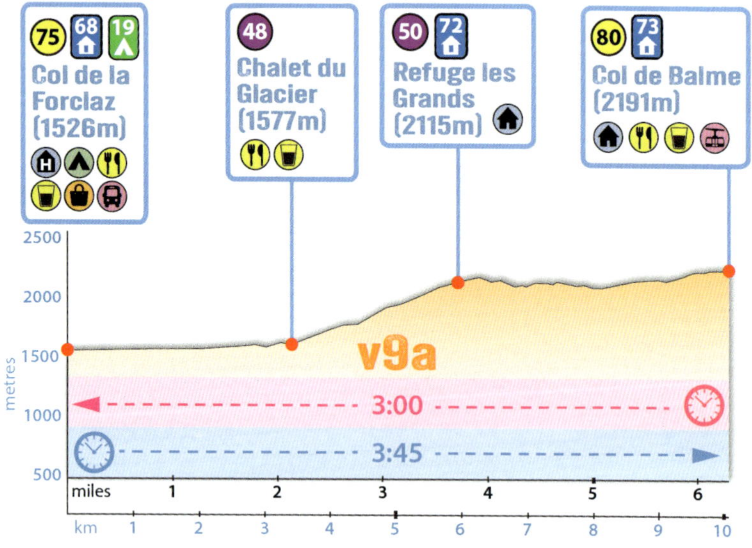

	Start	Finish	Time	Distance	Ascent (ACW)	Descent (ACW)	Max Alt
v9a	Col de la Forclaz	Col de Balme	3:45 3:00	10.1km 6.3miles	816m 2677ft	151m 495ft	2203m 7228ft

Terrain	Stage v9a is harder than the main TMB route: the long climb to Refuge les Grands is steeper than the climb to Col de Balme on Stage 9b. Furthermore, just E of Refuge les Grands, take care on an exposed section of path cut into the cliffs and protected with a cable. W of Refuge les Grands, the balcony path is harder than it appears on paper: relentless undulations with significant height gain/loss; narrow, exposed, rocky and uneven; sections of rocks to clamber over. Avoid Stage v9a in snow, bad weather or low visibility.
Route-finding	This is a high mountain route: although navigation is straightforward in good conditions (red/white waymarks), it can be more difficult in bad weather and low visibility. Sometimes snow remains on the high parts of the route until early July: in such conditions, the route is more challenging and navigation can be tricky.
Camping	Campsite at Col de la Forclaz. No official bivouac sites.
Transport	**Col de la Forclaz:** Bus 213 heads NE to Martigny; W to Trient and le Châtelard (MBE station). **Col de Balme:** Autannes/Charamillon ski-lifts between Autannes (0.7km from Col de Balme) and le Tour.

Stage v9a: Col de la Forclaz to Col de Balme

(75) See map on p145. Head S from the hotel at **Col de la Forclaz**, crossing a road to reach a yellow signpost. Keep SH ('Fenêtre d'Arpette') and continue on a path contouring around the hillside (shared with Stage 8b). Keep SH past (76) and (49). Soon, walk beside an old irrigation canal.

(48) 0:40: TR at a junction (just before **Chalet du Glacier**) and cross a bridge. Immediately afterwards, TL and start to climb generally SE. After a while, the path bends right and climbs SW. At a junction, take the higher path and climb steeply. Later, climb an exposed section of path, cut into the cliffs: cable to assist.

(50) 2:20: 5min later, arrive at **Refuge les Grands (2115m)**. Climb NE on the path above the refuge: in places, the trail is rocky and harder to follow. There is a steep (but short) rock section to climb with a chain to assist.

(51) 2:40: The path gradually bends left and heads NW, contouring around the hillside. The views of the Swiss Alps to the N are magnificent.

(52) 3:15: Bear left, now heading SW.

(80) 3:45: Arrive at **Refuge du Col de Balme (2191m)**.

Stage v9a: Col de Balme to Col de la Forclaz

(80) See map on p145. From **Refuge du Col de Balme**, cross into Switzerland and head E on a path ('les Grands'). The path contours around the hillside with magnificent views of the Swiss Alps to the N. Soon the path becomes rougher and there are short sections of rocks to cross.

(52) 0:30: Bear right, contouring around the hillside, generally SE. After 30min, incredible views of **Glacier du Trient** suddenly appear.

(51) 1:00: The path gradually bends right and heads SW; this section is challenging.

(50) 1:15: Descend some steep rocks using a chain. Shortly afterwards, arrive at **Refuge les Grands (2115m)**. Descend SE from the refuge. After a few minutes, descend an exposed section of path cut into the cliffs: cable to assist.

(48) 2:20: TR at a junction. Immediately afterwards, cross a bridge to arrive at another junction (beside **Chalet du Glacier**): TL to head to Col de la Forclaz; alternatively, TR for Arpette (Stage v8b). Walk along a beautiful balcony path beside an old irrigation canal. Keep SH past (49) and (76).

(75) 3:00: Arrive at the road at **Col de la Forclaz (1526m)**.

v9b Le Peuty/Col de Balme (via Croix de Fer)

View from Croix de Fer

Although this is the least hiked of the three routes between Trient/Col de la Forclaz and Col de Balme, we think that it is the most beautiful. The main attraction is Croix de Fer, the summit next to Col de Balme which (as its name suggests) is topped with an iron cross. Although Croix de Fer is considered to be a minor peak, its position (just N of the MB massif) ensures that the 360° panorama from the top is sublime: to the S, peering directly down the Chamonix valley, the views of MB and the Aiguilles Rouges are completely unimpeded; to the W, Lac d'Émosson and Mont Buet; to the SE, Glacier du Trient.

In fact, Croix de Fer's summit is a short distance OR: the round-trip to the summit from 54 takes about 45min and leads you along a thrillingly exposed knife-edge ridge with sheer drops on either side. If the weather is fine, the extra distance is well worth the effort but the side-trip is not essential because the views along the rest of the stage are also superb.

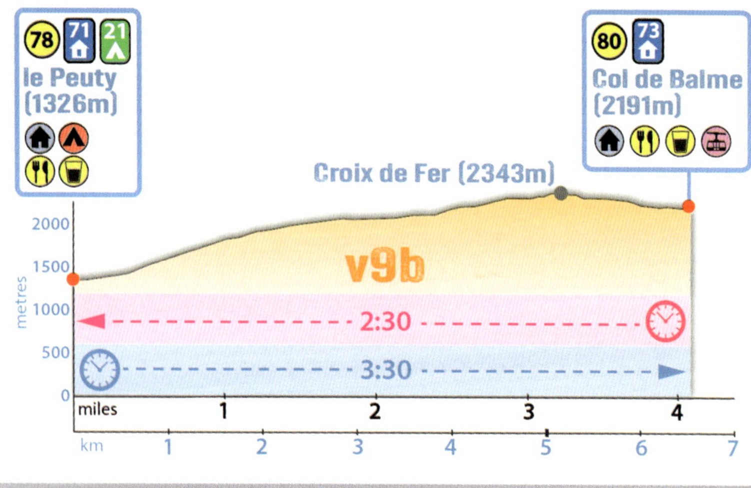

	Start	Finish	Time	Distance	Ascent (ACW)	Descent (ACW)	Max Alt
v9b	Le Peuty	Col de Balme	3:30 2:30	6.6km 4.1miles	1055m 3461ft	190m 623ft	2343m 7687ft

Terrain	Stage v9b is longer and harder than the main TMB route. Between (54) and the summit of Croix de Fer, the route is narrow and exposed; sections of rocks to scramble over. Otherwise, paths/tracks are clear and well maintained. ACW trekkers have a long, steep climb; for CW trekkers, the descent into le Peuty is hard on the knees. Avoid Croix de Fer in high winds, foul weather, low visibility or snow: it is very exposed and a fall would be serious.
Route-finding	This is a high mountain route: although navigation is straightforward in good conditions, it can be more difficult in bad weather/low visibility. Sometimes snow remains on the high parts of the route until early July: in such conditions, the route is more challenging and navigation can be tricky.
Camping	Official bivouac site at le Peuty. Bivouac prohibited W of Trient/le Peuty.
Trail notes	The original route from (53) headed N to Trient (avoiding le Peuty). However, at the date of press, this was closed due to rockfall. The route had been diverted E down to le Peuty. It is unclear if this diversion is permanent. We describe the new routing below.
Transport	**Col de Balme:** Autannes/Charamillon ski-lifts between Autannes (0.7km from Col de Balme) and le Tour.

Stage v9b: le Peuty to Col de Balme

(78) See map on p145. Head S from **Refuge du Peuty** on a broad path. Shortly afterwards, TR and climb on a path. TL up a track. Shortly afterwards, TL up a path, climbing steeply through trees.

(53) 1:00: TL at a junction, still climbing: the path coming from the right is the old route (see above). Soon the path emerges from the trees, contours around the slopes of **Carraye** and then climbs S.

(54) 2:30: TL at a **junction** to climb Croix de Fer; alternatively, continue S to head directly to Col de Balme (avoiding Croix de Fer). Climb along an exhilarating ridge with sheer drops on either side. When the path drifts to the left of the ridge's crest, there are rocks to scramble over.

(55) 2:55: Reach the cross on the summit of **Croix de Fer (2343m)**. After admiring the views, retrace your steps.

(54) 3:15: At the **junction**, TL and descend.

(80) 3:30: Arrive at **Col de Balme (2191m)**.

Stage v9b: Col de Balme to le Peuty

(80) See map on p145. From **Refuge du Col de Balme**, head N ('Croix de Fer'). Shortly afterwards, the path bends left and reaches a fork: TR (no signpost).

(54) 0:15: TR at a **junction** to climb Croix de Fer; alternatively, keep SH to continue to le Peuty (avoiding Croix de Fer). Climb along an exhilarating ridge with sheer drops on either side. When the path drifts to the left of the ridge's crest, there are rocks to scramble over.

(55) 0:40: Reach the cross on the summit of **Croix de Fer (2343m)**. After admiring the views, retrace your steps.

(54) 1:00: At the **junction**, TR and descend. 10min later, TR at a junction ('Trient'). The path contours around the slopes of **Carraye**.

(53) 2:00: TR at a junction; the path on the left is the old route (see above). Later, TR down a track. Shortly afterwards, TR down a path. TL down a track.

(78) 2:30: Just afterwards, reach **Refuge du Peuty (1326m)**.

v9c Col de Balme/Tré-le-Champs (via le Tour)

The path to le Tour

This variant is an easier alternative to Stage 9c (p152). It travels close to the floor of the l'Arve valley instead of crossing the challenging summit of l'Aiguillette des Posettes: this makes it a good choice in bad weather or for those with tired legs. It is not as dramatic as Stage 9c but it is still extremely beautiful.

Itinerary option: to save time, you could use the Autannes and/or Charamillon-Balme ski-lifts to descend to le Tour (www.chamonix.net).

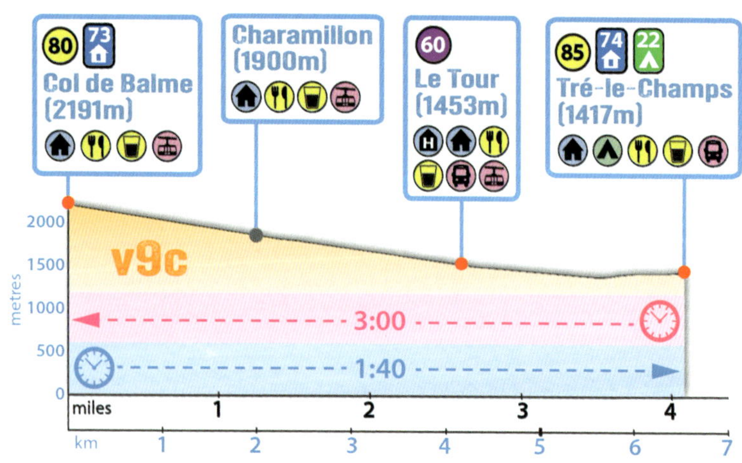

	Start	Finish	Time	Distance	Ascent (ACW)	Descent (ACW)	Max Alt
v9c	Col de Balme	Tré-le-Champs	1:40 3:00	6.5km 4.0miles	52m 171ft	826m 2710ft	2191m 7188ft

Terrain	Good paths/tracks. Walk along the road between (60) and (61). CW trekkers have a long steep climb between (60) and (80).
Route-finding	There is a confusing labyrinth of paths and tracks between (80) and (60): follow signs carefully. Otherwise, navigation is straightforward in good conditions. Sometimes snow remains on the high parts of the route until early July: in such conditions, the route is more challenging and navigation can be harder.
Camping	Bivouac permitted at Auberge la Boerne in Tré-le-Champs. Campsite at Argentière (OR). Otherwise, there are no places to bivouac legally.
Trail notes	There is only one place to stay in Tré-le-Champs, however, Gîte le Moulin in les Frasserands is only a short distance OR from Montroc (61). There is also a gîte/restaurant near the top of the Charamillon ski-lift (58). You can also stay in the village of Argentière: hike from le Tour (Argentière Link Route; 3.9km; p167) or Tré-le-Champs (1.6km); alternatively take the bus from Tré-le-Champs to Argentière.
Transport	**Col de Balme:** Autannes/Charamillon ski-lifts between Autannes (0.7km from Col de Balme) and le Tour. **Charamillon:** Autannes/Charamillon ski-lifts (see above). **Le Tour:** Autannes/Charamillon ski-lifts (see above); bus along the Chamonix valley between le Tour, Argentière and Chamonix.

Stage v9c: Col de Balme to Tré-le-Champs

(80) See map on p145. From **Refuge du Col de Balme**, head S on a path. Shortly afterwards, TR at a junction and descend SW: alternatively, TL and head S for the top of the **Autannes ski-lift** (0.7km).

(56) 0:05: Keep SH across a track (SW). Shortly afterwards, TR at a junction.

(57) 0:30: TL down a track.

(58) 0:35: TR at **Charamillon cable car station** and descend on a track. Shortly afterwards, keep SH on a path.

(59) 0:55: TL and descend on a track. At the bottom of the ski-lift, keep SH and descend on a road.

(60) 1:05: Shortly afterwards, pass the hamlet of **le Tour (1453m)**. Head SW along the road.

(61) 1:30: At **Montroc (1365m)**, TR on **Via des Cutes**. A few minutes later, TL onto a lane (heading SW). Just before reaching the main road, TL on a track.

(85) 1:40: A few minutes later, reach **Tré-le-Champs (1417m)**.

Stage v9c: Tré-le-Champs to Col de Balme

(85) See map on p144. From, **Tré-le-Champs**, head N up the track. Soon, TR on another track. After a while, it bends left to head NE. TR on **Via des Cutes**.

(61) 0:10: Shortly afterwards, TL at **Montroc (1365m)** and head NE on **Route de Montroc**.

(60) 0:40: Pass the hamlet of **le Tour (1453m)**. Just afterwards, pass to the right of the **Charamillon cable car station** and climb on a track ('Col de Balme').

(59) 1:00: TR onto a path ('Sentier Piétons').

(58) 1:45: Keep SH at a track. Soon afterwards, TL at a cable car station. Just afterwards, TL at a fork ('Col de Balme'). A few minutes later, TL at a fork.

(57) Shortly, TR on a path, climbing quite steeply. At the next junction, TL ('Col de Balme').

(56) 2:55: Keep SH at a crossroads.

(80) 3:00: Arrive at **Refuge du Col de Balme (2191m)**.

10 Tré-le-Champs/ Refuge de la Flégère

MB viewed from la Tête aux Vents

Stage 10a (Tré-le-Champs/la Tête aux Vents): this stage is an exhilarating delight. MB, just across the valley, keeps you company all the way up: ACW trekkers will get progressively closer to it as they continue through Sections 10 and 11. At the distinctive, pointy Aiguillette d'Argentière, the TMB delivers a much-discussed twist: the notorious sections of metal ladders bolted into the rock, enabling you to climb vertically up the cliffs (or descend if travelling CW). For many, this is a highlight of the TMB but others find it daunting. For ACW trekkers, the reward at the end of the stage is the epic viewpoint at la Tête aux Vents: the entire NW side of the MB massif is displayed in all its glory.

Stage 10b (la Tête aux Vents/la Flégère): the route cuts along the face of the slope between la Tête aux Vents and la Flégère cable car station. The views of the MB massif are exquisite throughout. ACW trekkers can stay at the beautifully situated Refuge de la Flégère (just below the cable car station): it faces the massif and the alpenglow on MB at sunset can be incredible. For CW trekkers, the stage finishes at la Tête aux Vents: there is nowhere to stay here so you have to continue to Tré-le-Champs (along Stage 10a/v10a).

Itinerary options: if you do not have a head for heights then consider using our Ladder-free Route (Stage v10a; p170) instead of Stage 10a. In our opinion, v10a (which travels a path known as the '*Grand Balcon Sud*') is scenically superior to Stage 10a.

From la Tête aux Vents (88), both ACW and CW trekkers have a choice of routes. ACW trekkers can continue SW on the main TMB to la Flégère (Stage 10b) or follow the Stage v10b variant W to Lac Blanc. CW trekkers can head NE towards the ladders on the main TMB (Stage 10a) or N on the Ladder-free Route (Stage v10a): both go to Tré-le-Champs. All options are fabulous.

	Start	Finish	Time	Distance	Ascent (ACW)	Descent (ACW)	Max Alt
10a	Tré-le-Champs	La Tête aux Vents	2:10 1:10	3.4km 2.1miles	716m 2349ft	0m 0ft	2135m 7004ft
10b	La Tête aux Vents	Refuge de la Flégère	1:00 1:20	3.5km 2.2miles	22m 72ft	278m 912ft	2135m 7004ft

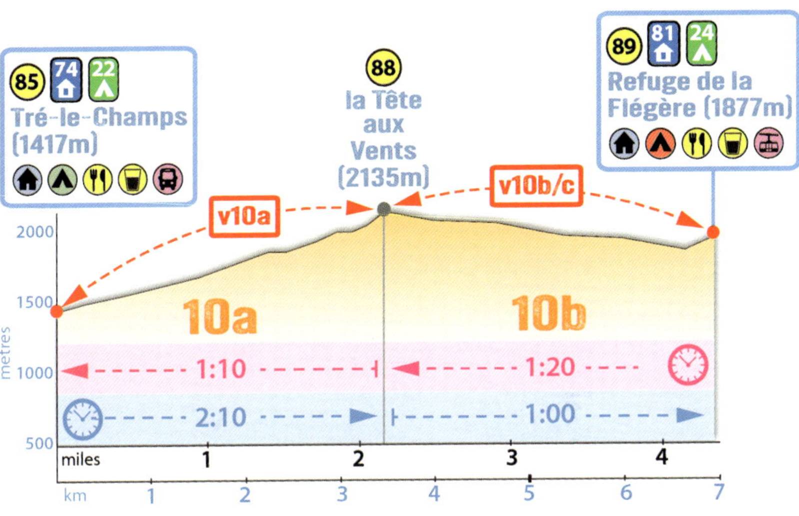

Terrain	**Stage 10a:** steep, rocky paths. ACW trekkers have a long climb; CW trekkers descend. The sections of ladders at Aiguillette d'Argentière are the stuff of legend for TMB hikers but, in fact, if you have a head for heights, they are quite straightforward; on some parts, there are chains/railings bolted into the wall; take great care as the drops are sheer and a fall would be serious. Arguably, the ladders are more intimidating for CW trekkers who face towards the drop as they descend. Do not attempt the ladders in snowy/icy conditions or high winds. **Stage 10b:** paths and tracks are clear and well maintained but they are sometimes rocky. ACW trekkers travel downhill and CW trekkers climb: the gradients are rarely steep.
Route-finding	Navigation is straightforward in good conditions.
Camping	Most of Section 10 lies within the Réserve Naturelle des Aiguilles Rouges where bivouac is prohibited except in certain places (see p33): bivouac is permitted in the zone around Lac Chéserys (1km W of (88), along Stage v10b); booking essential (see p33). Bivouac is also permitted at the lake near Refuge de la Flégère (which lies outside the reserve): campers can have dinner at the refuge with advance reservation. CW trekkers can bivouac at Auberge la Boerne in Tré-le-Champs.
Transport	**Tré-le-Champs:** bus between Tré-le-Champs and Argentière. **La Flégère:** ski-lift to/from les Praz (near Chamonix).

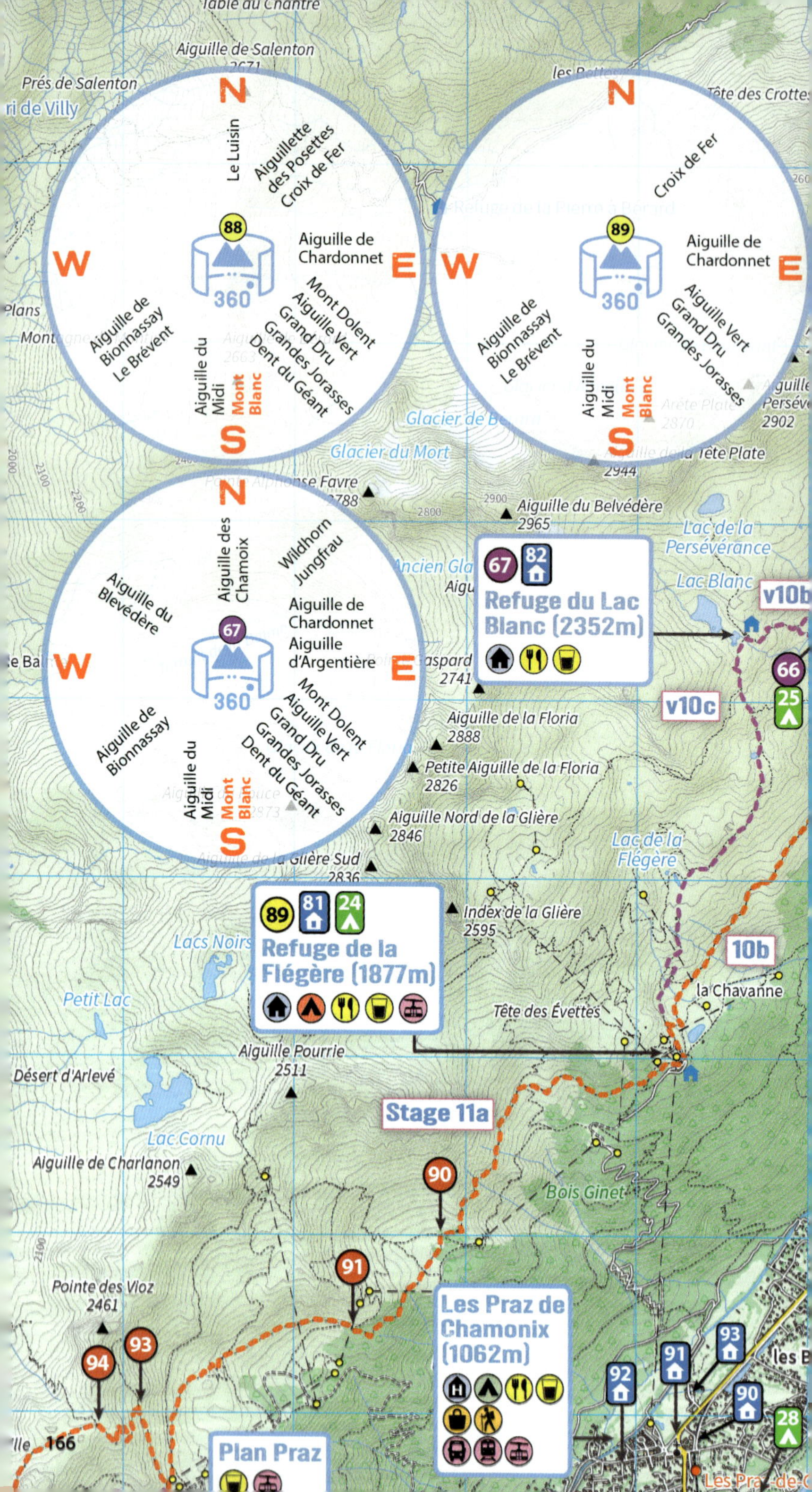

Aiguille de Salenton
2671
Prés de Salenton
N
Le Luisin
Aiguillette des Posettes
Croix de Fer
88
Aiguille de Chardonnet
W
E
360
Aiguille de Bionnassay
Le Brévent
Mont Dolent
Aiguille Vert
Grand Dru
Grandes Jorasses
Dent du Géant
Aiguille du Midi
Mont Blanc
S
N
Croix de Fer
89
Aiguille de Chardonnet
W
E
360
Aiguille de Bionnassay
Le Brévent
Aiguille Vert
Grand Dru
Grandes Jorasses
Aiguille du Midi
Mont Blanc
S
Glacier du Mort
2902
Tête Plate
2944
Aiguille du Belvédère
2965
N
Aiguille des Chamoix
Wildhorn
Jungfrau
Aiguille du Blevédère
67
Aiguille de Chardonnet
Aiguille d'Argentière
W
E
360
Mont Dolent
Aiguille Vert
Grand Dru
Grandes Jorasses
Dent du Géant
Aiguille de Bionnassay
Aiguille du Midi
Mont Blanc
S
Lac de la Persévérance
Lac Blanc
67
82
Refuge du Lac Blanc (2352m)
v10b
66
25
v10c
2741
Aiguille de la Floria
2888
Petite Aiguille de la Floria
2826
Aiguille Nord de la Glière
2846
Lac de la Flégère
2836
89
81
24
Refuge de la Flégère (1877m)
Index de la Glière
2595
10b
Lacs Noirs
Petit Lac
la Chavanne
Tête des Évettes
Aiguille Pourrie
2511
Désert d'Arlevé
Stage 11a
Lac Cornu
Aiguille de Charlanon
2549
Bois Ginet
90
91
Pointe des Vioz
2461
94
93
Les Praz de Chamonix (1062m)
93
91
92
90
28
166
Plan Praz

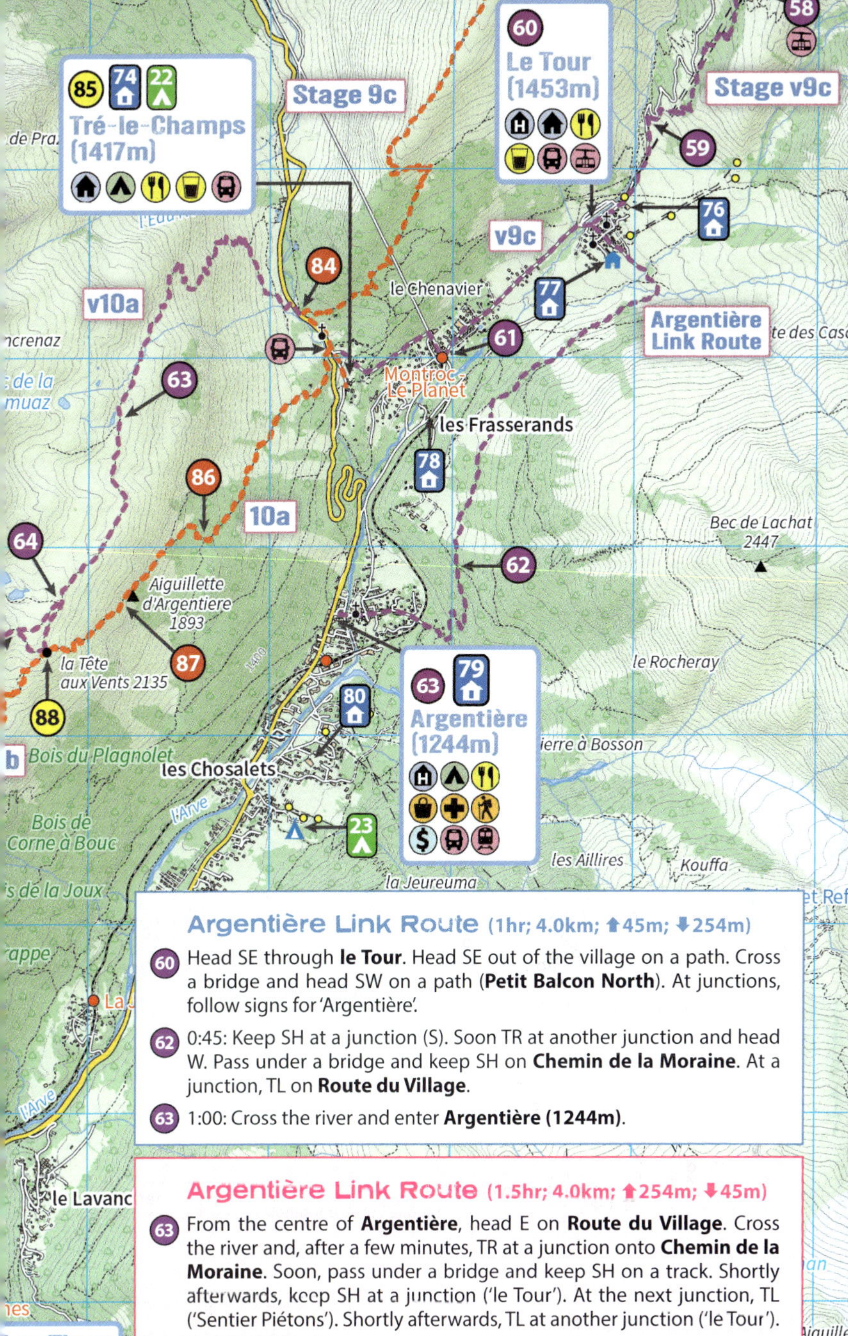

Argentière Link Route (1hr; 4.0km; ⬆45m; ⬇254m)

60 Head SE through **le Tour**. Head SE out of the village on a path. Cross a bridge and head SW on a path (**Petit Balcon North**). At junctions, follow signs for 'Argentière'.

62 0:45: Keep SH at a junction (S). Soon TR at another junction and head W. Pass under a bridge and keep SH on **Chemin de la Moraine**. At a junction, TL on **Route du Village**.

63 1:00: Cross the river and enter **Argentière (1244m)**.

Argentière Link Route (1.5hr; 4.0km; ⬆254m; ⬇45m)

63 From the centre of **Argentière**, head E on **Route du Village**. Cross the river and, after a few minutes, TR at a junction onto **Chemin de la Moraine**. Soon, pass under a bridge and keep SH on a track. Shortly afterwards, keep SH at a junction ('le Tour'). At the next junction, TL ('Sentier Piétons'). Shortly afterwards, TL at another junction ('le Tour').

62 0:35: Keep SH at a junction ('le Tour'). At the next two junctions, keep SH ('le Tour'). Descend gently, cross a bridge and keep SH on a path. Enter **le Tour (1453m)**.

60 1:30: Shortly afterwards, arrive at the main road. TR and reach a restaurant and a hotel.

Views of MB at Aiguillette d'Argentière (Stage 10a)

Stage 10a: Tré-le-Champs to la Tête aux Vents

85 See map on p167. From **Tré-le-Champs**, head N (back up the track travelled on Stage 9c). Cross the main road and climb on a path.

86 1:10: TR at a junction.

87 1:40: After a long ascent, climb the first section of the famous ladders at **Aiguillette d'Argentière**. Afterwards, continue climbing on a steep path. 10min later, climb another section of ladders, metal steps and railings.

88 2:10 : At **la Tête aux Vents (2135m)**, reach a junction with a large cairn. TL (SW) for Stage 10b ('la Flégère') or keep SH for Stage v10b to Lac Blanc.

Stage 10b: la Tête aux Vents to Refuge de la Flégère

88 See map on p167. From **la Tête aux Vents**, head SW on a path and descend ('la Flégère'). 10min later, keep SH at **Chalet des Chéserys**: continue SW on the main path all the way to the restaurant at **la Chavanne** (normally closed in summer). From there, follow a track SW. Soon, TL at a junction and pass **la Flégère cable car station**.

89 1:00: Just afterwards, reach **Refuge de la Flégère** (1877m; just below the cable car station).

Stage 10b: Refuge de la Flégère to la Tête aux Vents

89 See map on p166. From **Refuge de la Flégère**, head N on a track and pass **la Flégère cable car station**. Soon, TR at a junction and head NE on a track. Keep SH past the restaurant at **la Chavanne** (normally closed in summer): climb NE on a path. Keep SH at **Chalet des Chéserys**, still climbing NE.

88 1:20: At **la Tête aux Vents (2135m)**, reach a junction with a large cairn. TR (NE) for Stage 10a or keep SH (N) for Stage v10a.

Stage 10a: la Tête aux Vents to Tré-le-Champs

88 See map on p167. From **la Tête aux Vents**, descend NE on a path. After 5-10min, descend the first section of the famous ladders: the harder ladders come later. Then keep descending NE.

87 0:20: At **Aiguillette d'Argentière**, descend the main section of ladders. Then keep descending NE.

86 0:40: TL at a junction and continue descending. Later, cross the main road and TR on a track heading S. Shortly, ignore a path on the left.

85 1:10: Shortly afterwards, enter **Tré-le-Champs (1417m)**.

v10a Tré-le-Champs/la Tête aux Vents (Ladder-free Route)

If you do not have a head for heights then the ladders on Stage 10a can be a terrifying experience. Fortunately, Stage v10a offers a ladder-free alternative between Tré-le-Champs and la Tête aux Vents. However, do not think for a moment that this safer, ladder-free option is scenically inferior to the main route because it is one of the finest hikes in the Chamonix valley. It follows a spectacular ridge on a path known as *'Grand Balcon Sud'*. The views of the MB massif are sublime and ACW trekkers walk directly towards it: the Aiguille Verte is particularly beautiful when viewed from here. This route is also one of the best places on the trek to spot ibex (see image above). This is one of our favourite parts of the TMB but it is a little longer than the main route.

Terrain	Steep, rocky paths. ACW trekkers have a long climb; CW trekkers descend.
Route-finding	Occasionally, the path disappears across rocks: follow waymarks/cairns carefully. Otherwise, navigation is mostly straightforward in good conditions. Because this is a high altitude route, avoid it in bad weather or low visibility. Often, snow lies on parts of the route until early July, making navigation difficult.
Camping	Stage v10a lies within the Réserve Naturelle des Aiguilles Rouges where bivouac is prohibited except in certain places (see p33): bivouac is permitted in the zone around Lac Chéserys (1km W of (88), along Stage v10b); booking essential (see p33). CW trekkers can bivouac at Auberge la Boerne in Tré-le-Champs.
Transport	**Tré-le-Champs:** bus between Tré-le-Champs and Argentière. **La Flégère:** ski-lift to/from les Praz (near Chamonix).

	Start	Finish	Time	Distance	Ascent (ACW)	Descent (ACW)	Max Alt
v10a	Tré-le-Champs	la Tête aux Vents	2:30 1:30	4.9km 3.0miles	744m 2441ft	28m 92ft	2135m 7004ft

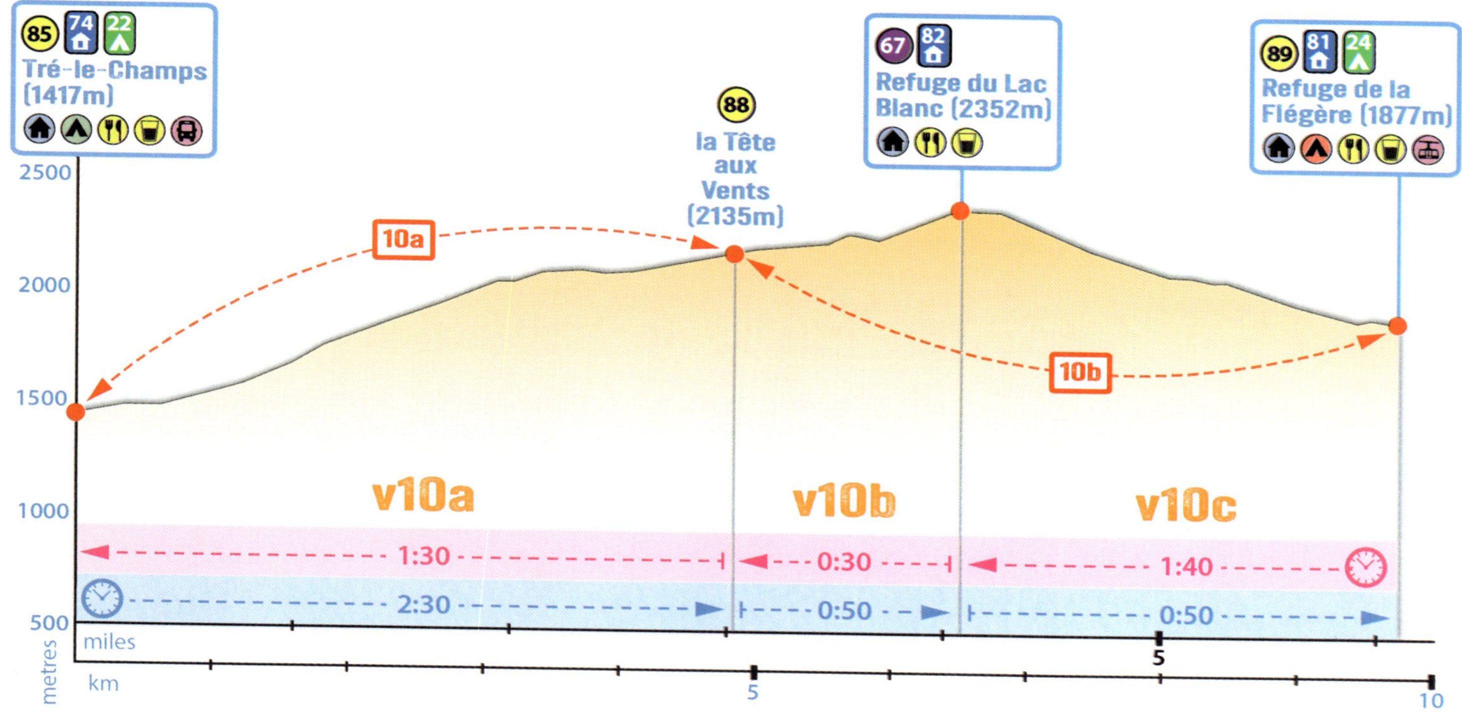
85
74
22
Tré-le-Champs (1417m)
88
la Tête aux Vents (2135m)
67
82
Refuge du Lac Blanc (2352m)
89
81
24
Refuge de la Flégère (1877m)
10a
10b
2500
2000
1500
1000
500
metres
v10a
v10b
v10c
1:30
0:30
1:40
2:30
0:50
0:50
miles
km
5
5
10

Stage v10a: Tré-le-Champs to la Tête aux Vents

85 See map on p167. From **Tré-le-Champs**, head N (back up the track travelled on Stage 9c). TR up the main road. After 5min, TL on a botanical path. TL at the next two junctions and climb on the **Grand Balcon Sud**.

63 1:50: TL at a **junction (2060m)** and soon pass a cairn. The path now levels out and you get your first glimpse of MB. Shortly afterwards, cross a section of boulders: watch your footing.

64 2:25: Reach a junction; TL to head to la Tête aux Vents (where you can join Stage 10b to la Flégère); alternatively, TR for Stage v10b to Lac Blanc.

88 2:30 : At **la Tête aux Vents (2135m)**, reach a junction with a large cairn. Head (SW) for Stage 10b ('la Flégère') or W for Stage v10b to Lac Blanc.

Aiguille des Grands Charmoz & Aiguille de Blaitière (Stage v10a)

Stage v10a: la Tête aux Vents to Tré-le-Champs

88 See map on p167. From **la Tête aux Vents**, head N on a path.

64 0:05: Keep SH (NE) at a junction. Cross a section of boulders: watch your footing.

63 0:25: Keep SH at a junction and descend N along the ridge. Later, the path zigzags steeply down to the E. Approaching the main road, TR at a junction. Soon TR at another junction. TR along the main road. A few minutes later, TL on a track heading S. Shortly, ignore a path on the left.

85 1:30: Shortly afterwards, reach **Tré-le-Champs (1417m)**.

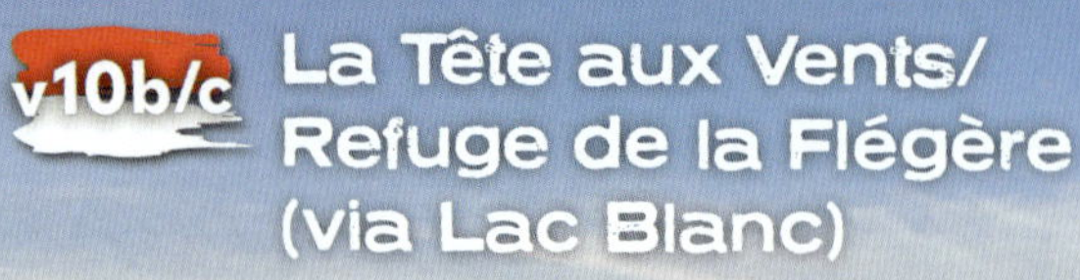

v10b/c La Tête aux Vents/ Refuge de la Flégère (via Lac Blanc)

Lac Blanc

This variant is another highlight of the TMB. The reflection of the MB massif in Lac Blanc on a calm day is a sight to behold. The balcony of the refuge (beside the lake) overlooks MB and is a superb place for lunch. However, the finest viewpoints often require a little extra effort and so it is with Lac Blanc (which sits well above the level of the main TMB route): if you have spent the previous night at Tré-le-Champs, you have a hefty 974m of ascent to endure before reaching Lac Blanc; the climb to Lac Blanc is more manageable for CW trekkers who have spent the previous night at la Flégère.

Stage v10b is the route between la Tête aux Vents and Lac Blanc: it is uphill for ACW trekkers and downhill for CW trekkers; it leads you past another collection of spectacular lakes (Lacs des Chéserys). Stage v10c travels between Lac Blanc and Refuge de la Flégère: it is a knee-jerking descent ACW and a stiff climb CW.

Terrain	A high-altitude route with steep, rocky paths. On Stage v10b, between 66 and 67, the route is very steep and there is a section of metal ladders: they are not as difficult as those on Stage 10a but some may find them intimidating; take great care. Sometimes snow/ice lies on the route until early July, making progress more difficult: in particular, the route between 66 and 67 can be treacherous.
Route-finding	Follow waymarks carefully between 66 and 67. Otherwise, navigation is mostly straightforward in good conditions. However, avoid Stages v10b/10c in bad weather, low visibility or snowy conditions when navigation can be difficult.
Camping	Most of Stage v10b/c lies within the Réserve Naturelle des Aiguilles Rouges where bivouac is prohibited except in certain places (see p33): bivouac is permitted in the zone around Lac Chéserys 66; booking essential (see p33). Bivouac is also permitted at the lake near Refuge de la Flégère (which lies outside the reserve): campers can have dinner at the refuge with advance reservation.
Trail notes	Because Lac Blanc is such a beautiful place, the refuge books up fast. As a side route, follow the fabulous trail around Lac Blanc (20-30min): watch for chamois and ibex, especially early in the morning.
Transport	**La Flégère:** ski-lift to/from les Praz (near Chamonix).

	Start	Finish	Time	Distance	Ascent (ACW)	Descent (ACW)	Max Alt
v10b	La Tête aux Vents	Refuge du Lac Blanc	0:50 0:30	1.6km 1.0miles	230m 755ft	11m 36ft	2352m 7717ft
v10c	Refuge du Lac Blanc	Refuge de la Flégère	0:50 1:40	3.2km 2.0miles	12m 39ft	487m 1598ft	2352m 7717ft

Stage v10b: la Tête aux Vents to Refuge du Lac Blanc

88 See map on p167. From the cairn at **la Tête aux Vents**, head W on a path.

65 0:10: TL at a junction onto a superb balcony path, rising above Lacs des Chéserys. From the top of a rocky spur, descend towards the most westerly of these lakes.

66 0:25: Follow the path around the S side of the most westerly of **Lacs des Chéserys (2211m)**: you could also take the path heading around the N side (to view the stunning reflections of the mountains in the lake). To the W of the lake, the two paths meet: now climb W on a steep path. A few minutes later, climb some metal ladders.

67 0:50: Arrive at **Refuge du Lac Blanc (2352m)** with its incredible setting beside Lac Blanc.

Stage v10c: Refuge du Lac Blanc to la Flégère

67 See map on p166. From **Refuge du Lac Blanc**, head S on a path. After 10min, keep SH at a junction. At the next junction, TR: the descent is steep at times. After a long descent, reach a plateau near the restaurant at **la Chavanne**. Follow one of the tracks uphill to the S.

89 0:50: Arrive at **Refuge de la Flégère** (1877m; just below the cable car station).

Stage v10c: la Flégère to Refuge du Lac Blanc

89 See map on p166. From **Refuge de la Flégère**, head N on a track and pass **la Flégère cable car station**. A few minutes later, keep SH at a junction and head N on a path. At any junctions, continue climbing N on the main path.

67 1:40: After a long climb, reach **Refuge du Lac Blanc (2352m)**.

Stage v10b: Refuge du Lac Blanc to la Tête aux Vents

67 See map on p166. From **Refuge du Lac Blanc**, descend E on a path. Descend some metal ladders.

66 0:10: Follow the path around the S side of the most westerly of **Lacs des Chéserys (2211m)**: you could also take the path heading around the N side (to view the stunning reflections of the mountains in the lake). To the E of the lake, climb briefly: cross a rocky spur, continuing E on a superb balcony path.

65 0:25: Reach a junction. TR to head to la Tête aux Vents (where you can join Stage 10a to Tré-le-Champs); alternatively, TL for the Ladder-free Route to Tré-le-Champs (Stage v10a).

88 0:30: At **la Tête aux Vents (2135m)**, reach a junction with a large cairn. Head NE for Stage 10a or N for Stage v10a.

11 Refuge de la Flégère/ les Houches

Stage 11a (la Flégère/Refuge Bellachat): for ACW hikers, the end of the TMB is in sight but fortunately, some of the best scenery has been saved for last. Stage 11a takes place on wonderful balconies high above the Chamonix valley, directly opposite MB: in fact, this is the closest you will have been to the mighty peak since Stage 5b. The hike between la Flégère and the ski station at Plan Praz is an epic traverse, providing continuous views of MB. Between Plan Praz and le Brévent, the terrain is wilder and the views only get better: the viewpoint at the summit of le Brévent provides one of the TMB's classic panoramas.

Finally, the finest balcony of the day travels between le Brévent and the fabulous Refuge Bellachat: its incredible outlook ensures that a stay there is unforgettable. However, although this part of the route is sublime and provides some of the TMB's finest views of MB, an urban myth seems to have materialised which leads prospective trekkers to believe that the section is inferior and should be skipped (by descending from le Brévent to Chamonix by cable car). Without any hesitation, we can tell you that this is a mistake: in our opinion, this small part of the TMB is unmissable (which is why it features on the cover of this book).

Stage 11b (Refuge Bellachat/les Houches): if travelling ACW, a long descent stands between you and the end of the TMB. You may be tired but grit your teeth and think of the celebrations ahead when you reach LH. As you leave the refuge, enjoy the last of the breathtaking views of MB because soon you enter the forest. For CW trekkers, Stage 11b is a brutal climb (see p10). Watch out for chamois on this part of the route.

Itinerary options: if Stages 11a and 11b are combined, as is common, it is a long and tiring day (especially for CW trekkers who have to endure more than 1600m of ascent).

	Start	Finish	Time	Distance	Ascent (ACW)	Descent (ACW)	Max Alt
11a	Refuge de la Flégère	Refuge Bellachat	4:10 3:30	10.1km 6.3miles	790m 2592ft	531m 1742ft	2525m 8284ft
11b	Refuge Bellachat	Les Houches	2:45 4:00	7.9km 4.9miles	36m 118ft	1155m 3789ft	2152m 7060ft

Stage 11a's epic balcony

Instead, consider breaking the stage by overnighting at Refuge Bellachat: this enables ACW trekkers to rest before Stage 11b's knee-jerking descent; CW trekkers would be splitting up Section 11's mammoth climb.

Terrain	**Stage 11a:** between la Flégère (89) and Planpraz (92), there are undulating rocky paths which are not too steep (except for the steep steps near (89)). Between (92) and (94), paths are steep and exposed. Between (94) and (95), the route enters wilder terrain: very steep in places; section of exposed metal ladders (easier than the Stage 10a ladders but some may find them intimidating). Between (95) and (97), wild remote terrain and rocky paths. Sometimes snow/ice remains until early July, making progress difficult: in such conditions, the route between (92) and (95) can be treacherous; for a safer alternative, climb/descend directly between (92) and (95) using a track (coloured purple on the map on p179). **Stage 11b:** clear paths/tracks. Steep gradients.
Route-finding	Between la Flégère (89) and Planpraz (92), there is a complicated labyrinth of paths/tracks: follow waymarks/directions carefully. Between (92) and (97), the route crosses wild, high terrain: avoid it in bad weather/low visibility/snow when navigation can be difficult; route-finding can be particularly tricky in the rocky terrain between (94) and (95).
Camping	Part of Section 11 lies within the Réserve Naturelle des Aiguilles Rouges where bivouac is prohibited except in certain places: bivouac is permitted around Lac du Brévent and Col de Bellachat; booking essential (see p33). CW trekkers can bivouac at la Flégère (see p165). For general rules on bivouac outside the reserve's borders, see p33.
Transport	You can use the Brévent cable car to travel directly between (92) and (96): useful if you are tired or the weather is bad. You can also leave the TMB at (92) or (96) by taking the Plan Praz/Brévent cable car down to Chamonix: some trekkers descend to Chamonix, overnight there and then use the cable car to return to the TMB the following morning. Others start/finish the TMB at le Brévent/Plan Praz using the cable car to get to the start and to return to Chamonix at the end of the trek.

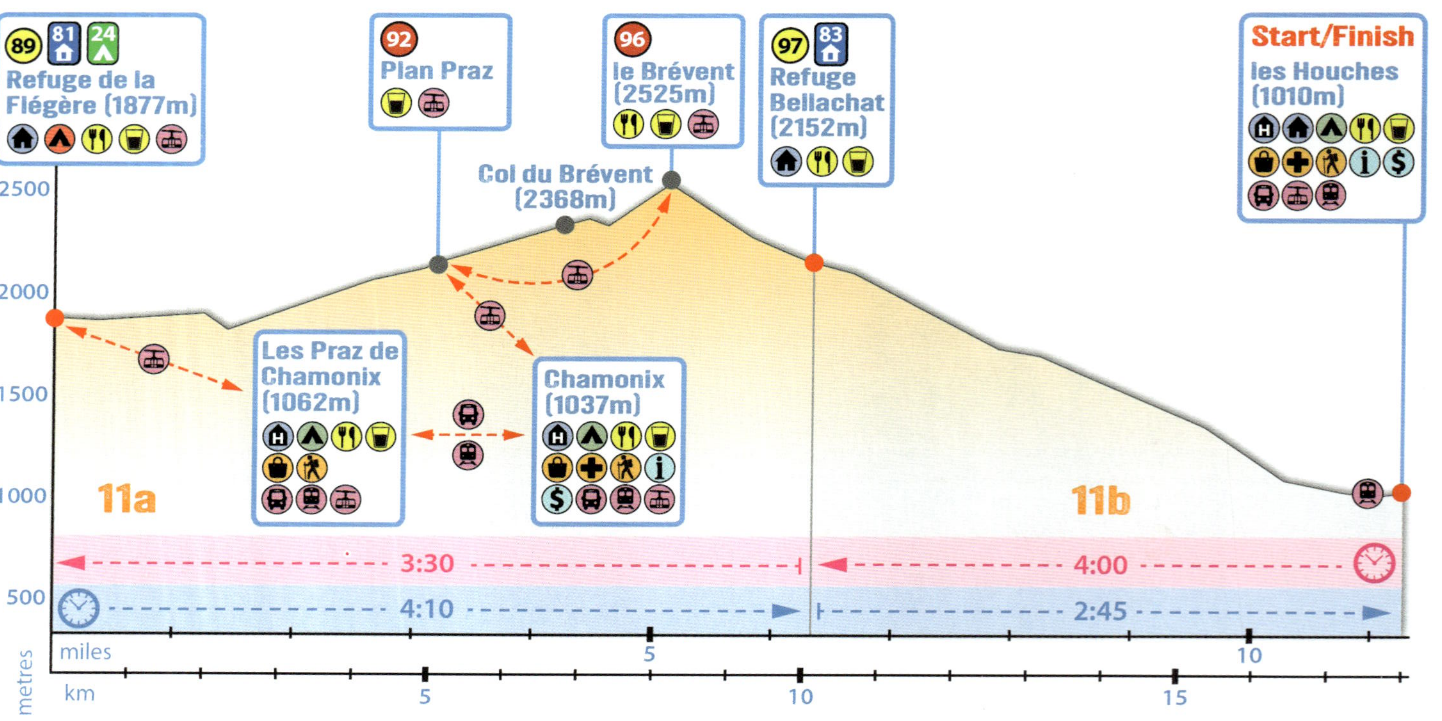

89
81
24
Refuge de la
Flégère (1877m)
92
Plan Praz
96
le Brévent
(2525m)
97
83
Refuge
Bellachat
(2152m)
Start/Finish
les Houches
(1010m)
Col du Brévent
(2368m)
Les Praz de
Chamonix
(1062m)
Chamonix
(1037m)
2500
2000
1500
1000
500
metres
11a
11b
3:30
4:00
4:10
2:45
miles
5
10
km
5
10
15

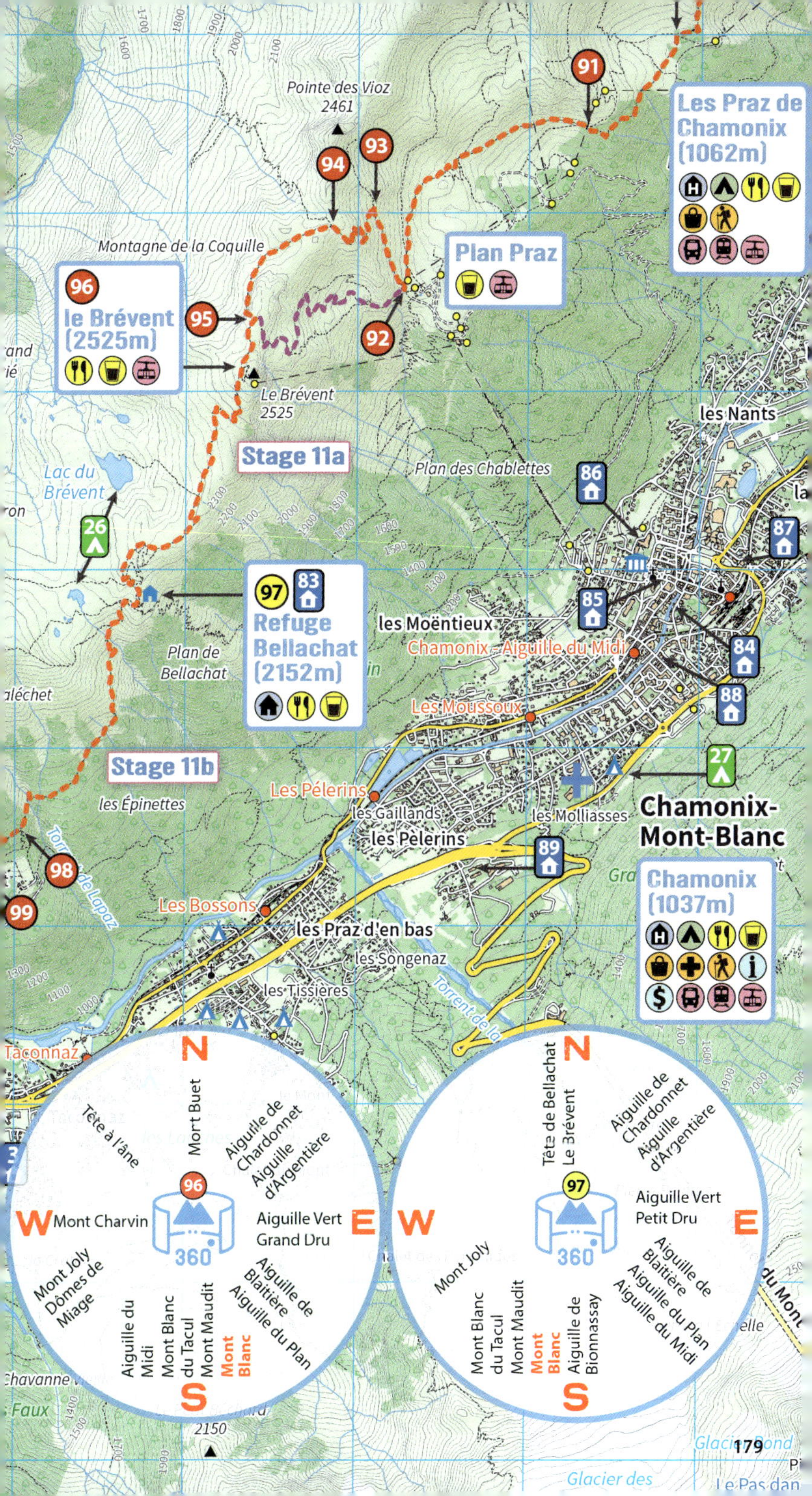

Pointe des Vioz
2461
Montagne de la Coquille
Les Praz de Chamonix (1062m)
Plan Praz
le Brévent (2525m)
Le Brévent
2525
Stage 11a
Lac du Brévent
Plan des Chablettes
les Nants
Refuge Bellachat (2152m)
Plan de Bellachat
les Moëntieux
Chamonix - Aiguille du Midi
Les Moussoux
Stage 11b
les Épinettes
Les Pélerins
les Gaillands
les Pélerins
les Molliasses
Chamonix-Mont-Blanc
Chamonix (1037m)
Torrent de Lapaz
Les Bossons
les Praz d'en bas
les Songenaz
les Tissières
Torrent de la
Taconnaz
Mont Buet
Tête à l'âne
Aiguille de Chardonnet
Aiguille d'Argentière
Mont Charvin
Aiguille Vert
Grand Dru
Mont Joly
Dômes de Miage
Aiguille du Midi
Mont Blanc du Tacul
Mont Maudit
Mont Blanc
Aiguille de Blaitière
Aiguille du Plan
Tête de Bellachat
Le Brévent
Aiguille de Chardonnet
Aiguille d'Argentière
Aiguille Vert
Petit Dru
Mont Joly
Mont Blanc du Tacul
Mont Maudit
Mont Blanc
Aiguille de Bionnassay
Aiguille de Blaitière
Aiguille du Plan
Aiguille du Midi
Chavanne
2150
Glacier des

Stage 11a: Refuge de la Flégère to Refuge Bellachat

89 See map on p166. From **Refuge de la Flégère**, head W on a path, contouring around the hillside. After 5min, TL onto a track. Immediately afterwards, TR at a junction. Soon, take care descending steep steps. Then climb gently over rocks and continue contouring around the hillside on an exquisite balcony path.

90 0:40: Keep SH across a track and take a path heading S on the other side (poor waymarking). Soon, keep SH at a junction.

91 1:00: TL onto a track. Immediately afterwards, TR onto a path contouring around the hillside: at junctions, stay on the main path following cairns/waymarks.

92 1:40: See map on p179. Arrive at the ski station of **Plan Praz**. At the top of **la Parsa chairlift (2075m)**, TR onto a small path climbing NW.

93 2:00: TL at a **junction (2197m)** and climb SW on a path.

94 2:30: TL at **Col du Brévent (2368m)** and follow a marked path which zigzags up a ridge. A few minutes later, the path drifts to the right of the ridge. Soon the path heads down the right side of a broad gully. Eventually, leave the gully and climb again (waymarks/cairns). 5-10min later, scramble up a short section of rocks and then climb fixed metal ladders: take care. Afterwards, continue climbing on a clear path. A few minutes later, follow waymarks up over rocks.

95 3:05: TR at a large cairn and climb more gently up a track.

96 3:15: Reach a junction: keep SH up the track for the magnificent viewpoint at the cable car station on the summit of **le Brévent (2525m; 5min return from junction)**; to continue on Stage 11a, descend S from the junction (on a path). Soon, the gradient eases and the path traverses around the slopes, directly in front of MB. After a while, start to descend more steeply.

97 4:10: Arrive at **Refuge Bellachat (2152m)**.

Stage 11b: Refuge Bellachat to les Houches

97 See map on p179. From **Refuge Bellachat**, head initially W on a path: do not follow signs for 'Chamonix'. Soon, descend steeply S: take care crossing a waterfall in a gully (chains to assist). Start to dip below the tree-line. Take care on exposed sections with railings.

98 0:45: Keep SH at a junction: do not descend to the left.

99 0:55 : TL at a fork and descend steeply beside the fence of a wildlife sanctuary. See map on p79. At the next junction, TL (still descending beside the fence). TL at the following two junctions.

100 1:20: TR onto a road at a car park. After a few minutes, TL on a path. At the next junction, keep SH. 5min later, TL at a fork.

101 1:45: At the statue of **le Christ Roi**, either TL or keep SH: both paths meet up later. Now follow signs for 'les Houches' at junctions. Nearing the valley floor, keep SH along a lane, ignoring offshoots: the lane becomes a road.

102 2:25: Eventually, TL on a road and descend. Just before **les Houches train station**, TL and cross a bridge over the river. Follow the road up to a junction at LH's main street: TR ('les Houches Centre').

2:45: Walk under the TMB arch in **les Houches (1010m)**. Congratulations! You have completed the trek.

Stage 11b: les Houches to Refuge Bellachat

See map on p79. From the **TMB arch** in **les Houches**, walk NE out of the town. A few minutes later, TL down **Route de la Gare**. Cross a bridge and TR at a junction: alternatively, TL for **les Houches train station**.

102 0:10: Shortly afterwards, TR at a fork. Keep SH on a lane: near the end of it, pick up a path and climb N.

101 0:45: From the statue of **le Christ Roi**, climb N on a path. TR at a junction, climbing E.

100 1:20: TR onto a road. After a few minutes, TL on a path. 5-10min later (at around 1500m), TR at a junction. At the next few junctions, keep SH (NE).

99 2:05: See map on p179. At a junction, keep SH (NE).

98 2:20: At a junction, keep SH (N). Take care on exposed sections with railings. Rise above the tree-line. Take care crossing a waterfall in a gully (chains to assist).

97 4:00: Arrive at **Refuge Bellachat (2152m)**.

Stage 11a: Refuge Bellachat to Refuge de la Flégère

97 See map on p179. From **Refuge Bellachat**, climb N on an exquisite balcony path (directly facing MB).

96 1:20: Reach a junction: TR up a track for the magnificent viewpoint at the cable car station on the summit of **le Brévent (2525m; 5min return from junction)**; to continue on Stage 11a, descend N from the junction.

95 1:25: TL at a large cairn and descend. Follow waymarks down over rocks. Afterwards, continue descending on a clear path. Soon, climb down fixed metal ladders: take care. Then scramble down a short section of rocks. Descend N. Climb the left side of a broad gully. Descend E along a ridge.

94 1:55: TR at **Col du Brévent (2368m)** and descend SE on a path. Soon zigzag down to the E.

93 2:05: TR at a junction and descend S on a path.

92 2:15: TL at the top of **la Parsa' chairlift (2075m)** and descend N on a path contouring around the hillside: at junctions, keep on the main path (following cairns/waymarks).

91 2:40: See map on p166. TL onto a track. Immediately afterwards, TR onto a path. Keep SH at a junction.

90 2:55: Keep SH across a track and pick up a path on the other side (poor waymarking). Contour around the hillside on an exquisite balcony path. Later, take care climbing steep steps. Soon, TL onto a track. Immediately afterwards, TR at a junction and head E on a path.

89 3:30: Reach **Refuge de la Flégère** (1877m; just below the cable car station).

Climbing above Plan Praz

Facilities along the route

Stage	Place	Hotel	Hut/Gîte/ Hostel	Campsite	Meals/ Drinks	Shops	ATM/Info	Transport
Start/Finish	Les Houches							
v1c	Le Prarion							
1a/v1a	Col de Voza							
1a/1b	Refuge du Fioux							
1b	Bionnassay							
v1a/v1b	Refuge de Miage							
v1b	Auberge du Truc							
1b,v1b/ 2a, v2a	Les Contamines							
2a	Le Pontet							
v2a/v2b	Refuge de Tré-la-Tête							
2a,v2b/2b	Refuge de Nant-Borrant							
2b	La Rollaz							
2b/2c	Refuge de la Balme							
2c/2d,v3a	Refuge de la CB							
2d/3a	Les Chapieux							
3a	La Ville des Glaciers					Cheese for sale		
3a,v3a/3b	Refuge des Mottets							OR
3b/4a	Rifugio Elisabetta							
4a/4b,v4b	Combal							2.8km OR
4b/4c	Rifugio Maison Vieille							

Stage	Place	Hotel	Hut/Gîte/Hostel	Campsite	Meals/Drinks	Shops	ATM/Info	Transport
v4b	La Visaille							
v4b	Val Veny			Dormitory			$	
v4c	Rifugio Monte Bianco							
4c	Dolonne	H						
4c,v4b,v4c/5a,v5a	Courmayeur	H					$ i	
5a/5b,v5b	Rifugio Bertone							
5b,v5b/6a	Rifugio Bonatti							1.5km OR
v5a	Entrèves/la Palud	H						
v5a	Italian Val Ferret	H						
6a/6b	Chalet Val Ferret							
6b/6c	Rifugio Elena							
6c/6d	Alpage de la Peule							
6d/6e	Ferret	H						
6e/7	La Fouly	H					$ i	
7	Praz-de-Fort							
7	Les Arlaches							
7	Issert							
7/8a,v8a	Champex	H					$ i	
8a	Champex d'en Haut							
8a	Plan de l'Au							

Stage	Place	Hotel	Hut/Gîte/ Hostel	Campsite	Meals/ Drinks	Shops	ATM/Info	Transport
8a	Bovine							
8a,v8b/ 8b,v9a	Col de la Forclaz					Basic		
v8a/v8b	Arpette							
v8b,v9a	Chalet du Glacier							
v9a	Refuge les Grands							
8b/9a	Trient							
9a/9b,v9b	Le Peuty							
9b,v9a,v9b/ 9c,v9c	Refuge du Col de Balme							0.7km OR
v9c	Charamillon							
v9c	Le Tour							
9c,v9c/ 10a,v10a	Tré-le-Champs							
10a,v10a/ 10b,v10b	La Tête aux Vents			OR (p33)				
10b,v10c/ 11a	Refuge de la Flégère							
v10b/v10c	Refuge du Lac Blanc							
11a	Plan Praz							
11a	Le Brévent							
11a/11b	Refuge de Bellachat			OR (p33)				
Finish/Start	Les Houches							

We thought hiking guidebooks were boring so we decided to change them. Mapping is better than it used to be. Graphics are better than they used to be. Photography is better than it used to be. So why have hiking guidebooks remained the same?

Well our guidebooks are **different**:

- **We use Real Maps.** You know, the **large** scale maps that walkers actually use to navigate with. Not sketch maps that get you lost. Real maps make more work for us but we think it is worth it. You do not need to carry separate maps and you are less likely to get lost so we save you time!
- **Numbered waypoints** on our Real Maps link to the walk descriptions, making routes easier to follow than traditional text-based guidebooks. No more wading through pages of boring words to find out where you are! You want to look at incredible scenery and not have your face stuck in a book all day. Right?
- **Colour, colour, colour.** Mountains and cliffs are **beautiful** so guidebooks should be too. We were fed up using guidebooks which were ugly and boring. When planning, we want to be **dazzled** with full-size colour pictures of the **magnificence** which awaits us! So our guidebooks fill every inch of the page with beauty: big, **spectacular** photos of mountains, etc.
- **More practical size.** Long enough to have Real Maps and large pictures but slim enough to fit in a pocket.

Now all that sounds great to us but we want to know if you like what we have done. So hit us with your feedback: good or bad. We are not too proud to change.

Follow us for trekking advice, book updates, discount coupons, articles and other interesting hiking stuff.

 www.knifeedgeoutdoor.com

 info@knifeedgeoutdoor.com

 @knifeedgeoutdoor

 @knifeedgeout

 @knifeedgeoutdoor